George F. (George Fox) Bacon

The Leading Business Men of Concord, and Vicinity

Embracing Penacook, East and West Concord

George F. (George Fox) Bacon

The Leading Business Men of Concord, and Vicinity
Embracing Penacook, East and West Concord

ISBN/EAN: 9783744778794

Printed in Europe, USA, Canada, Australia, Japan

Cover: Foto ©Suzi / pixelio.de

More available books at **www.hansebooks.com**

THE

LEADING BUSINESS MEN

OF

CONCORD

AND VICINITY,

EMBRACING

PENACOOK. EAST AND WEST CONCORD.

BY GEO. F. BACON.

ILLUSTRATED.

BOSTON :

MERCANTILE PUBLISHING COMPANY,

No. 258 Purchase Street.

1890.

PREFACE.

In this historical and statistical review of the commercial and manufacturing interests of Concord, it has been our purpose in as thorough a manner as was possible to justly describe those enterprises which have contributed so largely during the last half century to the material advancement of the city. History plainly shows that many large cities owe their prosperity and growth chiefly to advantages of situation, great influx of foreign people, and similar causes; the present prosperity of Concord, however, is due mainly to the genius and efforts of its people. A study of these facts, and of its varied mercantile interests, which are presented herewith, must show clearly, we think, the rich harvests that have been reaped from the exertions and foresight of the past, the present flourishing and influential position of Concord as a commercial center, and its bright outlook for many lines of growth in the time to come.

MERCANTILE PUBLISHING CO.

[For Contents see last pages.]

CONCORD AND ITS POINTS OF INTEREST

INTRODUCTORY.

THE history of Concord as a city dates from 1853, for it was on the tenth of March in that year that the city charter was adopted, it having been granted July 6, 1849, and rejected three times by popular vote, finally being accepted by a majority of 269 in a total vote of 1387. The history of the parish and town is of deep interest but does not properly come within the scope of the present work, which deals especially with the Concord of to-day and may be considered as a sort of appendix to the complete, authoritative and admirable history of Concord from 1725 to 1853, written by the Rev. Nathaniel Bouton and published in 1856. This is a standard work whose value steadily increases with the passage of time, and we wish here to express our obligations to it for many of the facts presented in the introductory sketch, which by summarizing Concord's development in the past may lead to a more complete understanding of her probable growth in the future. The "History of Merrimack and Belknap Counties," published by J. W. Lewis & Co., of Philadelphia, in 1885, has also been of great service by reason of its clear presentation of facts concerning Concord's later history, and it is to be regretted that the necessarily high cost of that handsomely and substantially gotten up volume of nearly 1000 pages should prevent a copy of it from being owned by every family in the large and important section of which it treats so interestingly and accurately.

THE FIRST SETTLEMENT.

"Where once the savage Penacook
Took deadly aim at beast and bird,
And all the silent valley heard
His whizzing arrow, where to-day
Whistles the engine on its way."

The first settlers of New England found it inhabited by five distinct Indian nations, among these being the Pawtucketts, concerning whom Daniel Gookin wrote in 1674 as follows : "Their country lieth north and northeast from the Massachusetts, whose dominion reaches so far as the English jurisdiction or colony of the Massachusetts doth now extend ; and had under them several other smaller sagamores ; as the Pennakooks, Agowames, Naamkeeks, Pascataways, Accomintas, and others. They were a considerable people heretofore, about three thousand men, and held amity with the people of Massachusetts. But they were almost totally destroyed by the great sickness that prevailed among the Indians, so that at this day they are not above two hundred and fifty men, beside women and children. This country is now inhabited by the English, under the government of Massachusetts."

The "Pennakooks," or Penacooks, to use the accepted style of spelling, occupied the tract of land on which Concord is located, and are said to have taken their name from the erratic course pursued by the Merrimack river in flowing through the township, Penacook meaning "the crooked place." When first known to the English their chief was Passaconaway, who had a great reputation as a sorcerer, and was credited with the ability to turn water into ice in the heat of summer and do many other wonderful things. In spite of the superstitious awe with which he was regarded, even by the English, he foresaw that armed opposition to them would result in the ruin of his people, and hence was as friendly as circumstances would allow. Passaconaway was induced to embrace Christianity by the apostle Eliot, in 1648, and when the great chief died some twenty years later, at the age of more than one hundred, his farewell command to his son Wonolancet, who succeeded him in the leadership of the Penacooks, was, "Never be enemies to the English ; but love them and love their God also, because the God of the English is the true God and greater than the Indian gods." This command was faithfully obeyed, for although Wonolancet suffered many privations and finally lost all his property by reason of unjust suspicions, he never injured the English by word or deed, but on the contrary interposed several times to save them from attack.

The last sagamore of the Penacooks was Kancamagus, a grandson of Passaconaway, but totally unlike him in character. Kancamagus was concerned in the attack upon Dover, in 1689, and was among the six "eastern Indian enemy, sagamores" who signed a treaty of peace with the Massachusetts government, November 29, 1690. The power of the Penacooks as a tribe was then at an end, and such as were hostile to the English joined other tribes, the rest remaining in the vicinity of Penacook and rendering valuable aid to the early settlers by supplying them with food in winter and doing them other services.

The first petition for a grant of land in "a place which is called Pennecooke," was presented in 1659, but this and several others which followed amounted to nothing, for although the grants were made they were forfeited on account of breach of conditions, and it was not until June 17, 1725, that the decisive petition was presented to the authorities of Massachusetts Bay Province. This was granted January 17, the petitioners being given a tract "to contain seven miles square" upon certain conditions, among which were the building of a meeting-house within three years, the cutting of a road through the wilderness to the plantation, and the division of the land into one hundred and three equal parts or shares, of which one hundred were to be given to one hundred desirable persons or families on the payment of five pounds for each lot, the remaining three shares being reserved : one for the first settled minister, one for a parsonage, and one for the use of the school forever.

The land having been duly surveyed and apportioned to the settlers, they set actively to work to fulfill the other conditions and by 1728 had erected a meeting-house and made arrangements for building a saw mill, a grist mill, and for establishing a ferry. In 1730 the proprietors petitioned the General Court to be given the rights and privileges of a town, but the result was not altogether satisfactory, and in December, 1732, another petition was presented, by the granting of which the inhabitants of Penacook were enabled to hold legal meetings for the choice of officers and the raising of money for town purposes. But the General Court appointed the moderator of these meetings and it was not until February 27, 1733, that the bill was passed which made the plantation of Penacook the town of Rumford. Why this name was chosen is not definitely known, but probably it was because some of the proprietors came from the English parish of that title. In 1740 the town was greatly excited by the terms of the settlement of the long-disputed question as to the division line between Massachusetts and New Hampshire, for the decision arrived at had the effect of placing Rumford under New Hampshire's jurisdiction, whereas both sentimental and practical considerations attached the townspeople to the Massachusetts government. Every effort was made to bring about

THE MERRIMACK RIVER FROM BLUFFS.

a continuance of the existing condition of affairs, but without avail, and the passage of what was called the "District Act" by New Hampshire, made Rumford a district and subjected her to the indignity and expense of taxation without representation.

From 1742 to 1754 Indian warfare very seriously interfered with the development of New England frontier settlements, and before these troubles were over Rumford became involved in legal complications with the town of Bow, so that between the two opposing forces her very existence was imperilled. The tract of land granted by Massachusetts in 1725 was covered in part by a grant made by New Hampshire in 1727, this latter grant conveying eighty-one square miles of territory to one hundred and seven proprietors and their associates and forming "a town corporate by the name of Bow." In November, 1750, an action of ejectment was brought against Dea. John Merrill, one of the Rumford proprietors, by the Bow proprietors, this being the first of a series of similar actions against different parties. The Rumford proprietors combined to defend these suits, but every case brought to trial in New Hampshire was decided against them, and only a firm belief in the justice of their cause gave them faith to continue the apparently hopeless struggle. Agents were sent to England to present the points at issue before His Majesty in Council, and the result was that the adverse judgment was reversed and the position of the Rumford proprietors endorsed. This was in 1762, but it was not until 1772 that the controversy was finally terminated.

In May, 1765, the "parish of Concord" was created, the name being given in commemoration of the "concord" of action which had characterized the residents of Penacook and Rumford from the very beginning. The territory was known as a parish until January, 1784, when a small portion of Canterbury and London was annexed, and it was "enacted that the parish of Concord be henceforth called the town of Concord, any law, usage or custom to the contrary notwithstanding."

The town steadily grew and prospered, and in 1790 had become of such importance that it became necessary to provide a house for the accommodation of the General Court, and the sum of five hundred and fifty-five dollars was raised by private subscription, one hundred pounds additional being afterward appropriated by the town for the purpose. The structure was known as the Town House and was utilized by the General Court until the completion of the State House in 1819, which year is also memorable as the date of the appearance of the first steamboat on the river at Concord. It was designed to tow loaded boats up the river but lacked the power necessary to overcome the rapids and hence the company by whom it was controlled had to depend upon the primitive methods of sails, oars, and "setting-poles." The first boat arrived at Concord in the fall of 1814, but it carried only a small cargo as the river-locks were not then completed. The first boat, with regular freight from Boston to Concord, through the Middlesex Canal, arrived June 23, 1815. The rates for freight from Boston to Concord during the first four years, were $12 per ton of 2,240 pounds; the rate from Concord to Boston being $8 for the same weight. The charges were gradually reduced and in 1841-42 had fallen to $4 per ton of 2,000 pounds, whether carried up or down the river. The largest business done in any one year was in 1839, the receipts being $38,169. The average receipts were about $25,000 per annum, the company doing a very profitable business until the opening of the Concord railroad in the fall of 1842.

The first train from Boston to Concord arrived at quarter of seven, Tuesday evening, September sixth, and consisted of three passenger cars drawn by the "Amoskeag." Such an arrival was an event indeed, and the whole town turned out to honor the occasion. Amid shouting, cheering and the thunder of cannon the train came to a stop, and when it was announced that such as could be accommodated would be given a "free ride," a tremendous rush was made and every available inch of sitting and standing room was occupied. A regular service of two passenger trains per day was inaugurated, and the following week three trains per day were run.

The first omnibus to run in Concord was owned by George Dame, of the Pavilion Hotel, and began its trips between the north end of Main street and the depot in 1852. It was gorgeously painted and upon the panels were views of the State House, depot and Main street, and a likeness of Franklin Pierce.

By this time Concord had become a wealthy and populous town, the United States census of 1850 giving the valuation of real estate as $3,015,286, and of personal estate as $573,624, making a total valuation of $3,588,910. The population was 8,584, having increased to that figure from 4,903 in 1840. Although many disliked to abandon the system of government which had served so well in the past, the great number of voters rendered some change imperative, and the popular conviction of this fact finally overcame all opposition and secured the adoption of a city charter, March 10, 1853. The first election under this charter occurred March 26, 1853, but no choice of mayor was made, there being three candidates and the most popular receiving twenty-one less votes than his two opponents. At a second election, held April 5th, he was elected by 192 majority out of a total vote of 1,466, and the following day the city government was formally organized by the induction to office of the mayor elect and the two branches of the city council, the following gentlemen having been chosen :

Mayor — Joseph Low.

Aldermen — Ward 1, John Batchelder ; ward 2, John L. Tallant ; ward 3, Joseph Eastman ; ward 4, Robert Davis ; ward 5, Edson Hill ; ward 6, Matthew Harvey ; ward 7, Josiah Stevens.

Common Council — Ward 1, Jeremiah S. Durgin, Eben F. Elliot ; ward 2, Samuel B. Larkin, Heman Sanborn ; ward 3, George W. Brown, Moses Humphrey ; ward 4, Ezra Carter, George Minot ; ward 5, William H. H. Bailey, Cyrus Barton ; ward 6, Ebenezer G. Moore, Thomas Bailey ; ward 7, Moses Shute, Giles W. Ordway.

And now, having sketched Concord's history from the time when the territory was but a savage wilderness until it became Penacook Plantation, Rumford town, Rumford district, Concord parish, Concord town, and finally Concord city, let us proceed without further preface to a consideration of the Concord of to-day, and see how far it has fulfilled the hopes of its founders and what are the opportunities held out to the manufacturer, the merchant, the workingman and all the members of that wonderfully intricate and interdependent body known as "society."

THE CONCORD OF TO-DAY.

"Such Concord is ! but who may see
A vision of the town to be?"

Concord is located in the southern central part of Merrimack County, and is bounded on the north by Webster, Boscawen, and Canterbury ; on the east by London, Chichester, and Pembroke ; on the south by Pembroke and Bow ; on the west by Dunbarton and Hopkinton.

It is the capital of the State of New Hampshire and the county-seat of Merrimack County, and is also a very important manufacturing and mercantile centre; its representative products being well and favorably known throughout the United States and in many foreign countries, while the enterprise and the advantages of position possessed by Concord merchants have made the city the purchasing centre for all the country adjacent. Many of its products are shipped to Boston for export and for domestic distribution, that city being but seventy miles distant, and the railway facilities for the transportation of freight and passengers being excellent. Concord is directly on the line of communication between the representative industrial and commercial centres of the East and the important and rapidly developing market in the great Northwest, and the remarkable prosperity of the city's manufacturing enterprises during the past five years, affords an indication of what may reasonably be expected in the near future, and has had the effect of calling the attention of capitalists and practical manufacturers to the opportunities here presented for the profitable establishment of extensive manufacturing plants. In spite of the immense amount of water power now in use in Concord, there are undeveloped privileges having sufficient capacity to supply power for the driving of machinery, the direction of which would necessitate the employment of thousands of operatives ; and it may be added that the policy of the city concerning the establishment of new industries is very liberal, and will be referred to more in detail under the head of "The Commercial and Industrial Outlook."

By the United States census of 1880, Merrimack County is given a population of 46,300, that of Concord being stated as 13,845. The valuation of the county, April 1, 1879, was $24,882,550, and the valuation of the city the same year was $10,604,465.

The census of 1890 will show a very marked increase over these figures, especially those relating particularly to Concord, for the growth of that city is very steady and permanent, as the great majority of those who take up their abode within its limits "come to stay," all the conditions being favorable to the development of an intelligent, public-spirited, and law-abiding population.

The opportunities for remunerative employment are many and varied, and the cost of living is moderate, especially when the industrial, mercantile, educational, and social advantages available are taken into consideration. Houses and tenements may be rented at reasonable rates, the most of them being in excellent condition and having pleasant, healthful, and convenient locations. During the past three years more than one hundred and seventy houses have been erected, including several palatial private residences, but the constant growth of the city creates a steady demand for desirable tenements, and those built to rent at from $8 to $14 per month are especially popular and prove a very safe and profitable investment.

The stores of the city are generally large, well lighted, finely equipped, and neat and attractive in appearance within and without, but what is of more interest to purchasers is the fact that unsurpassed advantages are offered to retail and wholesale buyers. The markets contain a full assortment of seasonable food products at all times of the year, and in the line of country produce offer inducements which very few cities can parallel, for Concord is in the midst of a region which produces an abundant supply of vegetables, fruits, grains, eggs, butter, cheese, etc., and under existing arrangements these commodities are furnished to consumers in a very fresh and appetizing condition. Wood and coal are obtainable at reasonable rates, the former coming from the surrounding country, which also supplies large quantities of hay, corn and feed in general, much of the money received for these and other products being paid out to Concord merchants for farming tools, hardware, clothing, dry goods and the many other commodities they are prepared to furnish at especially favorable rates. An extensive wholesale trade is also carried on, as the country merchants for miles around obtain the bulk of their supplies in this city.

THE STATE CAPITOL BUILDING AT CONCORD.

EDUCATIONAL FACILITIES.

Under existing conditions a good common school education is practically indispensable to success in business life, and the excellent opportunities Concord offers for obtaining such, deserve prominent mention in even a brief summary of the advantages of the city as a place of residence. It is true that many men have won distinction as inventors, as manufacturers, or as merchants, in spite of an almost total lack of early educational advantages, but they were enabled to do so by the possession of great natural ability, indomitable perseverance and the favoring conditions which prevailed before competition had raised the standard in every field of effort and materially narrowed the chances for individual success. Parents owe it to their children to see that they are equipped at all points for the struggle of life, and a good general education is of no less importance than sound health and sound morals. It is the fashion of the day to judge schools by the practical results they attain, and not by the claims they make or the magnitude of the field they essay to cover, and certainly the results attained by the Concord schools justify us in giving them a leading place among New England educational institutions. The graduates of the grammar schools have a good, sound English education, fitting them to take places in offices, stores, and factories, with minds prepared to receive knowledge relating to the special duties they have entered upon ; to reason logically, and in short to gain that practical education to which a school education is merely preparatory. The high school graduates who enter colleges, or other institutions of learning, make records and assume positions in their classes which conclusively prove that their preparatory training has been intelligent, faithful, and valuable. " By their fruits ye shall know them," and the knowledge the citizens of Concord possess of what their schools have done and are doing, compensates them for their liberal expenditure of time and money for their support.

The pioneer school of Concord was established in 1731, its support being assumed by the town in 1733. For more than thirty years it was kept in four sections of the town—East Concord, West Concord, Hopkinton road and Main street—but after 1766 a winter school was maintained at each of these places. The first school house was built in 1742, and at the beginning of the Nineteenth century there were about nine school houses in the town's possession. These were all small and rude structures, and no better method could be devised to gain an adequate idea of the enormous increase in the wealth and culture of the community since their erection, than to compare the best of them with the poorest school building Concord has to-day.

In 1807 the town was divided into sixteen school districts, and in 1818 the first visiting committee was appointed ; but the act which had by far the most beneficial effect upon local schools was the establishment of the Union School District, in 1853, for from that date the improvement in schools, school buildings and systems of instruction and supervision has been rapid and continuous. A Board of Education was appointed in 1859, nine representative citizens, elected September tenth of that year, constituting it. As the population of city increased and the questions to be considered multiplied in number and importance, the duties of the Board became too exacting to be performed satisfactorily under existing arrangements, and the result was the passage, in 1874, of an act authorizing the appointment of a Superintendent of Schools. The original incumbent was Daniel C. Allen, and he and his successors deserve a good share of the credit for the marked improvement in the efficiency of the school system which has since been brought about.

During the years 1888 and 1889 the city expended about $140,000 for new school buildings, the High, Franklin, and Kimball school houses being erected during that period. These are model structures for the purposes for which they are utilized, both in design and construction, being commodious, excellently lighted and heated, thoroughly ventilated and very conveniently arranged. Other school buildings are the Tahanto, Walker, Chandler, Rumford, and Bow Brook. The Tahanto and Walker houses have recently been thoroughly renovated and equipped with improved ventilating appliances, and it is within the bounds of truth to say that, taken as a whole, the school buildings of Concord will now compare favorably, as regards heathfulness and convenience, with those of any other New England city.

Liberal appropriations are regularly made for the support of the school system ; there is none of that overcrowding so common in most of the larger cities, but every child of suitable age is given abundant opportunity to gain a good education under favorable conditions, and is supplied with all necessary text books free of expense.

There are various private schools in the city, prominent among them being St. Mary's day and boarding school for young ladies, but by far the most important of these institutions is St. Paul's School, which, like St. Mary's, is conducted under the auspices of the Episcopal church. This is one of the best-known church classical schools in the world, for although of recent origin when compared with other famous institutions of a similar character, its management has been such as to have given it wide and honorable celebrity, and to have rendered frequent and extensive enlargement of its facilities absolutely necessary.

The school is located at Millville—a suburb of Concord—and is about two miles from the centre of the city, on the borders of a pretty little lake, in a beautiful valley with high hills on every side. The institution was founded by George Cheyne Shattuck, M. D., a wealthy resident of Boston, and the original school building was the country-seat of the founder. The school was first opened in 1856, and this building continued to be used for school purposes until its destruction by fire in 1878. It was replaced by a structure known as " The School," and pronounced by expert judges to be one of the most complete buildings of the kind to be found in the country. Long before this, however, it had become necessary to provide greatly increased accommodations, and these were furnished by the erection of the " Upper School," a handsome three-story granite building built in 1869 ; the " Lower School," in 1870 : the Rectory, in 1871 ; a large school house, in 1873, and the Infirmary or Sanitarium, in 1877. The school opened in 1856 with five pupils ; there are now nearly two hundred and fifty, and so anxious are some parents that their sons should profit by the advantages here offered, that they enter their names five and six years before they are old enough to be admitted. As the Reverend Hall Harrison has said, in writing of the institution, after eulogizing the personal characteristics and paying tribute to the efficiency of the methods pursued by those having its interests in charge :

"But after making all due allowance for these personal qualifications, which it might indeed be difficult to replace, it is quite certain that if anything like the wise judgment and unselfish labor of the past quarter of a century shall mark the administration of Dr. Coit's successors, St. Paul's,

GOVERNMENT BUILDING, CONCORD.

Concord, will more and more take a leading rank among those noted places of education which after all, are the true glory of our country, because they are the best security that we have for the cultivation of those virtues which lie at the foundation of the safety, honor, and welfare of our people."

The complete course of study covers seven years, and students are prepared to enter the freshman and sophomore classes of any American college, but many enter business life directly from this institution.

Schools and libraries are closely related, and in the Fowler Free Library Concord has an institution of which she may well feel proud, and which is destined to increase steadily in value and importance. The building was erected by William P. and Clara M. Fowler, in memory of their parents, and was dedicated in 1889. It is a handsome and substantial structure and is sufficiently commodious to provide for all probable demands upon its facilities for a long time to come. The several Shakespeare clubs of the city have a fine room allotted to them in this building.

There are a number of excellent private and semi-private libraries in Concord, the most important of them being that of the New Hampshire Historical Society, which was formed at

Portsmouth in 1823, for the purpose of discovering, procuring, and preserving matter relating to the natural, civil, literary, and ecclesiastical history of the United States in general, and the State of New Hampshire in particular. The society celebrated its semi-centennial anniversary May 22, 1873, a feature of the occasion being the dedication of its newly fitted-up building. There have been some ten volumes of valuable historical matter published by this association, whose library now comprises about 9,000 volumes, more than 12,000 pamphlets, over 100,000 newspapers, an extensive and valuable collection of manuscripts, together with many ancient and curious articles, some of which are associated with the most noted personages and decisive events in American history.

THE PRESS.

The newspaper press of Concord comprises two dailies and three weeklies ; the former being the *Concord Monitor* and the *People and Patriot;* the latter the *Independent Statesman, People and Patriot*, and *Concord Tribune.* The *Monitor* has the distinction of being the first permanent daily paper established in Concord, for although a number of efforts had previously been made in this direction all had ultimately failed. The *Monitor* made its initial appearance May 23, 1864, the publishers being Cogswell and Sturtevant. At that time the attention of the Northern people was of course concentrated upon the actions and fortunes of their soldiers in the South, and as the *Monitor* not only published full telegraphic reports but made a specialty of news concerning New Hampshire troops in the field, it made an instant and decided "hit." But the expenses of publication were heavy, and as no part of the subscribed guaranty fund of $3,000 was ever turned over to the publishers (who had contracted to print and publish the paper at a fixed compensation, without editorial responsibility), and as a large sum was owing to them, the paper and its accounts were given to them in part payment of their claim. This was in August, 1865, and Cogswell & Sturtevant continued the editorial and business management of the *Monitor* until January 2, 1867, when the *Monitor* and *Independent Democrat* offices were combined and the "Independent Press Association" formed. The "Republican Press Association" was organized October 1, 1871, and purchased the papers and the business of the Independent Association and of the *Republican Statesmen*, merging the two enterprises into one. From this time the *Monitor* has been solidly and steadily prosperous ; it has been enlarged several times, is constantly gaining in circulation, advertising patronage and influence, and is a "monitor" whose admonitions concerning municipal affairs are worthy of the most respectful consideration, and have saved tax payers many a dollar and wisely guided the expending of many more.

The *People and Patriot* was established by the Democratic Press Association in 1885, and has since very ably represented the principles of the democratic party as applied to municipal, state and national politics. Although the paper as now published is of comparatively recent origin, a full account of what may be called its pre-natal history would have to go back nearly half a century to trace its origin, for the first number of the *Daily Patriot* was issued June 2, 1841. The first prospectus for a daily paper in Concord was sent out by William P. and John M. Hill, in May, 1841, but the first number of their paper, *Hill's Daily Patriot*, did not appear until June third — one day later than the appearance of the *Daily Patriot*, which was published by Barton & Carroll. Both these papers were issued only during the sessions of the Legislature, and *Hill's Daily Patriot* suspended publication at the close of the second volume, in 1842. The publication of the *Daily Patriot* steadily continued in spite of various changes in ownership, and January 3, 1868, it began to be issued regularly throughout the year, so continuing until November 1, 1877, when it was stopped.

Charles C. Pearson & Co. had commenced the publication of a legislative paper, called the *Daily People*, in June, 1870, and it was continued until the completion of the ninth volume, in 1878. The following year Mr. Pearson began the publication of the *People and Patriot*, issuing it daily during the legislative session of 1879. December first of that year he resumed its publication, sending out six issues a week, and September 3, 1881, the enterprise was abandoned, but as before stated was revived by the Democratic Press Association in 1885. The *People and Patriot* now has a large circulation and a good amount of advertising patronage, fairly sharing honors with the *Monitor.* Both papers are ably conducted and although looking at many things from different points of view, both unquestionably have the best interests of the city, state and nation at heart. The *People and Patriot* publishes a weekly edition and one is also issued from the *Monitor* office, known as the *Independent Statesman ;* these have an especially large out-of-town circulation. Another weekly is the *Concord Tribune,* the successor of the *Weekly Blade,* which succeeded the *Concord Daily Blade,* established September 1, 1880. The *Tribune* occupies a field of its own and appeals successfully to the support of a large and important class of readers.

THE WATER SUPPLY.

The water supply of a city has so important a bearing upon its healthfulness, upon the cost of manufacturing, and upon the probable fire losses and consequently the insurance rates, that there is no other single advantage offered by Concord as a city to live and do business in, which will outweigh its magnificent water service. "Magnificent" is a pretentious word and may perhaps be legitimately objected to from a literary point of view when used in this connection, but it seems to describe, as no other word can, a service which, although not perfect, is doubtless as nearly so as that enjoyed by any New England city. Concord has expended about half a million of dollars on her water works, and the system is so arranged as to enable a heavy increase in the present consumption to be provided for at comparatively small cost.

The great fire of 1851 caused an awakening of the people to the imperative need of an additional water supply, and earnest efforts were made to provide such, but little or no progress was made, for all available money was needed in the development of private business interests, and the people objected strongly to material increase in the rate of taxation. Finally a committee was appointed to investigate the matter, and in a report dated December 16, 1859, it is stated :

"Our population is at present supplied in part from wells and in part by several aqueduct companies, the two principal of which are the 'Torrent Aqueduct Association' and that of Nathaniel White. In addition to these are several others of more limited capacities, each supplying from one or two to forty families."

The Committee examined five different sources of supply, comprising Merrimack River, Horse-shoe Pond, Ash Brook, Little Pond, and Long Pond, and very wisely gave their preference to the last on the list, summarizing its advantages and the attending conditions as follows : " Long Pond is distant three and one-half miles from the State House, has an area of two hundred and sixty-five acres, and is, in some places, seventy-five feet deep. Several small brooks enter it, but it is fed principally by springs. The land about it is of a granite formation, and rises pretty rapidly to a height of from three hundred to four hundred feet, and is mostly cleared. The Pond is surrounded by a water-shed of some 3,000 acres in extent. Its bottom is of white sand, overstrewn with granite boulders, and is free from sediment and aquatic weeds. There are no boggy meadows on its shores. Its water is soft, pure, perfectly transparent, and abundant in quantity."

Although issued thirty years and more ago, this report is a faithful description of the Long Pond, or rather the "Lake Penacook" of to-day, for no changes have occurred such as would exert a contaminating influence on the water. The outbreak of the Rebellion put aside all thoughts of expensive local improvements, and for some years after its close no decisive steps were taken concerning the water supply, but at a mass meeting of citizens held October 1, 1870, it was

" *Resolved,* that the safety, health, prosperity, and growth of our city absolutely demand a greater and better supply of water than it now has."

A committee was appointed to vigorously push the matter, and in August, 1871, they reported that they had obtained from the Legislature "An Act to authorize the city of Concord to establish water-works in said city." A Board of Water Commissioners was appointed in January, 1872, and the work of preparation and construction was very vigorously pushed. The right to draw water from the pond was bought of the owners of the water power at West Concord, for $60,000, and contracts were made with the American Gas and Water Pipe Company for the construction of the main line, distributing branches, and the furnishing and setting up of gates, hydrants, etc., at a total cost of about $144,000. The stock of the Torrent Aqueduct Association, and the water rights of Nathaniel White were bought for $20,000, and a little more than $16,000 was paid for other rights and for land damages. The contractors put a large force to work and hurried matters along so successfully that water was admitted to the pipes only eight months after the beginning of operations, or January 14, 1873.

Although done hurriedly, the work was done very thoroughly and has given excellent satisfaction from the first. In fact its very perfection soon made an extension of the delivery facilities imperative, for as the knowledge of the convenience and reliability of the service became more general, there was a constantly growing demand for water and the consumption reached a point where the fourteen inch main was unable to supply an adequate amount to the higher portions of the territory covered. The result was the laying of a second main, eighteen inches in diameter ; the work being completed in the summer of 1882, the total construction account being thus brought up to $492,000.

CONCORD FROM STATE HOUSE CUPOLA, LOOKING SOUTH.

Improvements have been made from time to time as circumstances required, and nearly every dwelling in the city is now supplied with an abundance of pure water, it having a good "head" in the pipes, as Penacook Lake is one hundred and twenty feet above Main street in front of the State House.

THE FIRE AND POLICE DEPARTMENTS.

A city having such a water service should have a fire department to correspond, and certainly Concord pursues a consistent policy in the matter, her fire department being as efficient as any in the State. Its mechanical equipment is generally modern in style and is handled by some two hundred trained firemen, who know their business and are commendably prompt and fearless in the discharge of their duty. On many occasions they have shown their ability to cope with all ordinary conflagrations, and although, in the light of recent experiences at Lynn and Boston, it would be presumptuous to claim that a disastrous fire in Concord is impossible, still it should be remembered that the character of local buildings and their contents, and the absence of the narrow streets, high walls and other conditions unfavorable to fire-fighting, which greatly aided to increase the loss at the cities named, all tend to justify the confidence which manufacturers, merchants, insurance companies and the citizens general repose in the Concord fire department.

At the Central station there are two second-class Amoskeag steamers and two first-class Amoskeag hose carriages ; all these pieces of apparatus being drawn by horses, of which six are always immediately available. There is also a hook and ladder wagon, manned by twenty men. At the north end is the "Alert Hose," and at the south end the "Good Will Hose," the former company using a modern department wagon and the latter a four-wheel Amoskeag carriage. Each house is equipped with a swinging harness, and horses are constantly in readiness in adjoining stables.

In Penacook there is a fourth-class Silsby steamer and a second-class Amoskeag hose carriage ; horses are available, but the steamer may be drawn by hand should circumstances require. At East Concord, is the "Old Fort" hand engine and hose company, and in West Concord is a similar organiaztion known as the "Cataract" Company. The electric fire-alarm service is wide spread and reliable, and a large number of hydrants are distributed throughout the city.

NEW HAMPSHIRE STATE'S PRISON AT CONCORD.

Concord's Police Department is worthy to be classed with the Fire Department, for although happily there is no occasion for it being maintained on anything like so large a scale, still it is amply sufficient to meet all demands upon it, and for a city of its population and amount of territory to be covered, Concord is remarkably free from disorder and from crimes against persons and property. The efficiency of any police force depends in a great measure upon the public sentiment behind it, and as the citizens of Concord, as a whole, are firm believers in the principle "Order is heaven's first law," they will not tolerate disorder, and are ready to lend financial and, if necessary, physical aid to the police in their efforts to repress it. It is this consciousness of popular support that makes Concord's policemen courteous in their dealings with the public, but prompt and fearless in preserving order when force is necessary ; while on the other hand those who have a disposition to break the law are in many cases restrained by the conviction that they are in a hopeless minority, and by the knowledge that the police have only to ask aid in order to get it instantly. A new Police Station of brick and stone is now in course of erection at an expense of about $20,000.

HOTELS.

Being the State Capital, as well as an important mercantile and manufacturing city, it is natural that the hotel accommodations of Concord should be at times heavily drawn upon, and should be superior to those available in almost all other cities of no greater population. Among the local hotels are the American House, Elm House, Commercial House, and the hotel of the Eagle and Phenix Hotel Co. The last named house is located opposite the State House yard, and is a very commodious and finely equipped structure, it having been rebuilt and newly furnished in 1890 at a cost of more than $35,000. It has one hundred and forty rooms, is supplied with elevators, electrical appliances and other conveniences, and is a worthy representative of Concord hospitality. All the hotels are well managed, and as a whole cater successfully to all classes of trade ; so it is not claiming too much to say that they have done their full share towards building up the favorable sentiment with which the city is regarded elsewhere.

CHURCH, BENEVOLENT, AND FRATERNAL SOCIETIES.

Although the temporal needs of Concord's residents are excellently provided for, their spiritual needs have by no means been neglected, for the city and suburbs contain many church societies, representing all the leading denominations and worshipping in edifices which, with scarcely an exception, are commodious and beautiful, while many have large and convenient chapels connected. Among societies in the city proper are the First and South Congregational ; the First Methodist Episcopal, and the Baker Memorial Methodist Episcopal ; the First Baptist, Pleasant street Baptist, and Free-Will Baptist ; the Universalist ; the Unitarian ; the Episcopal ; the Advent ; and St. John's, Roman Catholic. In East Concord there are the Congregational Church and the Episcopal Mission ; in West Concord, the Congregational Church ; and in Penacook, the Baptist Church, St. John's Catholic Church, and the Episcopal Chapel. There are many regular church-goers among Concord's population, and as strangers are cordially welcomed, there is usually a good attendance at divine service.

There are many fraternal and benevolent societies in the city, and the good-natured rivalry which exists between some of them is distinctly beneficial in its effects, as it is never carried to excess, and does much to stimulate interest in and to increase the membership of organizations which depend upon such increase for the means to carry out their helpful aims.

The Odd Fellows have a very large membership here, and in 1890 dedicated a handsome and commodious building erected at a cost of about $38,000. The Masonic orders also have beautiful rooms, and are in a most flourishing condition, while the Grand Army of the Republic is very strong and influential here, as would naturally be imagined by those familiar with Concord's record during the Rebellion. E. E. Sturtevant Post, No. 2, has its headquarters in the city proper ; William I. Brown Post, No. 31, at Penacook, and Davis Post, No. 44, at West Concord.

The Knights of Honor, Knights of Pythias, Ancient Order of United Workmen, Ancient Order of Hibernians, and other prominent secret societies, are all well represented.

The temperance movement has received no little aid from local organizations, for Concord has numbered many enthusiastic advocates of temperance among its residents from a very early period in its history, and the home societies now number about a dozen, and are very alert and efficient.

Among those organizations whose membership is limited to professional men, may be mentioned the New Hampshire Medical Society, the New Hampshire Homœopathic Medical Society, the Centre District Medical Society, the New Hampshire Dental Society, and the New Hampshire Pharmaceutical Association.

There is a Young Men's Christian Association in Concord and another at Penacook.

The oldest benevolent society in the city is the Concord Female Charitable Society, established in 1812. The Concord Female Benevolent Association was organized in 1835, and in 1852 the Rolfe and Rumford Asylum for destitute native female children of Concord was founded by the Countess of Rumford, it being opened for the reception of inmates in January, 1880. There is an Orphan's Home near Millville, and the Odd Fellows Home is situated upon the street leading to that beautiful suburb. The New Hampshire Centennial Home for the aged, is another institution which is accomplishing great good in its chosen field, and its location is on Pleasant street, opposite the grounds of the New Hampshire Asylum.

There are several Mutual Relief Associations in the city, and there is also the French Canadian Society, St. Patrick's Benevolent Society, and other helpful organizations, so that no person, whatever his nativity or creed may be, need lack sympathetic help when circumstances render aid of some kind essential.

PUBLIC BUILDINGS.

Among Concord's more prominent public buildings, the first which should be mentioned is, of course, the State House, which was first occupied by the Legislature at the June session in 1819, although the building was not entirely completed. Many improvements have been made in it since that date, and about a quarter of a century ago it was enlarged at an expense of nearly $200,000, the total cost of the work being paid by the city. The structure is massive and handsome in design and stands in the midst of spacious grounds containing many beautiful shade trees. It is built of the famous "Concord" granite, the stone being obtained from the quarries a little more than a mile distant, on the line of the Concord Electric Railway.

CONCORD FROM STATE HOUSE CUPOLA, LOOKING NORTHEAST.

The New Hampshire Asylum for the Insane was opened for the reception of patients in the latter part of 1842, and during the first seven months seventy-six patients were admitted, the original structure being capable of accommodating only ninety-six. New buildings have been added and old ones enlarged and improved, until now more than three hundred and fifty patients can be cared for without the least crowding. The institution is located in the heart of the city, the grounds having an area of about one hundred and twenty-five acres and being very highly improved. Special care is taken to make the surroundings and conditions as homelike as possible, and this has long ranked high among the model insane asylums of this country. From 1857 to 1883 it was in charge of Dr. Jesse P. Bancroft, and on his resignation the duties of superintendent were taken up by his son, Dr. Charles P. Bancroft, who has met with gratifying success in maintaining the high standing of the institution.

There has been a City Hospital in Concord since October, 1884, and the facilities offered have been of great public benefit, although the location and arrangement of the premises utilized have interfered somewhat with the efficiency of the service. This condition of affairs, however, will soon be a thing of the past, for, thanks to the generosity of George A. Pillsbury and his wife, Margaret, Concord will speedily possess a hospital building worthy of being classed with the best of her other public edifices. Mr. Pillsbury is a member of the great milling firm so famous throughout the country, and is a resident of Minneapolis, of which city he has been mayor. But he has also been mayor of Concord, and he has not allowed his later honors to banish the deep interest he has always shown in our city's welfare, a recent proof of this interest being the giving of $30,000 for the erection of a city hospital.

The United States Court House and Post Office building was completed in 1888 at a cost of $300,000, and is a very handsome and commodious structure, occupying a most eligible site and being very conveniently arranged for the accommodation of the post office, United States courts, pension agency, etc. The mail facilities of the city are excellent, the service being frequent, prompt and reliable. A very large amount of all classes of mail matter is handled monthly, and the reliability and general efficiency of the carrier service are of great benefit to the community in general and especially to manufacturers and other business men.

The Board of Trade Building was completed in 1873, and is now as ever an ornament to the city and a monument to the energy, enterprise and foresight of those who provided the money for its

CHASE'S BLOCK, NORTH MAIN STREET.

erection. Although the board of trade, as an organized body, did not erect the building, nearly all the subscribers to the stock were members of the board, and the completion of the structure was celebrated by a social festival, held October 20, 1873, under the auspices of that organization.

White's Opera House is a very popular resort among those seeking diversion in the mimic life of the stage, for many prominent dramatic and musical "combinations" appear here during the season. The house is conveniently appointed and has seating capacity for nearly one thousand.

There are other public halls, convenient in location and arrangement, among them being Grand Army Hall, Phoenix Hall and Chase's Hall.

CONVENIENCES.

The city is lighted by both gas and electricity, both being furnished by the Concord Gas Light Company, which was incorporated in 1854 and has a capital of $125,000. Some twenty miles of main pipe have been laid and gas is furnished to from 1,200 to 1,500 consumers; several hundred street lamps also being supplied. Electricity is also used for both exterior and interior illumination, and the stores along the principal streets present a brilliant appearance after night fall, as nearly all of them have great plate-glass show windows, and certainly the goods displayed in them do not suffer from lack of abundant light.

Another and most important application of electricity here has to do with the running of street cars, for what was the Concord "Horse" Railroad can claim that title no longer, the cars now being run by the Thompson-Houston system of electrical appliances—a system which has satisfactorily solved the famous "horse-car problem" in Boston, where it has been adopted by the only street railway company and applied to hundreds of cars. The system is even more satisfactory in Concord, where the streets are less crowded and the danger of accident greatly lessened, and as "rapid transit" is now an accomplished fact, the outlying districts on the company's line may be expected to increase in population and wealth more rapidly than ever. This road began running in April, 1881, and has considerably more than doubled its rolling stock since that time. The line runs from South Main street, or the "South End," through West Concord to Penacook.

DRAINAGE.

Many and important as are the hygienic advantages arising from an abundant supply of pure water, they are robbed of much of their effect unless reinforced by a comprehensive and efficient system of drainage, and the location of Concord together with the character of the soil is distinctly favorable to the easy and wholesome disposition of waste.

A large amount has been judiciously expended upon sewers and drains, and the present condition of the sewerage system is good, the drainage of the city being very efficiently accomplished; but further facilities have been rendered necessary by the growth of the community, and as the citizens realize that it is most economical to spend money freely in such a cause as this, and to provide for the future as well as the present, the city government will undoubtedly provide seasonably for the extension and general improvement of the sewerage system as may be required.

The streets of the city are as a rule, broad, well arranged, and well kept, notably Main street, in which the citizens are fully justified in taking pride, for it is the unanimous verdict of strangers, as well as residents, that this is without exception the finest business street in New England. It was laid out in 1785, and those who defined its limits must have had some conception of the probable growth of the community, for the street is of very generous width, even in the heart of the city, and can accommodate an enormous amount of traffic without crowding. It is paved, concreted or macadamized from end to end and is bordered by an abundance of shade trees, some of them being elms of magnificent proportions.

Concord's sidewalks are on a par with her streets, for they are of exceptionally fine quality, nearly all being concreted, as the city is the home of this industry. It is everywhere admitted that a first-class concrete walk is far superior to one made of any other material, and the concrete work employed in this city is equal to the best noticeable anywhere. The roads about Concord are maintained in generally excellent condition, and help materially to make the many picturesque drives thoroughly enjoyable. The country adjacent contains many attractive bits of scenery, and some of the views are justly entitled to rank among the most pleasant prospects in New England. The towns of Dunbarton, Hopkinton, Bow, Pembroke, and others that might be named, are within easy drive, and each has a reputation for natural beauty which is added to by the comments of every fresh visitor.

THE BANKING FACILITIES.

The magnitude and character of the banking facilities enjoyed by a community form a convenient standard by which its position as a mercantile and manufacturing centre may be determined, and as a general rule an intelligent judgment made on such a basis is extremely accurate, for although in exceptional cases the banks are unworthy of the community, or the community is unworthy of the banks, still these exceptions but "prove the rule," for on close investigation it will be found that they result from forced and unnatural conditions. The banks as truly represent the business methods and the mercantile standing of the people on whom they depend for patronage, as do the newspapers their intellectual and moral standing, and a people who support first-class financial institutions may, as a whole, invariably be depended upon to do business on sound principles and to be enterprising and intelligent in developing natural resources. Hence the high standing of Concord's banks, although gratifying and commendable, is the necessary consequence of the conditions which gave them birth and which have attended their development to the present time.

It is nearly eighty-five years since the first banking institution in this city was incorporated, and of course that was long before a city charter was ever thought of, for it was in 1806—only twenty-two years after Concord had changed from a "parish" to a full fledged "town." But, although only a town, it had its conflicting interests as truly as the largest city has, and in spite of the well-earned reputation for "concord" of action which had given it its name, its residents showed that they could oppose one another as vigorously and stubbornly as they, united, had fought the Bow proprietors.

MAIN STREET, CONCORD, LOOKING NORTH.

There was a "North End" interest and there was a "South End" interest, and after Timothy Walker, William A. Kent, and others, were incorporated "by the name of the President, Directors and Company of the Concord Bank," trouble at once arose in consequence of questions of location and management.

Hon. Timothy Walker was the champion of the "Northenders," and Colonel William A. Kent of the "Southenders;" and as no agreement could be arrived at, each side claiming that its position was clearly the just one, the upshot of the matter was the opening of two banks under the same charter, the Upper Bank and the Lower Bank, each of which claimed to be the "only and original Simon-pure Concord Bank, and denounced the other as a "base and fraudulent imitation."

The consequence of their not being able to even "agree to disagree" was ceaseless trouble and constant loss to both, for the competition was keen and incessant, and neither institution was very delicate in its choice of methods to overcome the other. At one time the Upper Bank forced a run upon the Lower, by demanding the redemption in specie of a large number of their bills, of which the former institution had secured possession. The Lower Bank kept the ball rolling by instituting suits against its rival for issuing bills without legal warrant, the result of this action being a long drawn out legal battle to decide which was the lawful Concord Bank. The lawyers profited by the contention if nobody else did, and among those who got a fee out of it was the early and famous legal antagonist of Daniel Webster, Jeremiah Mason. He was retained as cousel for Nehemiah Jones, who had brought suit against Timothy Walker, the indictment in the case containing more than one-hundred counts, being a sort of "drag-net" affair, covering all the points in dispute and designed to surely catch Walker in some of its many ingeniously contrived meshes. So able a lawyer as Mason at once perceived the hopelessness of settling the matter in Court and endeavored to effect a compromise. Those at all familiar with his career know that he did not mince his words when circumstances made plain-speaking advisable, and hence will readily accept the tradition which credits him with saying, when his client objected to the expense of the proposed settlement : " As you have got into gentlemen's company, you must expect to pay a gentleman's price."

After the banks ceased persecuting one another, they naturally rose in the esteem and confidence of the public, and both did a generally profitable business under the one charter until twenty years had expired, when the Upper Bank secured a new charter under the name of the " Merrimack County Bank." The Lower Bank had its charter altered and extended in 1826, and continued business until its failure in 1840.

Such a demoralizing and foolish conflict as that between these two banks would be impossible in the Concord of to-day, for although the interests involved are now vastly greater, and the prize so much the more worth the winning, our financiers, as well as our merchants and manufacturers, rigidly discriminate between competition and opposition, and recognize the fact that mutual aid confined to legitimate limits is the best policy to be followed by all parties concerned.

At the present time there are three National and four Savings Banks in Concord, all of which are in a sound and prosperous condition, while some among them are exceptionally strong, even in comparison with other leading financial institutions throughout the country.

As would be supposed from its name, the First National Bank was the pioneer Concord institution organized under the national banking laws, although the other two National banks in the city had been carried on under State charters for many years before the organization of the First National Bank in March, 1864. Asa Fowler was the first president, he being succeeded in 1867 by George A. Pillsbury, who resigned in 1878 and went West, where he was destined to win fame and fortune as a member of the great milling firm, now known throughout this country and England. He has had worthy successors in the office of president of the bank, and as the directors have also always been men of ability, it is easy to account for the exceptional prosperity the institution has enjoyed from the start. It has a capital of $150,000 and an extremely large surplus—so exceptionally large in fact that the bank has been reported by the comptroller of the currency to have the highest per cent. surplus of any New Hampshire bank.

The National State Capital Bank was not long behind the First National in beginning operations under a national charter, for it was re-organized under national banking laws, January 2, 1865, or only about ten months after the other institution. Its origin as a State bank dates back to 1853, the State Capital Bank having been organized January 26th of that year. The original capital stock was $100,000, and this amount was increased one-half in 1854, reduced to $120,000 in 1862, and a year later reduced to $100,000.

FIRST NATIONAL BANK.

After the obtaining of a national charter the capital stock remained at $100,000 only a little more than three months, it being increased to $150,000 April 17, 1865. A further increase to $200,000 was made May 31, 1872 ; the bonds and right of circulation of Carroll County National Bank, of Sandwich, having been purchased. The National State Capital Bank is worthy of its name and stands high in the financial and general business world, by reason of the wise conservatism of its management and the efficiency of its service.

LOAN AND TRUST SAVINGS BANK BUILDING.

The Mechanicks' National Bank was organized January 3, 1880, but from one point of view may be considered the oldest established bank of discount and deposit in the city, for as the Mechanicks' Bank it was first incorporated July 5, 1834. The original capital was $100,000, and the charter was extended June 22, 1853 ; the bank closing up its affairs in 1865. At the time business was stopped, Josiah Minot acted as president and Charles Minot as cashier, so that when these gentlemen began operations as a private banking firm under the style of Minot & Co., in January, 1866, it was in one sense a revival of the "Mechanicks'" business, and it steadily continued until its re-organization as the Mechanicks' National Bank in 1880. Josiah Minot was the first president of the new institution, and was associated on the Board of Directors with John Kimball, John M. Hill, B. A. Kimball, Joseph

B. Walker and other representative citizens. **This bank has a capital of $150,000, is very strong** financially and enjoys a goodly share of **the** patronage and the confidence of resident business men.

It is asserted by not a few eminent students of public affairs, that the number, importance, and condition of the Savings Banks in any given section of the country afford an accurate barometer of the state of industry and trade, besides giving valuable hints relating to the personal habits of members of the community, and the residents of Concord have certainly no reason to shrink from the application of such a test; for were not their industries and mercantile enterprises generally prosperous, and the community as a whole industrious, thrifty, and profitably employed, the local savings banks could never have reached their present development, and would not be able to safely challenge comparison with a like number of similar institutions anywhere, catering to no greater population.

Of the four Concord savings banks the New Hampshire Savings Bank is by far the oldest, it having been incorporated away back in 1830. The institution was organized July 21st, of that year, and during its sixty years of existence has paid its depositors more than one million and a half of dollars in regular dividends, and about $200,000 in extra dividends; the rate of interest thus far having averaged about four and a half per cent.—a very remarkable showing considering the pains the management have always taken to ensure the absolute safety of funds placed with them for investment.

BOARD OF TRADE BUILDING, NORTH MAIN STREET.

The Merrimack County Savings Bank was incorporated 1867, but was not organized until May 3, 1870, the first deposit being made June first. Lyman D. Stevens has been president of this bank from the beginning, and John Kimball has been treasurer for a like period. The record of this institution during the past five years goes far to establish the claim that savings banks accurately indicate the degree of prosperity a community is enjoying, for it is an open secret that Concord's representative industries have prospered remarkably since 1885, and during that time the deposits in and surplus of the Merrimack County Savings Bank have more that doubled, the amount now due depositors considerably exceeding a million and a half of dollars, and the surplus approximating $120,000.

The Loan and Trust Savings Bank was incorporated in June, 1872, and has proved a valuable addition to the savings institutions of the city and the State. The amount due depositors has increased to the extent of more than $700,000 during the last five years, and at present approximates two and a quarter millions of dollars. The guarantee fund amounts to $100,000 and the undivided profits considerably exceed that sum.

The Union Guaranty Savings Bank is by far the youngest institution of the kind in the city, it having been incorporated in 1887, but it is already firmly established in the confidence of the community, as it is managed in connection with one of the strongest of New England's financial institutions by men of ability and ripe experience. It has a perpetual guarantee fund of $50,000, has already accumulated a surplus of about one-fifth that amount, and now holds deposits amounting to about half a million dollars.

The facilities afforded by the National and the Savings banks of the city are supplemented by the admirable service offered by such representative financial houses as those of Crippen, Lawrence & Co., E. H. Rollins & Son, the American Trust Company and others, so that as regards opportunities for investment and the many other advantages arising from a comprehensive and ably conducted banking service, Concord stands high among New England cities.

NEW HAMPSHIRE ASYLUM FOR INSANE, CONCORD.

THE GRANITE BUSINESS.

A consideration of Concord's natural advantages must of necessity include the many valuable granite quarries there located, for these have long been a very important source of wealth, and yield stone of a quality which has made Concord granite the standard by which that from other localities is judged.

The local supply is almost inexhaustible, the large eminence known as Rattlesnake Hill being composed almost entirely of granite, while Oak Hill merits a similar description. A large amount of capital and many men are employed in the quarrying and working of the stone, and the most improved appliances and tools have been universally adopted, reducing the expenses of production to a minimum and enabling outside competition to be easily met. The exceptionally comprehensive United States census of 1880 included a close investigation by experts of the existing condition and future prospects of the quarrying industry, and the results arrived at concerning Concord granite are in the highest degree favorable, as will be seen from the necessarily limited quotations from the reports of the government agents which follow.

From a scientific point of view, the sort of stone found in this vicinity is a "massive, gray, biotite—muscovite granite." In spite of this formidable description we are told that "it is a good, safe, free stone to work and takes a high polish."

For commercial purposes it is divided into four classes :   No. 1, the best, for monumental work ; No. 2, for general building purposes ; No. 3, for underpinning, capping, etc.; No. 4, for foundation stones.

The Census Commissioners went very deeply into the subject of the durability of granite, and the several varieties were closely tested and compared.   Granite buildings and monuments throughout the country were minutely examined, and from the report made on those located in the City of New York we take the following:

"In the fine-grained granite from Concord, N. H., employed in the building on the southeast corner of 23d street and 6th avenue, many of the blocks are set on edge, but the only change yet seen is that of discoloration by street dust and iron-oxide from the elevated railway."

MAIN STREET, LOOKING SOUTH FROM OPERA HOUSE.

A complete list of the granite structures throughout the country is given, and a notable proportion of these are built of the Concord stone, among such being the Charter Oak Insurance Building, Hartford, Ct.; many New York structures, and numerous Boston edifices, as for instance the Security Bank, the Masonic Temple, the *Herald* building, the Life Insurance Building, the Germania Savings Bank, the City Hall, Horticultural Hall and others.   The monument to the discoverer of anæsthetics in the Boston Public Garden, is also of Concord granite, as is the Soldiers' Monument at Concord, Mass., the Cadet Monument in Mt. Auburn Cemetery, Cambridge, and the Soldiers' Monument in Manchester, N. H.

Of late years granite has become exceedingly popular as a monumental stone, and nearly all first-class cemetery work is now made from this material, a use to which the better grades of Concord granite is particularly adapted.   The demand for it as a building stone is also increasing as the country gains in wealth and culture, and the importance of the question of the permanence of this demand justifies the giving of space for the answer as it is stated by the distinguished scientist, Prof. N. S. Shaler, in the Census Reports of 1880.   The report is headed : "General Relations of New England Building Stones to the Markets of the United States," and, after stating in detail the important advantages possessed by New England quarries by reason of their nearness to tide-water and the effect of the glacial action, which stripped off the cap of decayed rock found encumbering deposits of crystalline rocks in other sections of the country, the report reads as follows :

"These two advantages — the neighborhood of, the crystalline rocks to the sea, and the absence of any worthless, decayed, upper part — will always give the New England rocks of the granitic group a very great advantage over those of any other part of the eastern United States. . . . It should also be noticed that the cost of quarrying granite of good quality is perhaps less than that of any other work of the same general utility, certainly much less than the cost of our other principal building stones, so that, for all large structures where rude strength is the only need, quarries of this stone are always likely to be at a great advantage in production. . . . There are no other sources of supply of granite that are ever likely to compete with this stone district of New England."

Prof. Shaler sums up the whole matter as follows :

"It is quite clear, therefore, that the position of the New England granite quarries is particularly favorable, and that they are likely to command the market for a great while in the future."

MAIN STREET, CONCORD, AT THE NORTH END.

MANUFACTURING INTERESTS.

Most prominent cities, like most prominent men, are many-sided in character — that is to say they are dependent upon no one feature for the maintenance of their importance, as that is the result of a harmonious combination of characteristics, all of which contribute to the sum total and afford a common but striking example of one of our main principles of government, "in union is strength."

Concord, for instance, is best known to some as the capital of the State ; to others, as a great purchasing centre where supplies may be bought to the best possible advantage, and to still others as the source from which come various manufactured articles, proved by practical test to be the best in the market. It is in the last-named capacity—as a leading manufacturing centre—that the city is best known outside the limits of New Hampshire, and it is a noteworthy fact of which every public-spirited citizen may well be proud, that the representative products of Concord owe their popularity to their quality rather than to their "cheapness ;" for it has long been, and is to-day, the policy of prominent local manufacturers to cater to the most intelligent trade, and, while giving unsurpassed value for the money received, to have that value represented by quality, not by quantity. Name a few of our leading products, and see what associations are connected with the list : "Concord Coaches," "Concord Axles," "Concord Harness,"—what is it that has made these goods well and favorably known throughout the civilized world ? Not cheapness, but uniform and unequalled excellence. The makers of them have the experience, the ability, the capital, the mechanical facilities and the skilled assistants necessary to enable them to attain the best possible results, and to easily meet all honorable competition ; that they accomplish both these ends, the reputation of and the demand for their products abundantly prove.

The immense business now carried on by the Abbott-Downing Company was founded many years ago, and would have developed even more rapidly than it did had not the founder refused to turn out more work than he could personally supervise the construction of. Nowadays, when the magnitude and variety of the interests involved make it absolutely necessary to entrust the carrying out of details to subordinates, such a policy as that may seem provincial and old-fashioned, but it indicates a sturdy honesty worthy of emulation in any age, and goes far to explain the world-wide fame of the "Concord Coach,"—a fame as well deserved now as ever. The present company utilize a most elaborate plant and employ an extensive force of help in the manufacture of light and heavy vehicles ; the goods being shipped to all parts of the world.

The "Concord Axle Company" was incorporated in 1880, with a capital of $50,000, to manufacture the original "Concord Axle," and kindred articles. Those having the direction of the company's affairs have been identified with the production of the goods in question since 1863, and we need hardly add that the reputation of the "Concord Axle" has been fully maintained. The factory is located in Penacook, and about seven hundred tons of wagon axles are turned out in the course of a year, besides three hundred tons of castings, and other articles.

It is fitting that a city producing first-class coaches, wagons and carriages, should also produce first-class harness, and the fame of the "Concord Harness" is on a par with that of the Concord Coaches and Axles. This harness is now made by the James R. Hill Harness Company, and is known and prized throughout the civilized world. Far from depending on past reputation, the present company spare no pains to keep the quality of the product fully up to the standard, while offering many new and attractive styles, and the result is to be seen in the steadily growing demand for the goods in this country and abroad. James R. Hill, the founder of this business, was a man of great force of character and distinguished ability, and literally "worked his way up" until he reached a leading position among New England manufacturers. The first shipment of harness to California from the east was made by Mr. Hill in 1849, and his enterprise in seeking out foreign markets, even at that early day, is shown by his having made a shipment to Chili in 1853. He had many things to contend with during his early business career, and met with serious loss by fire, but he had that ability and perseverance which command success, and as his capital increased he became interested in various enterprises which had such claims upon his attention that he found it inexpedient to retain sole control of his harness business, and hence in 1865 the firm of James R. Hill & Co. was formed, and the enterprise continued under that management until the organization of the present company.

A representative Concord industry, which, although of quite recent origin when compared with that carried on by the James R. Hill Harness Company, has still some eighteen years of prosperity to look back upon, is that conducted by the Page Belting Company, incorporated in 1872. This business was originally located in Franklin, where it was established by Page Brothers in 1868, and since its removal to Concord it has developed with a steadiness and rapidity which indicate that the claims made for this city as a most advantageous point at which to establish important manufacturing enterprises, are fully justified by the facts.

When the company began operations here in 1872, it had a paid-in capital of $75,000. In 1873 it was increased to $125,000 ; in 1878 to $200,000 ; and in 1887 to $250,000 — figures which tell their own story of the skillful utilization of favorable conditions. The company is authorized to have a capital of half a million, and present indications are that that amount will be reached before many years, as the demand for the product is apparently unlimited ; customers being found throughout the United States, and an extensive export business being done. Leather belting and lacing are the chief productions, an exceptionally complete line being manufactured. The plant covers an area of some ten acres, and has sufficient capacity to turn out 750 hides for belting and 1,200 sides of lace leather per week, employment being given to about 175 men.

There are various other prominent manufacturing enterprises which deserve careful consideration, but which, owing to the limitation of space, must be dismissed with mere mention. Among these are those conducted by the Holden Manufacturing Company, producing flannels and woolen dress goods ; the Haley Manufacturing Company, making curtain fixtures, skates and other articles ; the Concord Carriage Company, producing vehicles of standard excellence ; W. S. Davis & Son, manufacturers of wagons, hose trucks and carriages ; the New England Granite Company, doing stone-work for monumental and building purposes ; C. M. & A. W. Rolfe, makers of doors, sash, blinds, etc.; the Prescott Organ Company, producing instruments having a national reputation ; Ford & Kimball and Clapp & Co., brass and iron founders; the Concord Manufacturing Company, located at West Concord, and very extensively engaged in the production of all-wool flannels and heavy twilled goods ; William B. Durgin, manufacturer of solid silverware ; the Contoocook Manufacturing and Mechanic Company, located at Penacook, and producing an immense amount of print cloths ; the Penacook Mill, carrying on the same business on a still more extensive scale ; Stratton, Merrill & Co., located at Penacook, and operating the only Patent Roller Process flour mill in New England ; and C. H. Amsden & Co., also of Penacook, and proprietor of the largest furniture factory in New England, they using about a quarter of a million feet of lumber per month.

The above list is by no means complete, and yet it gives some idea of the variety, magnitude and standing of Concord's industries, and their distribution throughout the city and suburbs.

The Concord & Montreal and Northern Railroads both have well-equipped shops here, at which a great deal of repairing and constructing is done.

THE COMMERCIAL AND INDUSTRIAL OUTLOOK.

The outlook for the various industries located within the city limits is at this time most encouraging. For many years the establishments producing the world-famed Concord carriages and coaches, and the equally well known Concord harnesses, have given employment to many men. These concerns have deservedly won strong positions in the business world, and they have gradually grown from small beginnings into large and prosperous enterprises, yielding good profits to their owners, and continuous and remunerative employment to their very large numbers of employees. And what may be thus said of these two representative establishments, may with equal justice be applied to nearly, if not quite, all the manufactories within the borders of the city, including the most varied industries. Although not distinctively a manufacturing city, it produces very considerable quantities of flannels, cotton and woolen goods, furniture, carriages, leather belting, axles, pianos and organs, hubs and wheels, shoes, fire hose, brick, hammered and polished granite, wood-working machinery, churns, silverware, lumber, and other standard products.

During the past five years there has been a decided and noticeable increase in the volume of business, and many of the articles produced by the skilled workmen of Concord, find a ready and extensive sale throughout the United States and in many foreign countries. This is especially so of the goods produced by the Concord Axle Co., the Abbot-Downing Co., the James R. Hill Co., and the Page Belting Co., which are known all over the world.

The railroad facilities are such as to offer great advantages to Concord as a business and manufacturing center, as it is directly on the line of travel between the great Northwest and the commercial and manufacturing centres of the East, and only two hours ride from Boston. The expenses of living are moderate, rents are very reasonable for the accommodations afforded, and the mechanic, the artisan and the day laborer secure all the advantages of the larger cities, with but few of the drawbacks.

The policy of the city is very favorable to new industries, and toward a reasonable exemption from taxation for a term of years, for such enterprises as desire location and would give to the commercial and manufacturing forces of the city such additions as to make them desirable acquisitions.

There are still remaining in Concord undeveloped water privileges that are capable of supplying power for the employment of thousands of workmen when they shall be utilized by the erection of the proper manufacturing plants. But one by one the various mill-sites have been occupied on the Contoocook river, in that part of Concord known as Penacook, and the recent erection of the massive stone dam for the use of the woolen mill, now in process of construction in that village, reduces the

available sites there remaining so as naturally to turn attention to the Merrimack river.   Here
there are two most excellent water powers, the one at Garvin's Falls being partially developed while
that at Sewall's Falls will probably be developed at an early day.   The Sewall's Falls water power,
with its adjacent land, is situated only about four miles from the center of the city, and entirely
within the city limits.   It is capable of development so as to readily sustain a population of from
fifteen to twenty thousand.   Contiguous to the Falls there is a large area of land owned by the Water
Power Company, favorably situated for the erection of manufacturing establishments, and having equally favorable location for building the residences and houses of the hundreds finding employment within the establishments erected to utilize the power of the falls.   The land has already been
surveyed and is ready to be staked out for a village which will be one of the most delightfully

NEW DAM ON THE CONTOOCOCK RIVER AT PENACOOK.

situated and healthful in New England.   It will have all the advantages of cheap homes, cheap power,
excellent drainage, and the innumerable advantages which result from such an admirable location.
Not only can the power at Sewall's Falls be used for the neighboring manufactories, but the recent
discoveries in the transmission of power by electricity will make it possible to furnish power at a very
low rate in the central part of the city.   The possible advantages of the unused power at Sewall's
Falls can scarcely be overestimated, and at no distant day this power is to be utilized, and when
employed it will bring increase in population, in manufacturing, and in commerce, with all the
advantages that result from the regular distribution of large sums of money in compensation for
productive labor.

The preparation of this brief statement of facts bearing upon Concord's past, present and future, has been no easy task, for its very brevity added much to the difficulty of the work by necessitating careful selection and close condensation of the immense amount of material available. That the sketch as it now stands will give universal satisfaction is not for a moment to be expected, and indeed no one can appreciate more clearly than the writer that it falls far short of perfection and would have been more ably done had its preparation been entrusted to abler hands. But be did his best, and asks credit for honesty of intention, whatever may have been his errors of judgment.

This book is assured a very large circulation. It will be read even more generally outside the city than it will be in it, and in this hurrying age the systematic condensation which has been practiced in its compilation materially adds to its value by ensuring a much more thorough and general reading than it would otherwise have received. Primarily intended for business men, it is written from a business point of view, and contains much valuable information concerning one of the most enterprising cities in New England. The information is valuable, however faulty may be its presentation, and not only those living in other sections of the country but many residents of Concord may profit by a perusal of the story of New Hampshire's capital.

Men are prone to close their eyes to opportunities near at hand, and there is not a city in New England but what has suffered from this fact. We New Englanders build up the West, the South and the Northwest; we spend money like water to develop the resources of other sections; we take desperate risks in constructing railroads over and through mountain ranges, across miles of uninhabited prairie and over broad rivers, that the productions of some far-off city or town may find a market; we sink shafts thousands of feet through the solid rock on the bare chance of extracting paying quantities of precious metals; in short, in a hundred ways we maintain our world-wide reputation for magnificent enterprise and business audacity, and meantime we neglect dear old New England, that kind and lavish, if stern-appearing, old mother who gave us birth, who cherishes our friends and our homes, and who gives us the enormous sums we so freely spend elsewhere.

This should not be. "Boom New England," is a good motto if a new one, and its sound sense is lately being appreciated by many of those heavy investors who have enriched other sections without profit and often at a serious loss to themselves. The future of New Hampshire in general, and of Concord in particular, never looked brighter than now. The brief sketch headed "The Commercial and Industrial Outlook," should afford food, not only for thought, but also for congratulation, for it sets forth, despite the narrow limits to which it is confined, some of the things which have been and are being done to further develop local interests. Its reference to the possibilities offered by the electrical transmission of power, opens up a wide field of speculation, for truly, with that wonderful agent, "No man knows what a day may bring forth."

Concord has vast water powers undeveloped, besides those long and profitably utilized; she has pronounced advantages of position, a healthful location, an industrious and law-abiding population, numbering nearly 17,000 by the census of 1890, a disposition to cordially welcome and aid deserving new enterprises, and an international reputation as a manufacturing center. Surely the development so auspiciously begun is but an earnest of what may be expected in the near future, and every man living or working within the broad territory under Concord's jurisdiction owes it to his city, his family, and himself to do all he honorably can to hasten that development and keep Concord in the front rank of New England cities."

"And thus shall our beloved town,
Add to its wealth of old renown,
A name for strength and sterling worth,
Borne, like her coaches, round the earth."

Concord Commercial Club,

ORGANIZED SEPTEMBER 18, 1889.

Officers and Committees.

PRESIDENT,
Hon. EDGAR H. WOODMAN.

VICE-PRESIDENT,
GEORGE F. PAGE.

SECOND VICE-PRESIDENT,
CHARLES H. AMSDEN.

THIRD VICE-PRESIDENT,
JAMES H. CHASE.

TREASURER,
JOSIAH E. FERNALD.

SECRETARY,
AUGUST P. REIN.

DIRECTORS,

WILL M. MASON,   JAMES C. NORRIS,
EDSON J. HILL,   CHARLES E. FOOTE,
ARTHUR C. SANBORN.   GILES WHEELER.

Standing Committees.

ON NEW INDUSTRIES,

GEORGE W. ABBOTT,   WILLIS D. THOMPSON,
                          WILLIAM E. HOOD.

ON CITY IMPROVEMENTS,

EDMUND H. BROWN,   FERDINAND A. STILLINGS,
                          AI B. THOMPSON.

ON ENTERTAINMENT,

EDWARD E. PEARSON.   SOLON A. CARTER.

HOWARD A. DODGE,
FRANK W. ROLLINS,
PAUL R. HOLDEN.

GEORGE F. PAGE,
WILLIAM F. THAYER.

FRANK W. ROLLINS,
HENRY W. STEVENS.

EDSON J. HILL.

MEMBERS OF CONCORD COMMERCIAL CLUB.

STILLMAN HUMPHREY,
SAMUEL C. EASTMAN,
GEORGE F. PAGE,
GRANVILLE P. CONN,
GEO. D. B. PRESCOTT,
WARREN K. DAY,
EDWARD A. JENKS,
CHARLES S. PARKER,
LYMAN JACKMAN,
EDSON J. STILL,
GEORGE MAIN,
JAMES H. CHASE,
FRED'K S. CRAWFORD,
EDWARD N. PEARSON,
BENJAMIN C. WHITE,
ARTHUR C. SANBORN,
GEORGE H. EMERY,
WILLIAM F. THAYER,
EDWARD N. SPENCER.
JOSIAH E. FERNALD,
H. M. BRICKETT,
JOHN C. THORNE,
WILL M. MASON,
EDWARD DOW,
HENRY W. STEVENS,
LYMAN D. STEVENS,
EDGAR H. WOODMAN,
HENRY ROBINSON,
HENRY O. ADAMS,
LOUIS J. UFFENHEIMER,
FRED REED,
W. A. THOMPSON,
FRANK W. ROLLINS,
HARRY H. DUDLEY,
A. PERLEY FITCH,
P. B. COGSWELL,

S. C. MORRILL,
GEORGE A. CUMMINGS,
E. B. WOODWORTH,
F. A. STILLINGS,
W. ROBINSON,
FRANK E. BROWN,
H. E. CAMBERLIN,
M. J. PRATT,
JAMES C. NORRIS,
THOS. A. PILLSBURY,
C. H. DAY,
CHARLES H. MARTIN,
HENRY J. CRIPPEN,
CHARLES E. REMICK,
DAN'L B. DONOVAN,
JAMES MINOT,
WM. M. CHASE,
FRANK S. STREETER,
OBADIAH MORRILL,
HARRY G. SARGENT,
JOHN KIMBALL,
GILES WHEELER,
A. R. AYERS,
WM. E. HOOD,
JOSEPH T. SLEEPER,
HOWARD A. DODGE,
WILLIAM G. CARTER,
E. B. HUTCHINSON,
HENRY W. CLAPP,
H. W. FARLEY,
GEORGE E TODD,
WILLIS D. THOMPSON,
A. B. CROSS,
DAVID D. TAYLOR,
CHARLES FAIRBANKS,
T. A. HEATH,

GEORGE UNDERHILL,
WILLIAM P. FISK,
W. J. AHERN,
E. W. WILLARD,
FRANK H. GEORGE,
O. H. PHELPS,
GEORGE O. DICKERMAN,
WARREN CLARK,
CHARLES H. ALLEN,
ARTHUR C. STEWART,
EDSON C. EASTMAN,
CHARLES R. CORNING,
V. C. HASTINGS,
FRANK L. SANDERS,
J. B. WALKER,
S. S. KIMBALL,
JOHN P. GEORGE,
JOHN C. ORDWAY,
CHARLES H. AMSDEN,
JOHN H. PEARSON,
JOHN F. WEBSTER,
C. R. ROBINSON,
W. G. C. KIMBALL,
HENRY H. HUSE,
WILLIAM YEATON,
IRVING A. WATSON,
JOHN M. MITCHELL,
SOLON A. CARTER,
GEO. A. BLANCHARD,
JAMES C. BADGER,
DAVID E. MURPHY,
HENRY McFARLAND,

HENRY W. HAYDEN,
PAUL R. HOLDEN,
ADAM P. HOLDEN,
GEORGE W. ABBOTT,
CHARLES M. ROLFE,
EDMUND H. BROWN,
D. ARTHUR BROWN,
A. C. ALEXANDER,
CHARLES E. FOOTE,
STEWART I. BROWN,
NATH'L S. GALE,
B. O. KIMBALL,
CHARLES T. PAGE,
ENOCH GERRISH,
A. B. THOMPSON,
WOODBURY E. HUNT,
NATH'L E. MARTIN,
JOHN F. MOSELEY,
MOSES HUMPHREY,
JOHN F. JONES,
L. DOWNING, JR.,
G. B. EMMONS,
THEO. H. FORD,
PHILIP C. BEAN,
CHARLES H. SANDERS,
HIRAM O. MARSH,
M. W. NIMS,
GEORGE F. DURGIN,
THOMAS P. SULLIVAN,
CHARLES H. BARRETT,
H. C. BAILEY,
AUSTIN S. RANNEY.

LEADING BUSINESS MEN OF CONCORD.

JAMES R. HILL & CO.

ESTABLISHED 1840.

"THE CONCORD HARNESS"

The firm of **James R. Hill & Co**, the only makers of the "Concord Harness" and collars, is probably as well and favorably known as that of any other house in this country, as makers of the celebrated and world-renowned "Concord Harness," and the firm's business forms no small portion of the manufacturing industry of the capital city. The founder of the house, Mr. James R. Hill, commenced business, in a small way, in 1840, and by his indomitable energy and perseverance, attending strictly to business and making good work, soon gained for him a good reputation throughout the State. And as the railroads pushed out into the far West, necessitating connecting lines by staging, those who had used his harness in the East, wanted them in their new enterprises, and so as time rolled on, the business was increased. In 1851, the present senior partner of the firm entered the employ of Mr. Hill as an apprentice, commencing at the very foot of the ladder, learning all the details of every part of the trade, and in 1859 was placed in charge of the manufacturing department, and in 1865 was admitted to equal partnership with Mr. Hill and J. E. Dwight, the son-in-law of Mr. Hill, and since that time, the practical management has rested on his shoulders. On the decease of Mr. Hill in 1884, Mr. Emery and Mr. Dwight purchased the heir's interest and the business has since been managed under the same firm-name, in 1888 a stock company was formed continuing the same name, Mr. Emery becoming president and general manager and Mr. Dwight treasurer. A word in regard to the workshops, which are very extensive although the stranger passing by on Main street would not see the immense workshops in the rear. The building located on North Main street, comprises a three-story building and basement, 40 × 125 feet, with a three-story and basement building connected in the rear, 40 × 160, and a collar

shop building, two stories in height, 25 × 60 feet. The company has recently opened a store in Boston at 30 Sudbury street, 61-63 Portland street. Employment is given to 100 to 150 skilled workmen according to the season. The company does an extensive wholesale business, the largest probably of the kind in New England. No concern in the country gives more genuine value for every dollar received. The quality of the work manufactured by this concern stands unrivalled, being acknowledged not only to be the best to be had, but the Standard Harness of America. The trade of this house extends to every part of the inhabited globe where American or English enterprise has gained a foothold. The firm took the highest award at the Centennial in '76, special awards at Sidney in '79, and the only party receiving two awards at the Melbourne exhibition of '80. Their harness also took the first prize again at Melbourne in '88 and have always taken the highest awards when placed in competition. Barnum & Bailey are heavy patrons of this company's productions, and are using a complete outfit in all their departments of harness made by this firm. While express and coach harness are a prominent feature, yet a specialty of the house is the making of fine harness, including fine carriage harness, coupé, rockaway, gentleman's light driving and business harness of all sorts and descriptions. The customer can have his taste gratified in every respect, and in point of style they are surpassed by none.

The following editorial article taken from the *Coach and Saddlery Journal*, published in New York City, shows how the trade look upon the goods manufactured by this firm: "George H. Emery, senior member of the firm of James R. Hill & Co., Concord, N. H., paid a flying visit to this city last week for the purpose of buying stock for the firm, whose business is steadily increasing notwithstanding their factory is located in a city that of itself offers little inducement to business visitors. The value of a good reputation, honorable and square dealing, was never made more apparent than it is with the house of 'The Concord Harness,' their trade mark being an imperturbable barrier to rival houses, and especially to that class who have not the ability to invent new styles themselves, and can only copy and imitate others. There are such houses in the trade, and their reputations in this respect are well known. This house is among the pioneers and in the advance ground in getting up new styles, and probably there has been more copying from 'The Concord Harness' than all others in the country, as it seems to be the *ne plus ultra* of some harness manufacturers of the class we have mentioned to say they can make as good a harness as the 'Concord Harness,' made by James R. Hill & Co. It was Mr. Emery who first conceived the idea of making a standard harness, and obtained for his house their trade mark, which consists of the words 'The Concord Harness,' and also, at a later date, another in which music is made to appear, the significance of which has been a puzzle to many, as it was to us, to know what music had to do with a harness We asked Mr E. for the meaning, who said, —'Why, what is music but harmony, and what is harmony but a concord of sounds? And in all our harness we combine harmony in their proportions, one strap with another: hence they are "Concord Harness."' There is no danger of the good name of the house being sacrificed under its present management, as both members of the firm have had a long and practical experience, the senior from 1851, and the junior from 1865 Knowing how and what to buy is an attainment reached by comparatively few, but Mr. Emery is prominent among that few. He is looked upon by the New York harness leather manufacturers as one of the most competent judges of harness leather that visits this city. When David Moffat, the acknowledged leader in the manufacture of harness leather, says, as he did to the editor, of Mr. Emery,—'He is a thorough and critical judge of harness leather: he knows all about it. He knows good leather at sight, and, in buying, selects only the best: it is useless to offer him anything else. He buys close, but he buys good stock only,' —it speaks volumes in praise of the buyer, and gives assurance to those who buy 'The Concord Harness' that they will get harness made of good stock and in a workmanlike manner."

No higher endorsement can be had. The use of the firm's trade mark "The Concord Harness" is not limited to any one style of harness, but is and always has been applied and used by them for every description of harness of superior quality of stock and workmanship, meaning that the purchaser should become accustomed to rely upon the quality of any harness sold him under this name, and while the motto which is original with this house (although it has been copied by others) "Not how cheap but how good" when applied to the quality of "The Concord Harness," is wholly true, yet if a cheap harness is wanted, it can be obtained of them in any style desired, at prices lower than the lowest. Aside from the manufacturing of harness, the firm carry a line of all kinds of goods belonging to the trade, carriage and stable furnishings, horse clothing, trunks, travelling valises, and all sorts of saddlery hardware generally. On seeing the firm's trade mark where the music is made to appear the poet has furnished the following verses which state the facts very clearly

TUNE AMERICA.

I.

Come, drivers, let us sing,
Make all the welkin ring
With sounds of praise
Praise for the Harness fine,
Made in the best design,
Beauty in every line,
Strong in all ways.

II.

Not how cheap, but how good,
Long has our motto stood
Before all men
Surpassed by none e'er made,
No matter what the grade,
Of no fair test afraid,
By draft or pen

III.

In Afric's sunny clime,
Australia's land sublime,
O'er Europe's plains,
O'er Asia's boundless ground,
In fact, the world around,
Is "Concord Harness" found,
Where men draw reins.

IV.

So, with harmonious voice,
Proclaim the people's choice,
From near and far.
Shout, to the heavens blue
Shout, men of every hue!
Shout, for the "Concord," true!
Concordia!

Mechanicks National Bank of Concord.–The Mechanicks National Bank is one of the oldest established and most truly representative financial institutions in New Hampshire, and for nearly sixty years has steadily and powerfully assisted in the development of the manufacturing and mercantile interests of the State, giving particular attention to enterprises located in Concord and vicinity. Those who are attracted only by what is vaguely termed "brilliant" financiering will find but little to interest them in the record of this bank, but those who are old-fashioned enough to admire purely legitimate methods, and to appreciate a policy both conservative and progressive will heartily endorse its management from the beginning. The Mechanicks Bank was chartered under State laws in 1834 and was nationalized in 1880. It has a capital of $150,000 and is thoroughly equipped in every way for the carrying on of a general banking business, including the reception of deposits, the collection of drafts, the purchase and sale of standard securities and the discounting of approved commercial paper. The institution during the past season of 1889 has secured the extensive apartments on Main street in the corner of the Board of Trade Building, which have been rearranged—newly fitted, and furnished with special reference to the requirements of the bank so that, as completed, they are unsurpassed for their purpose, by any banking rooms in New England. The facilities it here offers are availed of by the leading manufacturers and mercantile houses of the city and vicinity. Its representative character is due not alone to its long and honorable career, but also to the character of the men identified with its management, for its officers and directors are gentlemen of such prominence as are rarely grouped together in a single institution, and on account of this fact we take the liberty to make personal mention of each as we record their names The position of president is held by Hon. Edgar H. Woodman, who for four years was mayor of this city, a lawyer by profession and holds many positions of trust, and is interested in the future development and prosperity of Concord and at the present time is active in this direction as president of the "Concord Commercial Club." The cashier is Mr. James Minot, and is a nephew of Mr. Geo. Minot, the first cashier of the old State Bank. Mr. Minot is one of the most experienced and best known of the cashiers of New England. He is also a veteran of the late war and prominent in Grand Army circles, having served two terms as Assistant Adjutant-General, Department of N. H. The board of directors is constituted as follows : Mr. Joseph B. Walker, a direct representative of the early settlers of Concord of the same surname, all of whom have been highly respected and successful citizens Hon. John Kimball has been mayor of the city for four years, a State senator and has occupied numerous positions of trust and confidence and is at present treasurer of the Merrimack County Savings Bank. Mr. John M. Hill, for twenty-five years the treasurer and general manager of the Concord Gas Light Co., and sufficiently well known throughout the State to be selected as a candidate for governor by the democratic party, with which he has always been identified. Hon. Benjamin A. Kimball, formerly a State senator and member of the governor's council, and now the managing director of the Concord & Montreal Railroad. Hon. Charles H. Amsden, a well known manufacturer at Penacook, in this city, has a wide reputation as an enterprising business man, was State senator, and recently selected as a candidate for governor by the democratic party. Ex-Mayor Edgar H Woodman has already been referred to as president. Frank W. Rollins, the youngest member of the board takes the place of his father, Hon. E. H. Rollins, the well-known senator from New Hampshire who is recently deceased, a rising young banker and business manager of the well-known firm of E. H. Rollins & Son. With such a board of management, there can be no question but that the old Mechanicks National Bank will continue to increase its prosperity and usefulness.

HARRY D. HAMMOND & CO..

THE

LEADING DRY GOODS HOUSE

IN CONCORD.

No one can treat Customers better with Price, Quality and Style.

Loan and Trust Savings Bank, 37 Main Street, Concord, N. H.—The chief incentive to and aid in saving money is now afforded by the various excellent savings banks distributed throughout the country, and one of the best of these worthy institutions is the Loan and Trust Savings Bank of this city. The design of this bank as outlined by the management is as follows: "The Loan and Trust Savings Bank is designed to afford a safe and profitable investment of all sums of money entrusted to its care, and is alike open to all classes in the community, thus enabling the industrious and frugal, by commencing early in life to make provisions for the future, and at the same time offering encouragement to those who have not been such to lessen their expenses and lay by something for a time of need." No one can deny that a well-managed institution having such aims is a great benefit to any community; and that this bank is well-managed is proved, first by the record made since its incorporation in 1872, second by the implicit confidence reposed in it by those conversant with its resources and methods, and third by the following figures from the statement of its condition, April 5, 1890; Deposits, $2,162,634.94; guarantee fund, $100,000; undivided profits, $123,112.72. As in all regular savings banks the guarantee fund and undivided profits as well as all income derived therefrom belong to its depositors. The complete list of officers is as follows: President, James S. Norris, vice-president, Lewis Downing, Jr ; treasurer, John F. Jones; teller, Fred N. Ladd; trustees, James S. Norris, Lewis Downing, Jr., Howard A. Dodge, John F. Jones, Silas Curtis, L. W. Cogswell, Paul R. Holden, Howard L. Porter, John M. Mitchell, John C. Linehan, James C. Norris, Josiah E. Fernald. Investment committee, James S. Norris, Lewis Downing, Jr., Howard A. Dodge, Howard L. Porter and John F. Jones. The interests of depositors are certainly secure under such guardianship, and we believe it would be impossible to point out an institution where small sums of money can be more safely and profitably invested.

E. W. Brooks, wholesale and retail dealer in Flour, Grain and Groceries, foot of West street, South End, Concord, N. H.—The business carried on by Mr. E. W. Brooks was founded in 1889. Mr. Brooks is a native of Portland, Maine, and has had long and varied experience in connection with the handling of flour, grain, groceries, etc., the result being that he is in a position to furnish strictly dependable goods at strictly bottom prices. The premises utilized are located at the foot of West street, South End, and comprise two floors each of which is about 22×60 feet in dimensions. This affords opportunity for the carrying of a heavy stock and it is fully improved, a large and complete assortment being constantly on hand. Particular attention is paid to the handling of such brands of flour as are especially adapted for family use, and as very low prices are named in this department housekeepers would do well to place a trial order with Mr. Brooks. The stock of groceries comprises staple and fancy articles of all kinds, and includes some of the choicest teas, coffees and spices to be found in Concord. Employment is given to two efficient assistants, and callers may safely depend upon receiving prompt and polite attention.

H. C. Bailey, Photographer, State Block, corner Main and School Streets, Concord, N. H.—Naturally the first question asked by those desiring to be photographed is: "Who does the best work?" We believe those who visit the new studio of H. C. Bailey, Main and School streets, will be well satisfied that they have chosen the right place. This studio was thoroughly remodeled and newly fitted up in the early months of the year 1888, and was taken possession of by the present proprietor the fifteenth day of May the same year. The premises occupied comprise two floors, utilized as reception and ladies' parlors, dressing rooms, printing, burnishing, solar and skylight rooms, the latter being conveniently fitted up with every modern improvement requisite to perfect portraiture, and the former elegantly furnished and adorned with hundreds of cabinets, imperials and life size portraits, which are well worthy a careful inspection. Mr. Bailey was born in Lisbon, N. H., but has resided in Concord the past thirty years, and has long been a well known business man in this city. He was the first photographer in this part of New Hampshire to totally discard the old wet plates and use exclusively the new instantaneous process, also the first to produce successful pictures at night by the flash light, and at the present time owns the exclusive right for Concord and vicinity of the celebrated Talcott glass mounts, the Gevelli stamp portrait, and the latest important improvement in modern photography—Snell's beautiful patented water colors. Mr. Bailey has a branch studio and art store in Woodsville, N. H., recently built expressly for him, which will compare favorably with any establishment in New England. This necessitates an increase of workmen and artists in the Concord studio, where all the photographic work is finished under Mr. Bailey's personal supervision, whose taste and experience in posing sitters and regulating light and shade are such as to accomplish the most satisfactory and life-like results, and well deserves the large patronage which this studio receives.

E. H. Rollins & Son (incorporated). A Legal Depository for Trust Funds, Financial Agents of the Courts, Boston, Mass., Concord, N. H.—The action of the legislature of New Hampshire in chartering the corporation of E. H. Rollins & Son at its June session, 1889, as the successor of the long established firm of E. H. Rollins & Son, was a handsome but deserved compliment to that representative concern, for the stock of the corporation was taken by those interested in the old firm, and it is an open secret that the favorable action of the legislature was largely due to an understanding that such was to be the case. The act was referred to both the banking and judiciary committee, each of which reported in its favor without one dissenting voice, and it provides that the affairs of the corporation "shall be under the supervision and control of the bank commissioners," thus subjecting the management to the same conservative restrictions as are exercised in the case of savings banks, etc. The company is especially authorized by its charter : To receive funds of trustees, guardians, administrators and others ; to act officially as financial agents of the courts of this and other States ; to act as trustees for individuals and corporations ; to execute all powers incident to a safe deposit and trust company ; to negotiate loans for itself and others and to issue its debentures ; to deal in money and securities and do a banking business. The loaning of its funds to any stockholder is forbidden by law. The former firm and the present company are identical in at least one very important principle of management : every important officer being so largely interested in the capital of the concern as to cause his personal interests to be the same as those of the company. The popular judgment of this and other principles of management is shown in the fact that the aggregate business of the several departments exceeds that of any other New Hampshire financial institution. In the banking department deposits will be accepted on conditions similar to those made by savings banks, interest at 5 per cent. per annum being paid. The trust department is entirely separate from all others, and has charge of the investment and disbursement of trust funds, and the performance of kindred duties attaching to legal financial agents. The bond department is devoted to the negotiation and sale of high-grade New England municipal bonds, and of those issued by Western counties and municipalities. In the bank stock department is handled a conservative line of national bank stock ; the leading commercial centers of the West being well represented. The investment department conducts all the vast amount of business incidental to loaning money on farm or city property in the West and negotiating securities founded thereon throughout New England. The placing of mortgage loans is confined to certain sections in Colorado and to the valley of the Red River of the North in North Dakota ; the Colorado loans being placed by the Rollins Investment Co., and the Dakota loans through the company's office in Grand Forks, the manager of which is a large stockholder, and personally examines every loan. Seven per cent., unguaranteed loans, six per cent. guaranteed loans and six per cent. debenture bonds are offered by the company, and perhaps the best evidence of the character of these securities is that afforded by the fact that the company's customers include the leading savings banks of the State and many other banks and institutions throughout New England. The American Loan and Trust company of Boston is the trustee for E. H. Rollins & Son debentures, and in this connection the statement of that company and of the Rollins Investment Company will be of interest :

AMERICAN LOAN & TRUST COMPANY.
TRUSTEE FOR E. H. ROLLINS & SON DEBENTURES.

Boston, Mass., April 29, 1889.

Assets.

Stocks and Bonds	$580,944.18
Loans (short time)	2,890,412.28
Expense Acc't	11,658.61
Cash	618,695.65
	$4,101,710.72

Liabilities.

Capital	$1,000,000.00
Surplus	125,000.00
Undivided Profits	53,674.11
Deposits	2,923,036.61
	$4,101,710.72

ROLLINS INVESTMENT COMPANY.
DENVER OFFICE OF E. H. ROLLINS & SON.

Denver, Col., March 31, 1889.

Resources.

Loans secured on Real Estate	$64,605.44
Loans on Personal Security	32,954.75
Stocks, Bonds and Warrants	166,326.22
Furniture and Fixtures	4,101.25
Current Expenses	10,411.66
Interest due	2,750.80
Due from Offices and Persons	59,029.07
Due from Banks and Bankers	72,625.63
Cash	1,388.05
	$414,282.87

Liabilities.

Capital Stock paid in	$200,000.00
Surplus Fund	30,000.00
Guarantee Fund	5,000.00
Undivided Profits	38,510.47
Loans paid, but not remitted for	5,834.78
Due Borrowers on Loans made	16,565.79
Deposits	113,006.83
Cashier's checks outstanding	5,365.00
	$414,282.87

The E. H. Rollins & Son Company has a paid up capital of $150,000, and its officers comprise the following representative citizens : President, F. W. Rollins ; vice-presidents, E. W. Rollins. Hiram A. Tuttle ; treasurer, H. H. Dudley ; secretary, H. B. Roby ; manager Boston office, Louis G. Hoyt ; manager Grand Forks office, George A. Batchelder ; directors, F. W. Rollins, E. W. Rollins, H. H. Dudley, H. B. Roby, Louis G. Hoyt, George A. Batchelder, John Laighton, J. Frank Seavey, Dr. W. G. Carter.

Oliver Racine, manufacturer and dealer in all kinds of Eastern Granite, Concord, Sunapee, Quincy, Barre, etc., Fine Cut and Polished Cemetery Work. Prompt Attention to Orders and Correspondence, Concord, N. H.—It is difficult to accurately forecast the future, but there seems to be no room for doubt that granite is to largely take the place of marble for cemetery work, building purposes, etc. Certainly such has been the tendency during the past score of years, and the popularity of granite is still constantly increasing. In our New England climate especially, it is far superior to marble and other soft stones for out-door use, and so far as beauty and variety are concerned it will compare favorably with any ornamental stone. If any of our readers are disposed to question this latter statement, we would respectfully request them to call at the establishment conducted by Mr. Oliver Racine, located on North State street, for he is a manufacturer of and dealer in all kinds of eastern granite, including Concord, Sunapee, Quincy, Barre, etc., and carries a large and varied stock at all times. A specialty is made of fine cut and polished cemetery work ; and where the grain of the stone is brought out by polishing, such beautiful effects are attained as no marble in the world can equal, while the polish is as durable as it is effective. Mr. Racine is a native of Canada, and became connected with his present enterprise in 1882, as a member of the firm of Racine & McGuire, assuming sole control in 1886. He does both a wholesale and retail business, and is prepared to furnish rough or finished granite in quantities to suit at the lowest market rates. Employment is given to from ten to fifteen assistants, and orders and all correspondence are assured prompt and careful attention ; estimates being cheerfully furnished on application.

F. A. Piper, dealer in Pianos and Organs ; Piano-Forte Tuner. Agent for Mehlin & Sons, Lawrence&Sons Pianos, Prescott Pianos. No. 92 North Main Street, Concord, N. H.—That there is "no home without music," has become almost a truism and really, it is wonderful how widespread, and indeed universal the love of harmony is. It has resulted in the manufacture of thousands of pianos and organs per annum, and as some of these are unfortunately made only to sell, and not to stand the test of years of wear, it behooves the purchaser to be very careful lest good money be given for a poor instrument. The best way of course, to guard against imposition is to deal only with houses of high and long established reputation, and in the line of pianos and organs we can recommend that conducted by Mr. F. A. Piper who occupies a part of a store with Mr. Oliver Ballou, at 92 North Main street. He deals in pianos and organs of various makes, which stand high in the estimation of the trade, but he makes a specialty of Mehlin & Sons, and Prescott Pianos, for which he is the agent in this section. He also deals in violins, banjos, guitars, sheet music and musical merchandise. This house was founded several years ago by Mr. A. J. Prescott who was succeeded in 1887 by Mr. F. A. Piper, and it was in November of the same year that he removed to his present location, where he is pleased to exhibit the various instruments and give all information as to their respective qualities in regard to tone, action, and capabilities for enduring the wear which they will have, and the changes of our climate which materially affect some instruments. Mr. Piper is also a piano-forte tuner, and is prepared to attend to all orders at short notice and warrants satisfaction in all cases.

J. D. Johnson & Son, manufacturers of Harnesses, Collars, Halters, Whips, etc., Concord.—Everybody knows that "practice makes perfect," and as Mr. Johnson has been engaged in the manufacture of harness for many years he certainly ought to be reasonably perfect by this time. As a matter of fact, the firm of J. D. Johnson & Son have the reputation of producing harness that has but few equals and no superiors in the market, and although they don't advertise to sell a first-class harness at less than the cost of the stock used in its manufacture, it is conceded by practical men that no concern in the State gives more genuine value for money received. The late Mr. J. D. Johnson, formerly the senior member of this firm, was a native of Wentworth, N. H., and began business in Concord in 1845. In 1876 the firm was changed by the admission of Mr. Fred. S. Johnson, who is a native of this city. The present firm name was then adopted, and since the death of J. D. Johnson in 1884 the business has been continued by his son, the surviving partner, Mr. Fred. S. Johnson. The premises utilized are located on Bridge street, and have an area of 800 square feet, exclusive of the rooms used for storage purposes. The high reputation of the firm's products is by no means confined to this city and vicinity, for large shipments were formerly made to Australia, New Zealand, San Francisco, etc., and doubtless by this time the export trade would have attained great magnitude had not the harness industry been introduced at all those points. The home demand however is quite extensive, and the firm carry a full line of harnesses, collars, halters, whips and horse furnishings in general, and have every facility at hand for the doing of custom work in a uniformly superior manner and at short notice. No fancy prices are quoted, and the goods are in every instance guaranteed to prove just as represented.

National State Capital Bank, 37 Main Street, Concord.—That commercial stability is largely dependent upon the facilities afforded by fiscal institutions is a fact too obvious to require demonstration here, and it goes without saying that the banks of Concord are intimately linked with the growth of every enterprise in this city and vicinity. Especially is this true of the National State Capital Bank, for this has ever been a favorite with the business world, its unusually extended line of deposits being largely those of active merchants and manufacturers, while it discounts a large proportion of the most desirable commercial paper on the market. This bank was organized in 1853, and received a National charter in 1865. It has a capital of $200,000, held by leading citizens as one of the choicest and most remunerative of investments, and the existence of a surplus of $100,000 attests the conservatism and general ability of the management. The board of directors is constituted of Messrs. Lewis Downing, Jr., James S. Norris, Lyman D. Stevens, John H. Pearson, John F. Jones and Henry J. Crippen—men prominent and influential in commercial circles, their names being synonymous with stability and integrity, so it is natural that no financial institution in the city should enjoy greater confidence than that with which they are so prominently identified. Mr. Lewis Downing, Jr., is president of the bank, and Mr. J. E. Feruald, cashier. It is located at No. 37 Main street, in a handsome, commodious and substantial building, erected by themselves in 1880, one of the architectural ornaments of Concord. The banking rooms are very conveniently fitted up and sufficient clerical assistance is employed to ensure the prompt and accurate transaction of all business submitted. The following statement gives a comprehensive idea of the resources of the institution and the extent to which they are utilized :

STATEMENT, APRIL 5, 1890.

Resources.

Loans and discounts	$536,579.44
Overdrafts	917.09
United States Bonds to secure circulation	50,000.00
Due from reserve agents	76,863.74
Due from other national banks	21,566.16
Banking house	25,000.00
Bills of other national banks and companies	12,736.62
Legal tender notes and gold	17,000.00
Redemption fund	2,250.00
Bond account	40,300.00
	$783,213.05

Liabilities.

Capital stock	$200,000.00
Surplus fund	100,000.00
Undivided profits	20,746.52
National Bank notes outstanding	44,160.00
Dividends unpaid	3,435.00
Deposits	414,871.53
	$783,213.05

ORGANIZED 1845

New York Life INSURANCE Co.

WILLIAM H. BEERS, PRESIDENT.

CROWELL & McKELLAR GEN'L AGENTS.

CHASE'S BLOCK 15 NO. MAIN ST. CONCORD. N. H.

What the lawyers call " the burden of proof," is now thrown on the man who is not insured, for such a revolution has occurred in public sentiment within a decade or so, that a man who can be insured but neglects to take out a policy, is regarded as careless and selfish unless he can prove the contrary to be the fact. Really the only question for a sensible man to consider is where he can place his insurance to the best advantage, and we can aid powerfully in an entirely satisfactory solution of that by directing our readers' attention to the facilities offered by the New York Life Insurance Company, whose State agency for New Hampshire is in Room No. 4, Chase's Block, No. 15 North Main street. Here may be found Messrs. Crowell & McKellar, who are the general agents for New Hampshire, and control sub-agents throughout the State. They established their agency in April, 1889, and have already written a great many policies, for not only do they understand how to bring the advantages of dependable life insurance home to every inquirer, but they are in a position to furnish the highest type of insurance at the lowest market rates. The New York Life is one of the strongest and most extensive life companies in the world, and the magnitude of its operations is most significantly shown by the record of a single year (1889):

INCOME ACCOUNT

From policy-holders	$24,585,921.10
" interest, rentals, etc.	4,577,345.14
Total income	29,163,266.24

DISBURSEMENT ACCOUNT

Death-claims and endowments	$6,252,095.50
Dividends, annuities and purchased insurance	5,869,026.16
Total paid policy-holders	12,121,121.66

These figures are impressive and would be even more so were it not for their magnitude, which prevents their being entirely comprehended. For instance the total income for the year of 1889, over twenty nine millions of dollars, is too large to be appreciated, but its significance becomes evident when it is learned that it amounts to nearly one fifth of the total income of all the life companies. Look for a moment at the summary for the 45 years' business. Received from policy holders in premiums $207,639,689.13 ; premiums for annuities, $15,846,595.06. Total from policy holders, $223,526,284.49. Payments to policy-holders and their representatives with assets now held as security for policies in force exceeds the amount received from policy holders, $10,871,375.34. Interest, rentals, etc., $52,868,649.94 ; death losses paid, $50,040,257.60 ; Interest and rents exceed death-losses paid, $2,827,812.34.

Assets, $105,053,600.96 ; surplus, $15,600,000.00. Some one may ask, who are the officers of this company responsible for the supervision of its affairs ? Wm. H. Beers, the president, has been connected with the company from its infancy, advancing step by step from clerk to cashier, actuary, vice president, to his present position. First vice-president, Henry Tuck ; second vice-president, A. H. Welch ; and actuary Rufus W. Weeks, have all reached their present position by advancement step by step. With such an administrative staff of officers, the company have and are always advancing the interests of its policy-holders and when we consider the fact, that the amount of its endowment and annuity policies is larger by more than forty millions of dollars, its forms of policies and the results more satisfactory than any other company, it speaks volumes for the executive ability of its officers. The New England Branch, located at Boston, Mass., comprising the New England States, excepting Vermont is under the supervision of Major Ben. S. Calef, one of the oldest and most prominent life underwriters of Massachusetts, with Hon. D. P. Kingsley late insurance commissioner of Colorado- as inspector of agencies Messrs. Crowell & McKellar will be happy to give full and detailed information upon application, and will gladly furnish the actual results of policies which have matured and been settled in 1889, and mail communications will be promptly and carefully attended to

D. M. Camp, successor to A. W. Gale, Ice Cream and Dining Rooms, Oysters, Home-made Bread, Rolls and Pastry, fine Confectionery and Cigars, 31 North Main Street, Concord, N. H.—The establishment now conducted by Mr. D. M. Camp is one of the most widely popular of Concord's "institutions," and it well deserves its popularity, for a better place to get a dinner, a light lunch or an ice cream is hard to find in the city. This enterprise was established in 1862, and after two or three changes in its management came into the possession of Mr. A. W. Gale in 1886, who was succeeded by the present proprietor in 1889. Mr. D. M. Camp is a native of Stowe, Vt., and is very well and favorably known throughout Concord. He conducts ice cream and dining rooms at No. 31 North Main street and a restaurant located at the Concord depot. The uptown establishment can seat seventy two guests at a time, and the one at the depot sixteen, they are very conveniently fitted up and always kept in a most attractive condition. Mr. Camp deals in oysters, home-made bread, rolls and pastry, also fine confectionery and cigars. He employs fifteen reliable assistants and is prepared to cater for balls, parties or any public occasion in a most able and satisfactory manner. The secret of the high reputation for delicacy and fineness of flavor held by his productions is easily explained, for it is the legitimate result of the use of the best obtainable materials and careful supervision of every process of manufacture. Success gained by such methods is as permanent as it is well deserved, and it naturally follows that Mr. Camp's business is steadily and rapidly increasing. Moderate prices are quoted in both establishments, and the largest orders can be filled at short notice.

Boston Branch, 17 Federal Street.—The enterprise conducted by the Page Belting Company was inaugurated in 1868 by Page Brothers, the original location being Franklin, N. H. The undertaking was removed to Concord in 1872, and the existing company was incorporated, with an authorized capital of half a million. The capital actually paid in was $75,000 in 1872, the following year it was increased to $125,000, again increased in 1878, to $200,000, and again in 1887, to $250,000,—figures which indicate to some degree at least the constant and rapid development of the business. Mr. George F. Page is president of the company, and Mr. C. F. Page is treasurer. Employment is given to 175 assistants, and the annual product is large in amount and extensive in value a great proportion of it consisting of high grade goods, in the manufacture of which the company especially excels. The goods are sold throughout this country, and are also exported to some extent, and during the past year several government contracts have been filled. The works are situated on two railroads, and are connected with the Concord & Montreal railroad, by private tracks. The total plant covers an area of about ten acres, and among the most prominent buildings it comprises may be mentioned a tannery, one story in height and 60 × 220 feet in dimensions; a two story belt shop measuring 45 × 250 feet; a two-story bark mill, measuring 35 × 45 feet, together with storehouses, tenements, out-buildings, etc. Three steam engines and boilers are included in the plant, and the works can consume 750 hides per week in the manufacture of belting, and 1200 sides of lace leather during the same period. The company manufacture four staple grades of belting and five special grades, the latter being known respectively as the Crown Extra, Page's Two Ply, the Dynamo, Hercules raw hide, and Agricultural. Each of these is adapted to a special work for which, either in price or quality, staple goods may not be exactly suited. A very popular specialty is the "Hercules" lacing, and another is the Acme link belt, constructed on entirely new principles and manufactured exclusively by this company, under a patent issued March 19, 1889. A stock of the sizes in most general request is constantly carried so that orders can be filled without delay. The Eureka Dynamo belting was also patented in March, '89, and is very highly thought of by practical electricians as it combines pliability, freedom from stretch, straightness in running, maximum traction and moderate cost. Standard kit cut laces and other specialties might be added to the list, but we will content ourselves with referring those interested to the handsome illustrated pamphlet issued by the company.

This little book should be in the hands of every manufacturer for it contains, besides a catalogue of leather and rubber belting, straps of all kinds, lace leather, etc., valuable practical rules for the purchase and use of belting, and a list of kinds and grades of belting to use for different kinds of work. It will be sent on application at the Concord works or at the branch offices in Boston, New York, Chicago and San Francisco. The following claims and warrants will be of interest to every belt-user and it should be remembered that they are issued by a concern of known and undoubted responsibility: Claims, *First*, leather of superior quality; *Second*, thorough stretching, belt to run very straight, and with a minimum of taking up. *Third*, the very best of workmanship. *Fourth*, attractive finish ; *Fifth*, liberal dealing with customers. *Sixth*, uniform quality in successive shipments. The care we exercise, and the accurate selection into various grades, our large and general trade, and our interests, all enable and incite us to send the same thing in quality every time. Warrant : *First*, we warrant our goods to be as represented, and to give satisfaction with proper usage. *Second*, we warrant our goods to run uniform in successive shipments of the same grades. *Third*, we warrant satisfactory dealings to our customers. *Fourth*, we warrant our prices to be as low as such quality of goods can be offered.

Thomas H. Dunstane & Son, Granite Monuments, etc., Main Street, Concord.—There are many granite monuments, headstones, etc., produced in Concord every year, for that city is a great centre for the granite trade and work is shipped to many distant points, but we risk nothing in asserting that no concern in this line of business gives more genuine value for money received than Messrs. Thomas H. Dunstane & Son, for the workmanship of their productions is first class in every respect, and their charges are uniformly moderate. The senior partner has been identified with the enterprise for about ten years, beginning in 1880 as a member of the firm of Hasking & Dunstane, who were succeeded in 1886 by Ola Anderson & Co., the present firm assuming control in 1889. It is made up of Thomas H. Dunstane and Thomas H. Dunstane, Jr., both of whom are natives of England, and are skillful workmen as well as successful business men. Granite monuments, headstones, tablets, curbing and cemetery work in general are manufactured, both a wholesale and retail business being done and employment being given to from four to six assistants. The premises utilized are located on Main street, and callers are assured prompt and courteous attention and will be shown a large variety of designs to choose from, varying from the simplest to the most elaborate and suited to all tastes and all purses.

F. E. Colburn, dealer in Ice Cream, Cake, Confectionery, etc., Oyster and Dining Rooms, 32 North Main Street, Concord, N. H.—Mr. Colburn has been the proprietor of this house since 1884, and it has become very popular, because he has striven to learn the wants of the public and has spared neither trouble nor expense in satisfying his patrons. He is one of the best known in this vicinity for the nature of his business favors the making of acquaintances, and after eating one of his finely-cooked dinners you feel as though he were a personal friend of yours. The premises are located at No. 32 North Main Street, and have seating capacity for fifty persons, and a first-class trade is carried on at his oyster and dining rooms. Mr. Colburn is a dealer in ice cream, cake, confectionery, etc., and he is also prepared to cater for parties, balls, etc., and those for whom he has provided on such occasions can testify to his capabilities and the purity and excellence of the edibles furnished by him. All orders are carefully and accurately filled, and satisfaction will be given in all cases. Mr. Colburn supplies his tables with choice food and plenty of it and those who go hungry from his establishment have only themselves to thank for it, for he is generous in his supplies, and his prices are low enough to come within the means of all. Good management prevails and the service is prompt and courteous.

William B. Durgin, Designer and Maker of Wares in Sterling Silver, Concord, N. H.—The increase in the wealth of the country and the decrease in the cost of silver, have combined to build up a great and constantly increasing demand for sterling silverware, and the value of the total annual production of such articles in the United States reaches well up into the millions. One of the best-known designers and makers of wares in sterling silver in New England, is Mr. William B Durgin of this city; for the business conducted by him was established in 1853 and has developed with even greater rapidity than has the demand for the class of goods he manufactures. When he began operations he employed but three men, and his facilities for manufacturing were correspondingly limited; at the present time he employs from ninety to one hundred assistants, and utilizes a spacious factory fitted up with the most improved machinery throughout, including a steam-engine of fifty horse power. The building is three stories in height, and some 40×100 feet in dimensions, giving a total floor space of about 12,000 square feet. About $300,000 worth of finished goods are produced annually, and the articles find a ready market among the most fastidious trade; they being unsurpassed for originality and beauty of design and fineness of workmanship. Mr. Durgin sells to the retail trade, and the best possible evidence that his productions are profitable and desirable to handle is afforded by his long list of regular customers and his steadily increasing business. His superior facilities enable him to fill orders at short notice, and to quote prices that will compare favorably with any named on goods of similar grade. He is a native of Campton, N. H., and is so well-known in social and business circles as to render extended personal mention altogether unnecessary.

Stratton, Merrill & Co., Roller Process Flour Millers, Manufacturers of Meal, Grain and Feed at wholesale, office, Railroad Square, Concord, N H. Mills at Pennacook, N. H.—Since the business carried on by Messrs. Stratton, Merrill & Co., was founded, nearly a third of a century ago, the flour and grain trade has undergone radical changes, which are too generally appreciated to require mention here; but the enterprise in question has been managed with marked ability, and in such a progressive manner that the present proprietors control the most perfectly equipped mill in New England and turn out a product which has no superior in the market. The mills are located at Pennacook, N H, and are fitted-up throughout with the latest improved machinery, driven by water-power. The corn-mill has a capacity of 2,500 bushels per day, and the flour mill has a capacity of 250 barrels per day; this being the only mill in New England manufacturing by the Patent Roller Process. Three water-wheels are utilized, giving a total of 310 horse power, nearly equally divided between the two mills. The office and storehouse are located in this city, in Railroad square, the premises occupied comprising three floors, each measuring 60×100 feet. An exclusively wholesale business is done, the bulk of the flour, meal and cracked corn produced being sold in this State and Massachusetts. With such facilities, it is hardly necessary to say that the most extensive orders can be filled at short notice, while the prices quoted are always in accordance with the lowest market rates on goods of similar grade. This undertaking was established in 1858 by John H. Pearson & Co., who were succeeded by Barron, Dodge & Co in 1861, and they by Whitcher, Stratton & Co. in 1872, the present firm dating from 1881. It is constituted of Mr. George L. Stratton, a native of Lancaster, Mass.; Mr. Henry C. Merrill, a native of Manchester, N. H.; Mr. William K. McFarland, a native of Concord; and Mr. John W. Johnston, a native of Pittsfield, N. H. Messrs Merrill and Johnston reside in Manchester, the former being a trustee of the Amoskeag Savings Bank of that city. All the members of the firm are widely and favorably known in business and social circles; and they have reason to be proud of their connection with the most truly representative enterprise of the kind in New England.

THE
New Hampshire Savings Bank
CONCORD, N. H.

INCORPORATED 1830.

OFFICERS.

SAMUEL S. KIMBALL, President.

WILLIAM P. FISKE, Treasurer.

TRUSTEES.

C. M. Boynton's Grand Depot, Dry Goods and Small Wares. Sign of the "Big Hand," 29 Central Block, opposite Depot Street, Concord.—No business man in town is more generally and favorably known than Mr. C. M. Boynton. He is a native of this city and won a host of friends while acting as clerk in the formerly well-known dry goods house of J. French in State Block, and as senior partner of the popular establishment of Boynton & Willard in Board of Trade Building, before he opened his present popular house in 1881. He is equally well known in social and fraternity circles, and is prominently identified with the Knights of Pythias, being secretary of the E. R. K. of P. of the World for section No. 11, the I. O. O. F., and the Springfield Mutual Relief Association, being a director in the latter company. He is also vice-president of Concord Building and Loan Association, belongs to the Masonic order, and is also a member of the Royal Arcanum. Mr. Boynton has had a long and prosperous career in the dry and fancy goods business, and is undoubtedly one of the most successful buyers as well as one of the very best salesmen in the entire State. The "Sign of the Big Hand" indicates the Concord headquarters for bargains in dry goods and small wares, and a call at No. 29 Central Block, opposite Depot street, will demonstrate the fact that whether you are in search of late novelties, dependable goods, polite attention or low prices you can find what you want here, and be so treated as to make it sure that you will repeat the visit when anything more in Mr. Boynton's line is required. It would be impossible to give a detailed description of the stock within our limited space, but suffice it to say, it is ever attractive, ever fresh and ever complete in all departments. A very large mail business is done, and samples and goods are mailed to every part of the State, so that the legend, "C. M. Boynton, Dry Goods, Concord, N. H." has become a household word throughout the entire commonwealth. Orders are assured prompt and careful attention, and Mr. Boynton spares no pains to fully satisfy every customer.

Geo. W. Jennings, Livery, Sale and Transient Stable. Feed, Twenty-Five Cents. Rear American House, North Main Street, Concord, N. H.—Although it is undoubtedly difficult if not impossible to carry on a livery stable (or any other enterprise) so as to satisfy everybody, still, as a general thing the public are not slow to appreciate liberal dealing, and show their approval by the support they give to establishments that are conducted in accordance with such methods. A case in point is that afforded by the livery, sale and transient stable of which Mr. Geo. W. Jennings is the present proprietor Mr. Jennings succeeded Messrs. Brown & Otis, who had conducted this enterprise for some time and a gratifying trade has been built up which is steadily increasing. He has some very desirable teams for livery service, and those who wish to hire a good horse and a stylish easy running carriage for a moderate sum, would do well to give him a call. Orders are filled at very short notice and the teams are kept in such first-class condition as to be presentable in any company. An extensive transient business is done for there are good accommodations for horses, the stable comprising twenty stalls. Mr. Jennings employs about four competent assistants, and every animal left in his care will receive the best of feed and treatment. The price of feed is twenty five cents. All who have dealings here can speak in praise of its present management.

Crippen, Lawrence & Co., Kansas Mortgages, Salina, Kansas; Denver, Col. Eastern Office, National State Capital Bank Building, Concord, N. H.—An immense amount of New Hampshire capital has been invested in the West during the past score of years, and where an equal amount of prudence has been exercised as would have been used in making investments in this State, the results have been in the highest degree satisfactory. It is now as true as it was ten years ago, that western farm mortgages placed through well-informed and reliable parties are unsurpassed by any securities in the market as regards security and profitableness. Such of our readers as reside in Concord or in fact anywhere in that section of the State, will inevitably be reminded of Messrs. Crippen, Lawrence & Co., when reference is made to western mortgages, for this firm have done more to make these securities popular among conservative investors than any other one concern in New Hampshire ; and the existing demand for them on the part of savings banks, insurance companies and other institutions of a kindred character is the direct consequence of the intelligent, honorable and enterprising methods which have been practiced by this representative firm from the very first. The inception of Messrs. Crippen, Lawrence & Co.'s business occurred about 1873 for it was at that time that the senior partner of the present firm began to invest for personal friends in western mortgages. He was then cashier of the State Capital Bank, and his previous career had been of a nature to give him a wide knowledge of men and affairs and an adequate conception of the future of this country in general and the western portion of it in particular. Being a man of exceptional natural ability and having made a study of financial matters, it naturally followed that Mr. Crippen's investments were well made and the results were so gratifying that in deference to the popular demand the firm of Crippen, Lawrence & Co. was formed to carry on operations on a larger scale, the partners being Messrs. H. J. and J. J. Crippen and George E. Lawrence. The latter had charge of the Concord office and at his death, in 1881, Mr. H. J. Crippen gave up his position as cashier and devoted his entire time to the firm. No change has been made in the name, but Mr. H. J. Putnam is now associated with Messrs. H. J. and J. J. Crippen in the business. Mr. H. J. Crippen is now State representative, and was prominently identified with the school board for twenty years ; still being deeply interested in educational affairs. He is a native of England, but both his associates in business are Massachusetts men by birth. The firm have an office in Salina, Kan., and in Denver, Col., besides the one in this city, and have unsurpassed facilities for the secure and profitable investment of both large and small sums, all business being assured prompt and careful attention, and no pains being spared to fully maintain the enviable reputation so long held.

Batchelder & Co., Grocers, 14 North Main Street, Concord, N. H.—Some genius or other has remarked, that "some proprietors run their stores, while some stores run their proprietors," and, whoever he was, no intelligent person can question his soundness on that subject, at least. System and order will accomplish a great deal, and when these are joined to experience as is the case at the establishment conducted by Batchelder & Co., success is assured. The grocery business was founded here in 1866, by N. S. Batchelder & Co., and the firm so continued until they were succeeded in 1871 by the present firm of J. T. and A. B. Batchelder, both of these gentlemen being natives of New Hampshire. Mr. J. T. Batchelder served in the late war for four years, and attained the rank of first lieutenant. He has also been an alderman. The premises occupied comprise one floor 22×85 feet in dimensions and a basement of the same size. As these gentlemen have been engaged for about a score of years in the retail grocery trade, it would indeed be strange if they were not able to offer their customers special advantages in many directions by this time. The stock which they carry is very large and varied, and consists of staple family groceries, flour and grain. Employment is given to six competent and polite assistants, and particular effort is made to serve all customers with promptness and cordiality. While all the goods are first-class, their prices will be found moderate, and the high reputation of this establishment for honorable dealing is well merited.

Geo. T. Comins Co., Manufacturers of Hardwood Bedsteads, Concord, N. H.—The George T. Comins Company is of comparatively recent origin, having been incorporated in 1889, but the business with which it is identified is of much earlier date, having been founded more than twelve years ago by Mr. George T. Comins. The company is engaged in the manufacture of hardwood bedsteads, and some idea of the magnitude and importance of the enterprise may be gained from the fact that from 70,000 to 80,000 bedsteads are produced annually. One might suppose it would be difficult for a single concern to dispose of so enormous a product of bedsteads alone, but the company find a ready market for all they turn out, as the product is uniform in quality, both of stock and workmanship, and the lowest market rates are quoted at all times. The office is located in the board of trade building, and a very commodious storehouse is utilized as a heavy stock is almost invariably carried. The company has a capital of $40,000, and some of Concord's leading business men are identified with it, the position of president being held by Mr. John Kimball, that of treasurer by Mr. Edward P. Comins, while Mr. George T. Comins acts as manager.

Eagle and Phenix Hotel Co., Edson J. Hill, Manager, Concord, N. H.—It has been said "there is nothing so good but what it could be better," and Mr. Edson J. Hill is evidently a believer in that principle, for although the Phenix Hotel has won a most enviable reputation during the past six years under his management, he has constantly endeavored to improve the service rendered, and the incorporation of the Eagle & Phenix Hotel Company puts him in a position to offer accommodations unsurpassed by the leading hotels of Boston and other great cities. This company was incorporated in 1890, with a capital of $120,000, Mr. Edson J. Hill being treasurer and manager, and Mr. Samuel C. Eastman also being prominently identified with it. It is the intention of the management to carry on a house which shall be strictly first-class in every respect, and neither trouble nor money is spared to carry out this intention to its fullest extent. The new Eagle Hotel can accommodate 100 guests, and is heated by steam, lighted by gas and electricity, supplied with a commodious elevator, and in short, equipped throughout with every modern convenience. Employment is given to from thirty to forty assistants, and the hotel is kept in the best of condition from roof to cellar, careful supervision being exercised and affairs being so thoroughly systematized as to enable everything to go on smoothly, and the large and rapidly growing business to be handled easily and efficiently. The *cuisine* is equal to the best, and the bill of fare always contains a complete variety of seasonable food, the best the market affords being utilized and provision being made for the most diverse tastes. The table service is prompt, intelligent and obliging, much less delay being experienced than at many houses doing a great deal smaller business. The Eagle Hotel is very pleasantly and centrally located, and is a prime favorite with tourists and others travelling for pleasure as well as with business men. Guests may safely depend upon being called promptly at any designated hour, and the facilities for transportation to adjacent points are first-class, prominent among them being those furnished by the excellent livery connected with the house, at which single or double teams with or without drivers can be obtained at short notice, at all hours and at reasonable rates. The citizens of Concord are to be congratulated on having such an establishment as this to represent their business methods, and those who appreciate how much the outside reputation of a community is affected by its hotel accommodations will agree with us that the best interests of Concord are materially aided by this liberally conducted enterprise.

W. G. C. Kimball, Photographer, Legislative Groups, Frames, etc., Chase Block, opposite Statesman Building, Concord, N. H.—Few people aside from those connected with the profession, have any idea of the number of things that must be attended to in order to produce a good photographic likeness, and if more were generally known regarding the difficulties that must be met and overcome, there would be much less surprise expressed at the rarity of really good photographs. Among the best equipped artists in this line in this section, is Mr. W. G. C. Kimball, whose studio is located in Chase block. This studio was originally started in 1850, by Messrs. W. H. & J. L. Kimball, the present proprietor, Mr. W. G. C Kimball, assuming full control of the business in 1860. Sixteen apartments are occupied, comprising reception and toilet rooms, operating, printing, developing, toning and mounting rooms and every attention is paid to the comfort and convenience of patrons, prompt attention being given to every caller, and every needful facility being at hand to enable orders to be filled at short notice, in an eminently first-class manner. Seven competent assistants are employed, and the work done at this studio is very carefully finished, and especial attention is given to securing a perfect likeness and at the same time preserving that softness of outline so indispensable to a really artistic picture. Mr. Kimball is remarkably low in his prices and courteous in his dealings. He is a native Concord, and served in the army during our late war of the rebellion receiving the promotion from sergeant-major to lieutenant-colonel at twenty-one years of age.

The American Trust Company, Concord, N. H.—The American Trust Company was incorporated in 1887 by a special charter from the legislature of New Hampshire, with a paid cash capital of $100,000 and an authorized capital of $500,000. Organized in 1888 it succeeded to the bond and loan business already established by Wm. Yeaton, and at once assumed a prominent position in the financial world, for its management is in the hands of men of experience, honesty and ability, who make themselves thoroughly familiar with any enterprise with which they are connected. Each one of the resident directors is identified with the prosperity of Concord, all owning real estate here, and all are successful business men ready and willing to help any enterprise likely to promote Concord's best interests. They combine successful business experience with an extensive acquaintance among financial men in New England, New York and the West, and guarantee careful, conservative management of the American Trust Company. It is authorized by its charter to do a general banking business; to act as trustee for individuals, estates or corporations, and to buy and sell investment securities. It is obvious that this company with experienced managers can offer efficient and valuable service to prudent investors and the general public, and it is gratifying to know that an extensive and rapidly increasing business is done in conservative investment securities, no investment being offered for sale until careful investigation shows the security to be ample and of solid merit. After sale each one is carefully watched until matured and paid off, each patron's interest being carefully guarded. As trustee the company has already large financial interests committed to its care. As the officers are thoroughly familiar with Concord's resources and with the standing of the many large manufacturing and mercantile enterprises carried in this section, they are excellently qualified to aid in the advancement of meritorious local interests, but worthless, windy schemes are not likely to receive much consideration at their hands. In its bond and loan business the company has very strong financial connections in New York and the west, and its facilities for investing large or small amounts in sound securities is not excelled by any company in the country. The president and manager, Mr. William Yeaton, had been treasurer of the Farmington Savings bank, and also the New England agent of the Dakota Farm Mortgage Company, before assuming his present position; he has made investments a study, personally visits each loaning field in the west, and started the business of the company upon the principle that business relations should be established and maintained only with firms and corporations having a good reputation in their own community. He is associated with F. S. Streeter as vice president and Mr. H. C. Brown as secretary, the board of directors being constituted as follows: W. N. Coler, Jr., William Yeaton, F. S. Streeter, John M. Mitchell, Edson J. Hill, James B. Edgerly and Austin S. Ranney.

J. J. Wyman, dealer in Tripe, Tallow, Swine, Neat's Foot Oil, Bones, etc., Rumford street, Concord, N. H.—The enterprise carried on by Mr. J. J. Wyman was inaugurated just about a third of a century ago, operations having been begun in 1857. The proprietor is a native of Concord and is so generally known in business and social circles as to make extended personal mention entirely unnecessary. He is a dealer in tripe, tallow, swine, neat's foot oil, bones, etc., doing both a wholesale and retail business and having such facilities as to enable him to fill the most extensive orders at short notice, and to quote prices in strict accordance with the lowest market rates. Several buildings are utilized, located on Rumford street, and power is furnished by a five horse steam engine. Mr. Wyman has had such extended experience in connection with his present line of business, that it goes without saying, he is thoroughly familiar with it in every detail and is prepared to carry it on to the best possible advantage, and to offer unsurpassed inducements to his customers. His productions have a high reputation for uniform excellence; the processes of manufacture being carefully supervised, and employment given to experienced assistants.

C. H. Martin & Co., wholesale and retail dealers in Drugs and Medicines, Paints, Oils, etc., 11 North Main Street, Concord, N. H.—The firm of C. H. Martin & Co. have carried on operations in this city for a full quarter of a century, and few houses in the State in a similar line of business are more generally known, while none have a higher reputation for absolute reliability. Operations were begun by Messrs. Allison & Brown, who gave place to Messrs James Morgan & Co., the present firm coming into possession in 1865. The partners are Mr. C. H. Martin, a native of Grafton, N. H.; Mr. R T. Crowell, a native of Hopkinton, N. H ; and Mr. Geo. L. Brown, who was born in Dunbarton, N. H. The latter gentleman has served as representative, and all the members of the firm are so well known as to make extended personal mention unnecessary. An extensive wholesale and retail business is carried on ; the premises being located at No. 11 North Main street, near Pleasant street, and comprising one floor and a basement of the dimensions of 30×70 feet and a rear room measuring 35×12 feet. A heavy and complete stock is constantly on hand, it being made up of goods chosen from the most reliable sources and guaranteed to be equal in every respect to the best the market affords. It includes drugs, medicines and chemicals, paints, oils, etc., and a full line of each of these commodities is always on hand to select from. Employment is given to four experienced assistants, and orders are assured prompt and careful attention, a prominent specialty being made of the compounding of physician's prescriptions, and no pains being spared to ensure absolute accuracy, while moderate charges are made in every instance.

S. G. Lane, Attorney-at-Law and Real Estate Agent, 60 North Main Street, Concord, N. H.—It is perfectly safe to make the assertion that no one in this section of the State is more prominent in connection with real estate matters than Mr. S. G. Lane, for this gentleman has been identified with such interests for nearly a third of a century, and was in fact the first one in Concord to advertise as a real estate agent, the inception of his business occurring in 1860. Mr. Lane was born in Chichester, N. H., but has been so long and is so prominently identified with Concord's interests as to be a Concord man by adoption, to say the least. No more competent authority on local real estate matters can be found anywhere, and his office at No. 60 North Main street is the headquarters for people wishing to buy, sell, exchange, rent or lease such property. Mr. Lane has constantly on his books a variety of desirable estates, town and country dwellings, stores, offices, factories, etc , and one may save a great deal of time and trouble by going directly to him, instead of proceeding in the hap-hazard fashion which so many who ought to know better follow.

T. A. Heath & Co., Crockery, China, Glassware, Lamp Goods, etc., 61 North Main Street, Concord, N. H.—This enterprise was established in 1880 by Mr. T. A. Heath and was conducted by him until in 1886, when Mr. Smith Tenney became associated with him. In 1887 the present firm of T. A. Heath & Co was formed, and the most significant evidence that can be given concerning the character and popularity of this house is that afforded by the fact that it is rapidly becoming known throughout this section as the headquarters for china, crockery, glassware, lamp goods, wall paper and draperies. So pronounced a success is not to be gained without hard and intelligent work, and Mr. Heath has certainly worked hard, but he has the satisfaction of knowing that his efforts are appreciated by the general public, and is therefore encouraged to continue his efforts with renewed vigor. The premises made use of comprise one floor and basement 23×75 feet in dimensions. The stock, which is extensive and varied, consists in part of fine china, glassware, etc. The styles designated as the Tournay, the Aberdeen and the Buckingham, are stock patterns, which can be had in separate pieces as well as in sets, and matched for years to come as readily as white ware. These are new and choice goods which will be shown with pleasure. They have also a large assortment of wall papers and draperies, of which they make a specialty, and can show many new and fashionable designs which must suit all tastes. Three competent assistants are employed and courteous attention is given to all customers, and orders are promptly filled.

H. N. Farley & Co., manufacturer of and dealers in Italian and American Marble, Scotch and American Granite, Monuments, Head Stones and Tablets of every description, Main, South Corner of Freight Street, Concord, N. H.—One of the oldest established business enterprises of the kind in the State is that conducted by Messrs. H. N. Farley & Co., for it was inaugurated more than eighty years ago, operations having been begun in 1818. The founder was Mr. Nathan Farley, and was succeeded by H. N. Farley & Co., consisting of Messrs. H. N. and George B. Farley, who assumed control in 1866. Both these gentlemen are natives of Concord and are too well known hereabouts to render extended personal mention necessary. They continued the business until April 1, 1890, when Mr. D. M. Spline was admitted to the firm without change of firm-name. Mr. Spline brings to the business a ripe and varied experience, having been connected with this line of business from apprenticeship, having been in business for himself at Petersborough, N. H., and and for the last three years as traveling salesman for the Valido Marble company of Fair Haven, Vt. Mr. Spline will be the traveling salesman for the firm of which he is now a partner. The firm are manufacturers of and dealers in monuments, head stones and tablets of every description, and can furnish them in Italian and American marble and Scotch and American Granite. Granite curbing will also be furnished at short notice and at the lowest market rates, and cemetery work of all kinds will be skillfully done at reasonable prices. The firm offer a great variety of designs to choose from, ranging from the simplest to the most elaborate, and thus are in a position to suit all tastes as well as all purses. The premises utilized are located at the south corner of Main and Freight streets, a few rods below the Elm House, on the same side ; and callers are assured prompt and courteous attention, estimates being cheerfully made and all desired information given. The work turned out by this concern is equal to the best, and we know of no establishment at which an order for monumental stone cutting can be placed to better advantage, or with more assurance of the results being satisfactory.

George W. Waters, practical Embalmer and Undertaker, and dealer in fine Caskets, Coffins. Robes, etc., warerooms 18 Pleasant Street, Concord, N. H. Also dealer in Light and Dark Concord Granite; Monuments, Tablets and Statuary a specialty, West Concord, N. H.—Among the most enterprising and successful business men of Concord may be found Mr. George W. Waters, who is a practical embalmer and undertaker, also dealer in light and dark Concord granite, which business was inaugurated in 1879 under the name of George W. Waters, the present proprietor. Mr. Waters has through his native ability and enterprise succeeded in building up his present prosperous industry The undertaking warerooms utilized by him are located at No. 18 Pleasant street, where orders for anything in the line of undertaking will receive prompt and careful attention. Fine caskets, coffins, robes, etc , are constantly carried in stock and will be found very reasonable in price. The granite works are located at West Concord, where light and dark granite is dealt in. Cemetery work of all kinds is done and a specialty made of monuments, tablets and statuary. A large business is done at these granite works, employment being given to fifteen experienced workmen, and as the product of the house has met with great favor among those interested, the annual output is constantly increasing. All orders in either department of Mr. Waters business will receive prompt and painstaking attention, and the goods are fully warranted to give the best satisfaction Mr. Waters is well known throughout Concord and vicinity and is highly esteemed for his many excellent qualities.

Welsh & Lovely, Dry Goods and Small Wares, 19 Main Street, Concord, N. H.—Among the leading houses devoted to the sale of dry goods and small wares there is none more worthy of prominent mention than that conducted since March 10, 1890, by Messrs. Welsh & Lovely who at that date succeeded Messrs. D. E. Clark & Son, Mr. Clark, the senior member, having successfully carried on the business for thirty-eight years. This house has for many years borne the reputation of handling the best lines of dress goods obtained only from perfectly reliable sources. The assortment embraces the latest styles and newest patterns all goods being marked at popular prices. The premises occupied are located in Chase's new Block and afford a fine store with an area of 20×60 feet. The individual members of the firm are Mr. H. Welsh, a native of Southbridge, Mass., and Mr. T. S. Lovely, a native of Concord. Mr. Lovely is particularly well adapted for the enterprise as he has had ten years experience in the dry goods business in this city, and hence is well and favorably known to the purchasing public in this vicinity. Mr. Welsh has also had about twelve years experience in general mercantile business. We commend this firm to our readers as one whose ambition is to merit the confidence and patronage of the public, who appreciate honorable and upright dealing.

Frank P. Mace, Bookseller and Stationer, and dealer in Photograph and Autograph Albums, Scrap Books, etc., No. 86 North Main Street, Concord, N. H.—The enterprise named above was originated by Mr. Wm. H. Fiske, who was succeeded in 1875 by the present proprietor, who is a native of this city. The premises occupied are 20×80 feet in dimensions, and are well filled with a choice collection of books and stationers' goods. A full supply of the latest novels is always at hand, as well as a fine selection of those standard works that will never lose their popularity, and book lovers who have not visited this store, will be both pleased and surprised when they do so, to find such a variety, as all tastes can be suited. He also carries a large supply of stationery in which he can show some novelties, as well as all the popular styles of paper with which the market is now so well supplied, and in which there is such a great variety. He deals largely in photograph and autograph albums, scrap books, etc. In fact you can find most everything which one would expect to find in a store of this kind. Goods will be shown with pleasure, and all information regarding them will be given in a courteous manner to all. Confectionery and soda will also be found here in good quality and condition. Mr. Mace having been established here for so long a time has become thoroughly acquainted with the tastes of his patrons, and they are sure to find just what they want, and his honorable dealings in the past are all the security he needs for future success

La Belle & Co., dealers in and manufacturers of Concord, Sunapee, Quincy and Barre Granites, Concord, N. H.—Granite, and in fact, any kind of stone, will not stand unskilled treatment, or in other words, there is something about stone which makes poor workmanship look a great deal worse when this is the material wrought, than is the case with wood, iron, or any other substance. For this reason orders for stone work should be very carefully placed, and if intelligent discrimination be exercised, gratifying results can be attained at no greater cost than attends much of the botch work too common in the market. La Belle & Co. have only carried on operations in Concord since 1889, but an enviable reputation has already been gained for producing first class work in their line of business. Fine cut and polished cemetery work of every description is executed in an artistic and thoroughly satisfactory manner. The individual members of this firm are Mr. L. La Belle, a native of Suncook, N. H., and Messrs. G. E. Le Blanc and T. Dailey, of Canada. These gentlemen are all practical stone workers of large experience. They are dealers in and manufacturers of Concord, Sunapee, Quincy, and Barre granites. They carefully supervise

every detail of the work entrusted to them. Ten competent assistants are employed, and all orders sent to Box 916 will receive prompt attention, and all work is fully warranted to prove as represented, while the prices quoted are as low as can be named by responsible dealers, and satisfaction is guaranteed in every particular.

George Goodhue, practical Plumber, Gas and Steam Fitter, Plumbers' Materials of all kinds, Gas Fixtures a specialty, No. 7 Capitol Street, Concord, N. H.—Within the past ten years or so the public have become alive to the importance of having plumbing work thoroughly and skillfully done and are well aware that a "cheap" job of plumbing is apt to cost dearly in more respects than one ; for doctors' bills count up heavily and, after all, the chances are that the work will have to be done over again. Mr. George Goodhue is universally known throughout this section of the State as a reliable, practical plumber, gas and steam fitter, and it is natural that he should be, for he has been engaged in this business in Concord for nearly a score of years, having begun operations in 1871. He utilizes spacious premises at No. 7 Capitol street, and carries a very heavy and complete stock, being a jobber of plumbers' materials of all kinds, together with iron and brass pipe and fittings, wash bowls, marble slabs, etc. A specialty is made of gas fixtures, and anything in this line, from the simplest to the most elaborate pattern, will be furnished at short notice and at the lowest market rates ; customers being given an opportunity to choose from the latest novelties. Particular attention is given to fitting up dwellings, stores, factories, etc., and estimates will be cheerfully furnished on application. Another very important department of the business is contracting for waterworks, sewers, etc., Mr. Goodhue being in a position to figure very closely on work of this kind, and, what is still more to the point, to faithfully carry out every agreement. Towns, corporations or individuals contemplating such improvements would do well to notify him ; and all communications by mail or otherwise are assured immediate and careful attention. Mr. Goodhue is ably represented when necessary by his superintendent, Mr. George S. Milton, who for nine years has held that position, and is thoroughly conversant with the business and whose counsel is appreciated by his employer.

Concord Carriage Co., Reorganized and Limited, Manufacturers of Heavy Trucks, Wagons, Caravans, Barges, Furniture, Job and Express Wagons. Jobbing promptly and neatly done. All Work Warranted to Give Satisfaction. Works at the Old State Prison Shops, Concord, N. H.—The Concord Carriage Co. began operations some fifteen years ago, but was reorganized in 1890, and now is better prepared than ever before to fill orders promptly and to quote the lowest prices possible on thoroughly first-class work. The gentlemen identified with it are well and favorably known in business circles, and may be depended upon to spare no pains to keep the service at the highest standard of efficiency. Mr. H. L. Worthington is a native of Connecticut, and Messrs. Lewis M. Brown and Guy S. Rix were born in this city. The company's works are at the old State's prison shops, and are commodious and well-arranged, fitted up with improved machinery, driven by an engine of thirty-five horse power. Employment is given to an adequate force of skilled assistants, and the manufacture of heavy trucks, wagons, caravans, barges, furniture, job and express wagons is extensively carried on, the vehicles being strongly and durably made in every part and equipped with the latest improvements. Jobbing is done in a neat and workmanlike manner at very short notice, and the charges are uniformly moderate. A large and varied stock of light and heavy wagons and carriages is constantly on hand, the vehicles, being fully guaranteed to prove precisely as represented, and the prices comparing favorably with those quoted by any dealer in articles of equal merit.

Thomas Woodward, manufacturers of Italian and Store awnings, Tents, Flags, Boat Sails, Sun Shades, Trunk Covers and Hammocks. Also, maker of Waterproof Oil Covers for wagons and horses, Coats, Hay Caps, Carriage Boots. All kinds of Rigging and Boat Splicing, etc. Rear of Masonic Temple, Concord, N. H.—Somebody has defined the temperate zone as "the place where you freeze in winter and roast in summer," and it must be confessed that there is more truth than poetry in this description, especially so far as New England is concerned. But, after all, our New England climate averages about as well as any, and if we will utilize the proper facilities we can easily make ourselves comfortable at all seasons. Awnings will do much to make houses and stores cool and comfortable in the hottest weather, and they are absolutely necessary to protect the goods in show windows from the effects of the sun. Their use is increasing every year; and as an ill-fitting awning looks as bad as an ill-fitting coat, everybody is interested in knowing where they can place orders and feel assured that the work will be so done as to be ornamental as well as useful. Well, Mr. Thomas Woodward certainly should be able to do work in this line equal to the best, for he has had long and varied experience in the business, maintains a well-equipped shop and employs skilled assistants. As a matter of fact, we feel assured that no awning maker in New England is better prepared to satisfy his patrons, and the residents of Concord will have no trouble in obtaining proofs of Mr. Woodward's skill, for he has carried on business here ever since 1873, and specimens of his work are to be seen on the leading public and private buildings throughout the city and vicinity. He is a native of England, and has made many friends by his enterprising and honorable business methods during his residence in Concord. His work was awarded a diploma in 1875 and a silver medal in 1876, and he refers by permission to the Abbott Downing Company of this city. The premises utilized are located rear of Masonic Temple, and have an area of about 5,000 square feet. Among the articles manufactured may be mentioned Italian and store awnings, tents, flags, boat sails, sun shades, trunk covers and hammocks, together with waterproof oil covers for wagons and horses, coats, hay caps, carriage boots, etc. All kinds of rigging and boat splicing will be done in a superior manner at short notice, and uniformly moderate charges are made in every instance.

E. H. Randall, dealer in Low Pressure Steam Heating Apparatus. Steam and Gas Fitter and Plumber, No. 166 North Main Street, Third Door North Free Bridge Road, Concord, N. H.—Competent judges concede that the most efficient, the most convenient, the most secure and the most economical method of supplying artificial heat is by the use of properly designed, constructed and arranged low-pressure steam-heating apparatus, so that really the only question for an intelligent man to consider when contracting for heating apparatus, is where to place his order. We have no hesitation in recommending Mr. E. H. Randall for he makes a specialty of supplying and setting up low-pressure steam heating facilities, and during the eleven years that he has carried on business in Concord has won an enviable reputation for skill, reliability and the quoting of moderate prices. He is prepared to contract to heat public or private houses by apparatus of his selection and setting up, and to guarantee that it will do all that is claimed for it if used in accordance with instructions, so that the purchaser assumes no risk whatever. Mr Randall utilizes one floor and a basement of the dimensions of 18×74 feet, located at No. 166 North Main street, third door north of the Free Bridge road, and carries a stock of steam and gas piping and fittings, together with plumbers' materials, etc. He employs from five to eight assistants and gives prompt and painstaking attention to orders for steam and gas fitting and plumbing, warranting all work to prove satisfactory and making uniformly moderate charges. His business is steadily increasing and will surely continue to do so as long as present methods of management are adhered to.

Carpenter Granite Co., manufacturers of and dealers in Granite, near State Prison, Concord.—Concord Granite is famous throughout this country, and as large as the demand for it in the past it is but an earnest of what may reasonably be expected in the future, for this stone has so many desirable qualities to recommend it that it is steadily and rapidly growing in popularity for both cemetery and building work. One of the best quarries in this vicinity is that controlled by the Carpenter Granite Co., whose office and yard are near the State prison. This company of which Mr. J. W. Carpenter is the principal is the successor to Mr. Ola Anderson, having purchased his interest in this quarry and business, Mr. Anderson being retained as superintendent. The granite obtained from this quarry has an established reputation for its superior quality and as a natural result they are doing a very extensive business with a large amount of contracts on hand, among which are the Watertown Soldiers' Monument, Palm's tomb, which is to contain the largest stone ever set up in this country. Also Gen. Alger's tomb is to be made by this company from this granite. A large business is done in supplying unfinished granite to dealers in any quantity desired, their facilities enabling them to fill the most extensive orders at short notice. Rough and finished granite for building purposes will also be furnished without delay, and at prices as low as the lowest. Employment is given to from fifty to sixty men and cemetery work of all kinds is largely manufactured, many beautiful and tasteful designs being shown, and original designs being made to order if desired. The workmanship is equal to the best in every respect, and the charges are as low as is consistent with the attainment of perfectly satisfactory results.

Merrimack County Savings Bank, Concord, N. H.— The average man has all he can attend to in gaining a mastery of his own business, and it would be absurd to expect the entire community to be versed in the practical details of finance, but there are certain fundamental principles so plain, and at the same time so important, that no person of average intelligence is excusable for ignorance of them. For instance, everyone should know that a high rate of interest means insecurity of the principal, when a banking institution, or a manufacturing company, or a railroad company, or a city, town or individual is obliged to pay more than the regular market rates for the use of money, the fact of such payment is equivalent to a confession that in the judgment of experts the security offered is not so good as it should be. This rule has no exception, and we wish every wage-earner in the country would bear it in mind when reading the seductively-worded advertisements so common in some of the public prints. We know that experts have made mistakes in the past and will doubtless do so in the future, but in the great majority of instances their judgment is correct, and no one having no money to throw away can afford to act in defiance of it. A well-established and conservatively managed savings bank affords by far the best facilities for the investment of small sums, and in the Merrimack County Savings Bank the residents of Concord and vicinity have as sound and deserving an institution of the kind as can be found in the State. Incorporated in 1867, it has steadily grown in usefulness and in the confidence of the public, until at the present time it has considerably more than a million dollars entrusted to it, the exact sum March 1, 1890 being $1,101,150.73. The guaranty fund amounts to $65,000, and undivided profits $40,569.31; and further evidence of able and careful management is afforded by the fact that the value of the securities held are worth $38,855 above their cost. Some of the leading business men of this section of the State are identified with this popular bank, as will be seen by a perusal of the annexed list of officers: President, L. D. Stevens; vice-president, Wm M. Chase; treasurer, John Kimball. Trustees: J. M. Hill, Wm. M. Chase, J. L. Mason, Daniel Holden, L. A. Smith, C. H. Amsden, L. A. Hill, W. Odlin, G. A. Cummings, L. D Stevens, H. W. Stevens, B. A. Kimball, John Kimball, F. T. Andrews, David D. Taylor.

O. S. Parker, manager for New Hampshire for the Ætna Life Insurance Company of Hartford, Conn., Concord, N. H. A man must be peculiarly constituted in order to enjoy reading tables, statistics, etc., no matter how carefully they may be prepared or how valuable the subject matter may be, and in calling attention to the facilities for insurance offered by the Ætna Life Insurance Company of Hartford, Conn., we have no intention of presenting such tables, but simply propose to inform our readers how they can obtain the most absolutely secure insurance at the most equitable rates. In no line of business is there more profession made of "giving something for nothing" than in the insurance trade; and every intelligent person should refuse to be deceived by the seductive but utterly fallacious "plans of insurance" submitted nowadays, by certain unscrupulous, or at the best, wonderfully sanguine parties. Every plan upon which the Ætna Life issues policies has been tried and proved; and during the forty years which this company has been in existence it has met every obligation, redeemed every promise and built up a business larger than that of any New England company. The following are a few good and sufficient reasons why the Ætna Life should be preferred by those seeking reliable insurance:

Because of its age, having had forty years of successful experience.

Because its contracts are liberal, and give to the insured full value for all the money paid.

Because its affairs are conducted upon business principles, which have stood the test of time.

Because it has a large capital stock, which acts as a bond for the proper conduct of the business.

Because it pays its claims upon the receipt of satisfactory proofs, without delay or discount.

Because its business is economically managed, and is confined to the object of its organization.

Because it pays large and increasing dividends to its insured, uniformly larger than those of other companies.

Because its policies are incontestable, so far as the beneficiaries are concerned, after three years from their date.

Because it gives advantages over purely mutual companies, with none of the liabilities incident to such management.

Because its policies are non forfeiting by their terms, so that in no event can there be loss to its patrons by reason of discontinuance of payment.

Because it not only pays its insured a constantly increasing dividend, but the ability of the company to continue the same has been increased each year.

Many others might easily be added, but we have certainly shown the claims made on behalf of the company to be mostly of careful investigation and Mr Charles S Parker, manager for New Hampshire, will cheerfully give whatever further information may be desired as to the plans of the company, of which some are specials and offered by the Ætna only. He is a native of Andover, Mass., has represented the company in Concord for about five years, and is widely known in insurance and general business circles. His office is conveniently located at 72 North Main street, and callers are assured careful and courteous attention and will do well to give him a call before insuring elsewhere.

Amos Blanchard, Variety Store, Dry Goods and Groceries 188 Pleasant Street, Concord, N. H.—This business was started in 1855 by the present proprietor on Main street, and in 1877 removed to his present site. He is a native of Methuen, Mass. It is not to be wondered at that Mr. Blanchard has a large and growing trade, for the advantages gained by dealing with him are so many that there is little chance of the most careless buyer failing to appreciate them. He occupies a large and attractive store that affords excellent facilities for the display and examination of goods. It is well lighted and has an area of 2,100 square feet. The stock is varied and desirable. It embraces dry goods and groceries, boots and shoes, hardware, agricultural tools, garden seeds and some clothing. It would be useless to attempt to describe this stock, as late novelties are continually being added, and the articles are constantly renewed. Particular attention is paid to the quality of the goods dealt in. They are selected with special reference to the demands of the many patrons of this store, with whom Mr. Blanchard, from his long acquaintance has become familiar. He employs three assistants, who are courteous to all. He guarantees his goods to prove as represented, and offers them at low prices in every department. Orders are solicited and promptly filled.

Humphrey & Dodge, Jobbers and Retailers in Hardware, Iron and Steel, Concord, N. H.—In every trade centre there are certain business undertakings which are conceded to be the leaders in their special lines, and a prominent example of such an enterprise is that conducted by Messrs. Humphrey & Dodge, it having been inaugurated more than sixty years ago, and having long since gained its present representative position. The original proprietors were Messrs. Porter, Rolfe & Brown, and the business has since been conducted and developed by the following proprietors: Messrs. Warde & Walker, David A. Warde, Messrs. Warde & Humphrey, Messrs. Warde, Humphrey & Co., Messrs. Warde, Humphrey & Dodge, Messrs. Humphrey & Dodge, Messrs. Humphrey, Dodge & Smith, and Messrs. Humphrey & Dodge, the existing style, being adopted in 1889. Mr. Stillman Humphrey is a native of Croydon, N. H., and being at present mayor of Concord, can scarcely need introduction to our New Hampshire readers, while Mr. Howard A. Dodge, who was born in Lempster, N. H., is a trustee of the Loan and Trust Savings Bank, is also too widely known in business and social circles to require extended personal mention. The firm employ ten assistants and are heavy jobbers and retailers of hardware, iron and steel, carrying a very extensive and complete stock, and being in a position to fill the largest orders at short notice. The premises made use of comprise one floor and a basement of the dimensions of 40×100 feet, another floor measuring 40×50 feet, a large storehouse in the rear of the warerooms, and another storehouse located on Bridge street. Careful supervision is exercised over every department of the business, and callers are assured immediate and painstaking attention.

Morrill Brothers, Fine Watches, Jewelry and Solid Silver Ware, Concord, N. H.—The taste for jewelry and the expression of art in personal adornment, is as old as the human race, and one of the most marked and universal of its characteristics, with the progress of civilization, is that it has assumed new and beautiful forms, and to-day the best jewelry stores are centers of the most delicate and lovely exponents of art. Such an honor must be unhesitatingly awarded the fine store and stock of Morrill Brothers, located at No. 55 North Main street, Concord. This establishment was inaugurated in 1863 by its present proprietors, who, since that date, have contributed a large share to the advancement of their department of trade in this section. They now supply one of the best and most valuable retail trades in this section, and their stock of fine watches, jewelry, solid silver ware, etc., is always maintained at the highest standards and sold on the most moderate terms. Bric-a-brac, Butterick's patterns, and pianos and organs are also dealt in, and if you are in want of a good piano don't fail to visit Morrill Brothers' rooms in the rear of the jewelry store. Special attention is given to fine watch and jewelry repairing in all its branches, and all work in this line may be entrusted to their care with perfect confidence that it will be most admirably and satisfactorily done. Both Mr. Samuel F. and John F. Morrill are natives of Dover, N. H., and are thoroughly conversant with all branches of their business, and rank among highly esteemed and reliable business men. Mr. Samuel F. Morrill has held the office of representative and both brothers are well known throughout Concord and vicinity. Their business has required more room, and larger accommodations have been obtained recently by building an addition in the rear of the store and connected with the same, which now affords them ample quarters, the addition being 40×23 feet and given up to the piano trade.

A. Perley Fitch, Drugs, Paints and Oils, Wholesale and Retail, Concord, N. H.—The gentleman whose card we print above is one of the largest dealers in drugs and paints in the State, and is also very extensively engaged in the manufacture of proprietary medicines, he having exceptionally complete facilities for ensuring absolute uniformity of quality in the various valuable remedies he prepares. The business is of very long standing, it having been founded by Messrs Allison & Eastman in 1859. In 1864 Messrs. Eastman & Co. assumed control, and in 1868 Mr. Chas. S. Eastman became sole proprietor, the present owner becoming connected with the enterprise in 1874, as a member of the firm of Eastman & Fitch, and assuming sole possession in 1882. He is a native of Enfield, N. H., and is widely known in Concord and vicinity, both in business and social circles. Mr. Fitch utilizes very spacious premises, including one floor and a basement of the dimensions of 25×65 feet, together with two outside basements and two storehouses. A very heavy and varied stock is carried, both a wholesale and retail business is done and Mr. Fitch proposes to always be in a position to fill the most extensive orders at short notice. Obtaining his goods from the most reputable sources, he can safely guarantee them to prove strictly as represented and the magnitude of his business enables him to quote the very lowest market rates at all times, while the employment of ten assistants assures immediate attention to every caller.

Sleeper & Hood, Gents' Fine Tailors and Furnishers, 90 North Main Street, Concord, N. H.—The demand for strictly first class gentlemen's clothing is increasing much faster than can be accounted for by the increase in population, and the explanation is to be found in the obvious fact that this country is gaining in culture as well as in wealth and that consequently a larger proportion of the inhabitants are fastidious in their tastes. One need not be rich in order to dress well, for fine custom garments are more durable in material and workmanship than those of inferior grade, and whatever difference there may be in their first cost is thus largely compensated for. In this connection we may properly call attention to the enterprise conducted by Messrs. Sleeper & Hood, at No. 90 North Main street, for this firm have a high reputation as gentlemen's fine tailors and furnishers, and are as moderate in their charges as they are skilled in their business. Operations were begun as far back as 1859, by Messrs. Critchett & Sleeper, who were succeeded by Mr. J. T. Sleeper in 1866, and in 1877 this gentleman became associated with Mr. William E. Hood, under the existing firm name. The senior partner is a native of Andover, N. H., while Mr. Hood is a native of Salem, Mass. Both members of the firm are very widely known throughout this section in business and social circles and Mr. Hood is connected with the board of aldermen. The premises utilized have a total area of 3200 square feet, and are equipped with every facility, employment being given to twenty five assistants. A carefully chosen and attractive stock of foreign and domestic fabrics for gentlemen's wear is constantly carried, embracing the latest fashionable novelties and being complete in every department. A full line of furnishings is also on hand to select from, and those wishing to dress correctly can do no better than to place their orders with this representative concern.

William F. Carr, dealer in Groceries, Flour, Teas, Spices, etc. Also, Fruits in their season. 185 North Main Street, Concord, N. H.—"The North End Cash Grocery" has been established for several years, but it was in 1887 that the present proprietor, Mr. William F. Carr, took possession of these premises. He is a native of this city, therefore he needs no introduction to the many readers of this history. He is an extensive dealer in groceries, teas, spices, meats, provisions, etc.; also, fruits in their season. That this store ranks with the most popular in town, and receives an increasing support every year, is convincing evidence of the high esteem in which it is held. A large stock of goods is carried, comprising choice grades of flour, teas, spices, etc. His meats and provisions are the best

that the market affords, while the extensive trade which he receives, enables him to keep his stock fresh by being daily renewed. This concern makes no pretense of selling cheaper than any one else, but offers first-class family groceries and provisions at reasonable rates, and can be depended upon, for Mr. Carr has won the confidence of his customers. Employment is given to three competent assistants, that every patron may be waited upon without delay. Orders are promptly and carefully filled.

Hunt & Greenwood, Books, Stationery, and Art Goods, 85 North Main Street, Concord, N. H.—The business carried on by Messrs. Hunt & Greenwood had its origin in two separate enterprises, one being conducted by Mr. D. L. Guernsey and the other by Mr. F. D. Batchelder. The former was a dealer in books and stationery, and the latter in art goods, and the two stores were combined by Messrs. Hunt & Wilson in 1887, the existing firm being formed in 1889. Mr. W. E. Hunt is a native of St. Johnsbury, Vt., and Mr. H. Greenwood of New London, N. H., both of these gentlemen giving their personal attention to the details of their business. The store is located at No. 85 North Main street, and comprises one floor and basement. Concord has long needed an enterprising firm in this line of business and their store seems destined to become the centre of literature and art in the capital city. "No matter what his rank or position may be the lover of books is the richest and the happiest of the children of men," and here he may find much to gratify his taste, and at reasonable prices. In their stationery department a specialty is made of selling writing paper by the pound, considerable success has been attained in this departure from the old-time method of dealing out by the quire. They also carry a line of blank books and miscellaneous stationery. In the art department a fine line of pictures is carried, including etchings, American and foreign photographs—photo reposets—and photogravure and mezzotype reproductions. An important part of their business is the manufacture of picture frames. Their factory is located in one of the Dow buildings where they enjoy superior manufacturing facilities, a large line of mouldings is carried and their wholesale trade extends to various points in the State and reaches into Vermont.

E. B. Hutchinson, Contractor and Builder, dealer in Lumber, Shingles, Laths, Clapboards, etc., manufacturer of Mouldings, Brackets and House Finish, Kiln Drying, Sawing and Planing done to order. Turnpike Street, Concord, N. H.—Mr. E. B. Hutchinson has been identified with his present business for more than thirty years, and the position he occupies as a contractor and builder, may be judged from the fact that he was entrusted with the construction of such representative edifices as the State Capital bank building, the Statesman building, the Public Library building, the Board of Trade building, the New Hampshire Savings Bank building; together with a number of school-houses, etc. He was born in Loudon, N. H., and began operations in Concord in 1859. Mr. Hutchinson has served as representative, but the character of his business interests has prevented him from giving much time to public affairs. Besides doing a general contracting and building business, he deals largely, both at wholesale and retail in lumber, shingles, laths, clapboards, etc., and is a manufacturer of mouldings, brackets and house finish of all descriptions, kiln drying, sawing and planing will be done to order at moderate rates, and the facilities are such as to enable the most extensive commissions to be executed at short notice. The shop and office are located on Turkpike street, and employment is given to from forty to sixty assistants usually, although at times seventy-five are required. Mr. Hutchinson will promptly and cheerfully furnish estimates on application, and considering his experience and facilities, it seems needless to add that he is in a position to figure very closely on plans and specifications submitted, or that every contract entered upon will be faithfully carried out to the satisfaction of all parties concerned.

Frank Coffin, dealer in Flour, Grain, Provisions, Hay, Lime, Cement, Plaster, etc., agent for Washburn, Crosby & Co's. Flour, Chicago Gluten Meal, warehouse rear Phenix Hotel, Concord, N. H.—Mr. Frank Coffin has been identified with his present enterprise for more than a quarter of a century, he having been a member of the firm of Quimby & Co., who began operations in 1863 and were succeeded in 1872 by Messrs. Coffin, Cochran & Co., the present proprietor assuming sole control in 1877. He is a native of Deerfield, N. H., and, considering his long and honorable business career, it is hardly necessary to add is very widely and favorably known in mercantile and social circles throughout this vicinity. Mr. Coffin is an extensive wholesale and retail dealer in flour, grain, provisions, hay, lime, cement, plaster, etc., and is in a position to quote bottom prices on all these commodities, while his facilities for the prompt and accurate filling of all orders, large or small, are unsurpassed. His business was removed to its present location in 1884; the premises now utilized comprising two floors of the dimensions of 80×40 feet, and a basement measuring 40×160 feet, thus affording ample room for the accommodation of a heavy stock. They are on the line of the Northern railroad, and flour, grain, etc., are received directly from the west, Mr. Coffin being agent for the sale of Washburn, Crosby & Co's., celebrated flour, Chicago Gluten meal, etc. Employment is given to three assistants, and all orders are assured prompt and painstaking attention.

J. M. Stewart & Sons, dealers in Furniture, Draperies, Curtains, Carpets, Rugs, etc., five doors north of Eagle hotel, Concord, N. H.—The business carried on by Messrs. J. M. Stewart & Sons may be said to have had its origin more than forty years ago, when operations were begun by Messrs. Brown & Young, they being followed by H. H. Aldich, he by Higgins & Patten, they by Messrs. Patten & Heath, they by Messrs. Patten & Young, they by Messrs. Young Brothers, who were succeeded by the present proprietors in 1887. In 1880, Messrs. J. M. Stewart & Sons succeeded. Mr. William B. Stearns in the carpet and crockery business, and added furniture, etc., on assuming control of the enterprise previously carried on by Young Brothers. As now constituted, the firm is made up of Messrs. A. C. and E. M. Stewart, both of whom are natives of this city. Spacious premises, located five doors north of the Eagle hotel, are utilized, comprising two floors measuring 60×80 feet each, one floor of the dimensions of 50×60 feet, three basements and store house, and a workshop thirty-five feet square. A very large stock is carried, made up of furniture, draperies, curtains, carpets, rugs, wall papers, crockery, lamps and other household goods, the assortment being exceptionally complete, the goods uniformly dependable and the prices low. This makes a strong combination of advantages, and it is therefore not surprising that the firm should do a business requiring the employment of from twelve to fifteen assistants. One result of the employment of this large force is the assurance of prompt and courteous attention to every customer, and another is the early and accurate delivery of all orders, large and small. The latest fashionable novelties are represented in the stock and the patronage is as select as it is extensive.

Concord Boot and Shoe Company, G. B. Johnson, manager, wholesale dealers in Boots and Shoes, and manufacturers' agents for Woonsocket Rubber Goods, Dow's block, Bridge Street, Concord, N. H.—It may seem at first thought as though the purchasing public not directly interested in such an enterprise as that conducted by the Concord Boot and Shoe company, who do an exclusively wholesale business, but a little reflection will show that as the retailer must buy to advantage if he is to sell to advantage; a concern that is in a position to supply him with dependable goods at bottom rates is capable of rendering valuable service to consumers. Such is the position held by the company in question, which was organized in 1885,

and has built up an extensive business; from two to five salesmen being kept on the road, and goods being sold throughout New Hampshire and Vermont and in a portion of Maine. The manager, Mr. G. B. Johnson, certainly needs no introduction to the residents of Concord, for he is a member of the board of aldermen, and is widely and favorably known both in business and social circles. The company utilizes premises located on Bridge street, in Dow's block, they comprising one room measuring 25×100 feet, and another 40 feet square. A heavy and varied stock is constantly carried, and the largest order can be filled at very short notice. Besides handling boots and shoes of all kinds the company are manufacturers' agents for the famous Woonsocket rubber goods, and are prepared to furnish those standard articles at the very lowest market rates.

Ford & Kimball, Car Wheels, Brass and Iron Founders. Office 29 Main Street, Concord, N. H.—The business carried on by Messrs. Ford & Kimball was founded nearly forty-five years ago, and for a long time has been classed among Concord's representative industries. Operations were begun in 1846 by Messrs. Ford, Pillsbury & Co., who were succeeded the same year by Messrs. W. P. and T. H. Ford. In 1850 the business was removed to the North End, and ten years later the present premises were bought. The existing firm was organized in 1865 and is constituted of Messrs. T. H. Ford and B. A. Kimball; the former a native of Sanbornton, and the latter of Boscawen, N. H. The manufacture of car wheels is the leading specialty, and the productions of this concern have an unsurpassed reputation for uniform excellence both of material and workmanship. The car wheels made here are highly thought of by practical railroad men, who say that as regards strength, durability and freedom from defects they have no superiors and few equals in the market. The premises comprise a moulding room, of the dimensions of 221×57 feet; a machine shop, pattern house, carpenter shop, fence shop, engine house, etc., and are very conveniently arranged. Employment is given to from forty to fifty assistants, and the most extensive orders can be filled at short notice. Brass and iron founding is extensively carried on, and estimates will be promptly furnished on application in person or by mail at the office, No. 29 Main street. Patterns will be made to order if desired and the firm are prepared to figure very low on any work included in their line of business.

Aldine Stable, Norris A. Dunklee, Proprietor. Livery, Boarding and Sale Stable ; Carriages Furnished for Parties, Weddings, Funerals, etc. Opposite Phenix Hotel, rear of First National Bank, Concord, N. H.—Mr. Norris A. Dunklee, the proprietor of the Aldine Stable, is a native of Virginia ; and to those who are familiar with the characteristics of the people of that historic State it is hardly necessary to add that he knows a good horse when he sees it, and thinks enough of such animals to allow no one to abuse them when he can prevent it. Mr. Dunklee has been in the stable business in this city for many years, and should a stranger ask an old resident of Concord where he could hire a first-class team at a fair price, the answer would almost certainly be, "At the Aldine Stable, opposite the Phenix Hotel and in the rear of the First National Bank." And this would be most excellent advice, too, for if there be a public stable in New Hampshire where better accommodations are provided, we have never had the good fortune to find it. The Aldine is a livery, boarding and sale stable, and contains twenty-seven stalls. Horses boarded here are assured comfortable quarters, good food and kind treatment, and the charges are uniformly moderate. Mr. Dunklee is prepared to furnish carriages for parties, weddings, funerals, etc., and can fill the most extensive orders of this kind at short notice. Experienced and courteous drivers are supplied and the carriages are of modern style and are kept in excellent condition.

The Capital Fire Insurance Co, Concord, N. H.—No insurance corporation in New Hampshire stands higher in the confidence of those thoroughly familiar with the methods and resources of the various state and foreign companies doing business here than the Capital Fire Insurance Co.; and if any of our readers be disposed to doubt this assertion we would respectfully refer them to the statement issued by the company January 8, 1890, for "facts are stubborn things," and the facts made evident by the figures presented indicate, as the management well say, that "this company has won the confidence of the people of New Hampshire, and has won it by deserving it." For instance, the insurance written in 1888 was $4,044,598,73 ; in 1889, $4,395,720.47, showing an increase of $351,121.74. The losses paid in 1888 were $22,737.46 ; in 1889, $31,001.85, an increase of $8,264.39. The assets January 1, 1889, were $97,879.55 ; January 1, 1890, $100,-876.15,—an increase of $2,996.60. The surplus, January 1, 1889, was $13,501.63 ; January, 1890, $14,807.76, an increase of $1,306.13. Certainly there is no need of extended argument to make manifest the deserving character of a company that makes such a showing, and the more widely these figures are disseminated the more rapidly will applications be made for policies by those seeking "insurance that insures." Any remarks concerning the ability of the management would be quite superfluous and we will simply state that the company numbers the following gentlemen among its officers : President, Hon. A. B. Thompson ; Vice-President, Henry McFarland ; Secretary, Lyman Jackman ; Treasurer, J. E. Fernald, Cashier Nat. State Capital Bank.

George B. Whittredge, dealer in Groceries, Fresh Fish, Oysters, etc., 101 South Main Street, Concord, N. H.—Mr. George B Whittredge is a native of Massachusetts, but as he has been in business in this city for about a quarter of a century, he could not be better known here had he lived in Concord all his life. He has carried on operations at his present location, No. 101 South Main street, since 1887, and has built up an extensive family trade: his stock being made up of articles especially selected for family use and comprising staple and fancy groceries, fresh fish, oysters, etc. Mr. Whittredge does not claim to quote lower prices than any other dealer in New Hampshire or even in Concord but he does claim to be in a position to meet all honorable competition and to name the lowest market rates on strictly dependable goods. Obtaining his supplies from the most reliable sources, he is prepared to fully guarantee them to prove as represented, and we have no hesitation in assuring satisfaction to the most fastidious among our readers who may favor him with an order. Prompt and polite attention is the rule to every caller, and the high reputation for fair dealing gained in the past will continue to be deserved in the future.

George A. Berry & Co., Pharmacists, 16 North Main Street, Concord, N. H.—This store has been known for a long time as one of the leading drug stores in this city. Business in this line was started here many years ago, and after passing through the hands of several proprietors when in 1889 it came under the control of Wyatt & Berry, but April 1st, 1890, the firm was again changed to George A. Berry & Co. It is the intention of the present firm to conduct a first-class prescription pharmacy, and merit the patronage of the purchasing public. Mr. George A. Berry is a native of this city, and is well known to the residents of this section. The premises occupied are 25×75 feet in dimensions, and are finely fitted and arranged for this business. They make a specialty of putting up physicians' prescriptions, and have an elegant case for this purpose fitted up with all the modern appliances. It is made of mahogany with a full length mirror, and is said to be the best of the kind in the city. A very complete stock of drugs, medicines and chemicals is carried, which are often replenished to secure their being fresh and in proper condition for use. Particular attention is paid to every detail of the business that no mistakes can occur. Employment is given to two competent assistants, and all orders are promptly and accurately filled.

Greeley & Todd, dealers in Domestic Dry and Fancy Goods, Family Groceries, Flour, Pork, Lard, etc.; also Crockery, Glass and Wooden Ware. 80 and 84 Washington Street, Concord, N. H.—One of the best stocked and most popular retail stores in Concord is that conducted by Messrs. Greeley & Todd, at Nos. 80 and 84 Washington street, and the popularity of this establishment is not to be wondered at, for the goods offered are excellent in quality and extremely varied in kind; the prices quoted are uniformly moderate, and the service is prompt and efficient in every way. This business was at one time carried on by Messrs. E. D. Clough & Co., who were succeeded by Messrs. Currier & Sleeper in 1885, and they by Mr. A. A. Currier in 1887, the present firm assuming control in 1888. Messrs. J. H. Greeley and W. H. Todd are both New Hampshire men by birth, and are evidently thoroughly familiar with the requirements of local trade, for the business has flourished under their direction and is still steadily increasing. The premises utilized are 60×75 feet in dimensions, and the available space is fully taken up by the exceptionally heavy and complete stock, which comprises domestic dry and fancy goods, choice family groceries, flour, pork, lard, etc., together with a full line of crockery, glass and wooden ware, including many late and popular novelties. Employment is given to two assistants, and no trouble is spared to assure prompt attention to every caller and to fully satisfy every customer.

Edward Dow, Architect, 72 North Main Street, Concord, N. H.—No one at all acquainted with building operations will deny that on the skill of the architect depends in a great measure, not only the convenience, but also the cost of the finished structure, and it may be accepted as an unvarying rule that it always pays to employ the best talent available in the architectural line. Experience is at least as valuable as skill, to the architect, for no knowledge coming from books is going to enable him to overcome the many minor difficulties, which he will encounter in practical business, and the readiness and judgment necessary to do so, are only the outcome of former trials of the same kind. Mr. Edward Dow opened this office in 1855, and after a while Mr. Wheeler became associated with him, and so continued for about ten years, but since 1886, Mr. Dow has been sole proprietor. He is a native of Lemington, Vt, and has become a prominent citizen of Concord, having been an alderman and a representative. He also served in our army during the late Rebellion. Mr. Dow will be found at all times willing to be consulted on anything pertaining to his profession, and we should certainly advise those contemplating the erection of a dwelling or business structure, to lay their plans before him and be guided by his advice.

Jackman & Lang, Insurance Agents, State Capital Bank Building, Corner Main and Warren Streets, Concord, N. H.—It is doing injustice to no one to speak of Messrs. Jackman & Lang as the leading insurance agents of Concord, for this position is accorded to the firm by common consent, and their office is regarded as the Fire Insurance headquarters of the city. The senior partner has been identified with the enterprise for more than a score of years, beginning operations in 1868 as a member of the firm of Hall & Jackman, who were succeeded in 1874 by Robinson & Jackman, and they by L. Jackman & Co. in 1875. In 1880 the firm of Jackman & Larkin was formed, and the existing style was adopted in 1883. Captain Lyman Jackman is a native of Woodstock, N. H., and served nearly four years in the army with the Sixth N. H. Regiment. During such service, he held several responsible positions such as Brigade Quartermaster of the Ninth Army Corps; Inspector General and Aid de camp of the Northern Central District of Kentucky, under Generals Boyle, Frye, Gibson, Nagle and Griffin. He is also a member of the N. H. House of Representatives in the year 1885. Mr. Thomas M. Lang is also an ex-soldier having seen two and one-half years service at which time he was obliged to leave the army on account of severe wounds received at the battle of Fair Oaks, Va. Also City Tax Collector for five years. He is a native of Georgetown, Mass. Both members of the firm are prominently connected with the Fire Underwriters Association, one of the most successful of Concord's insurance companies, Mr. Jackman being president and Mr. Lang secretary. Mr. Jackman is also identified with three other popular companies, in each of which he holds the office of secretary,—the Capital Fire Insurance Company; the Manufacturers and Merchants Mutual Insurance Company, and the Phenix Mutual Insurance Company. The home office of each of these organizations is at Messrs. Jackman & Lang's rooms in the State Capital Bank Building, and the firm not only act as agents for them but also represent the following foreign corporations:

California Insurance Co.....Assets,	$1,247,874.60
Orient, Hartford............ "	1,805,663.48
Springfield Fire and Marine.. "	3,410,982.94
American, of Newark....... "	2,048,584.12
Phenix Insurance Co. of London"	7,430,535.63
Norwich Union of England.. "	1,411,445.00
Sun Fire Office "	1,956,331.05

All business is assured prompt and painstaking attention, and we need hardly add that Messrs. Jackman & Lang are in a position to effect insurance to any desired amount on the most favorable terms.

William Wright's Stable, Livery, Boarding and Hack Stable; Carriages furnished for Parties, Weddings, Funerals, etc. Opposite Odd Fellows' new block, Pleasant Street, Concord, N. H.—The livery, boarding and hack stable, conducted by Mr William Wright on Pleasant street, opposite the Odd Fellows' new block, is worthy of liberal patronage, both from horse owners and the public in general, for the former may board their horses there in the full assurance that they will be given proper attention, while the latter may obtain first class teams at short notice and at very reasonable rates. This stable was opened by Messrs Bushey & Bowser, and after one or two changes in its management came into the possession of the present proprietor in 1889. He is evidently an excellent judge of horseflesh, for he has some universally good animals in his stable, and keeps them in the pink of condition at all times. There are twenty stalls on the premises, and a sufficient number of horses and carriages are on hand to properly accommodate the rapidly growing business. We are confident that those who may place a trial order with Mr. Wright will thank us for calling their attention to his facilities, for his teams are decidedly superior to those commonly devoted to livery purposes. Carriages will be furnished for parties, weddings, funerals, etc., and customers are assured prompt and polite attention, and the prices rule very low.

G. B. Emmons, Provisions, Beef, Pork, Mutton, Lamb and Veal, Poultry and Game. Also a Complete Stock of Vegetables. No. 4 North Main Street, Concord, N. H.—This is one of the best-known enterprises of the kind to be found in this section, it having been inaugurated many years ago, and since continued with steadily increasing success. We learn that after some changes had taken place in the management of this house the firm name in 1871 was Flanders & Emmons, and in 1875 the present proprietor, Mr. G. B. Emmons, assumed sole control. The business has materially developed since coming under his liberal and enterprising methods, which are evidently thoroughly appreciated by those conversant with them. The premises utilized are of the dimensions of 20×65 feet, and the stock carried is large and complete in every respect, being made up of beef, pork, mutton, lamb and veal, poultry and game, also a complete stock of vegetables. They sell the nicest lard to be found in the city. Only choice family goods which are of the best quality are offered to customers, who by long dealings with them trust implicitly to their judgment and honesty. Employment is given to seven competent assistants, and all orders are assured prompt and careful attention. Mr. Emmons is a native of Bristol, N. H., and is a highly respected citizen. He has been an alderman and is now a representative.

J. H. Morey, Pianos and Organs; also teacher on Piano and Organ. 3 North Main Street, Concord, N. H.—We believe that the public generally appreciate the fact that the cheapest piano or organ to buy is an instrument that is strictly first-class in every respect, and hence we will not waste space in urging us to the truth of this proposition. Those who think that the lowest priced instrument is invariably the cheapest are very decidedly mistaken, but as such people only learn (if they learn at all) from experience, we will not address them in this brief article. It is no harder to obtain one's money's worth in the purchase of a piano or an organ than in the buying of any other standard article of trade, but it is necessary to bear in mind the fact that to secure honorable treatment you must deal with an honorable establishment. The store conducted by Mr. J. H. Morey has gained so wide spread a reputation for entire reliability that few, if any, of the residents of Concord or vicinity can be ignorant of it. Mr. Morey deals in pianos and organs, and occupies a store 20×60 feet in dimensions at No. 3 North Main street. He handles only the best makes of pianos and organs, and is prepared to furnish either at the lowest market prices. Mr. Morey is a native of Franklin, N. H., and has conducted his present line of business in Concord since 1852, where he has gained a high reputation not only as a dealer, but also as a teacher of the piano and organ.

Thorne's Shoe Store, established 1835. John C. Thorne, successor to Calvin Thorne & Son, Boots, Shoes and Slippers. All work warranted. Opposite Opera House, Concord, N. H.—It would not require a great while for even an absolute stranger in Concord to gain a pretty correct idea of the estimation in which the establishment carried on by Mr. John C. Thorne is held. This store, which is popularly known as Thorne's shoe store, was founded in 1835 by Mr. Calvin Thorne and conducted by him until 1865, when the firm name was changed to Calvin Thorne & Son. In 1884 Mr. John C. Thorne, the present proprietor, assumed the entire management of the business. One floor and basement, 20×60 feet in dimensions, are occupied, and two competent assistants are always at hand to give courteous attention to all customers. Boots, shoes and slippers of all grades and sizes are kept in large quantity, and at all prices. Fine repairing, which is so hard to have executed to satisfaction nowadays, is made a specialty of. Mr. John Thorne, who is a native of Concord, understands the shoe trade thoroughly, and gives his business close attention. He is very well known throughout the city, and has held the office of alderman and councilman. All who will call at his establishment, located opposite the Opera House, can see for themselves the honorable way in which all parts of the business are carried on.

Manufacturers and Merchants Mutual Insurance Co., of N. H.—The Manufacturers and Merchants Mutual Insurance Company affords a striking example of what such a company should be, for it has been ably and progressively managed from the start, and its fourth annual statement made under the date of January 1, 1890, presents an array of figures which cannot but be gratifying to policy holders and management alike. No insurance organization in the State has experienced a more healthful and steady growth, as will be seen from the following figures taken from the statement in question : Cash assets, January 1, 1887, $21,-215.98 ; net cash surplus, $2,818.64. Cash assets January 1, 1888, $30,334.96 ; net cash surplus, $6,951.96. Cash assets, January 1, 1889, $53,123.75 ; net cash surplus, $21,094.65. Cash assets, January 1, 1890, $65,783.09 ; net cash surplus, $27,847.53. Further and more convincing evidence of the company's prosperity is afforded by the fact that the following dividends are now being paid on expiring policies: on one and two-year policies, 20 per cent ; on three-year policies, 25 per cent ; on four-year policies, 40 per cent ; on five-year policies, 50 per cent. No dividend is paid on policies written for a shorter term than one year, or on those cancelled before expiration As a feeling of uncertainty has existed in certain quarters concerning the effect of the return of foreign companies upon the business of New Hampshire insurance organizations our readers will be gratified to learn that the Manufacturers and Merchants Mutual Insurance Company makes the following favorable showing: Cash premiums on New Hampshire business written in January, 1890, $7,914.04 ; cash premiums written in January, 1889, $6,867.85; increase for the month, $1,046.19. The officers of this representative company are : president, Edward G. Leach ; vice-president, I. W. Hammond ; secretary, Lyman Jackman ; treasurer, John F. Jones.

J. C. Norris & Co., manufacturers of Crackers, Biscuit and Confectionery. Established in 1823. No. 18 South Main Street; Retail, 17 North Main Street, Concord, N. H. —The development of the industry of which J. C. Norris & Co. are now the proprietors, is as interesting as any of Concord's enterprises, for it is not only one of the oldest-established undertakings of the kind in New Hampshire, but is also one of the most extensive and truly representative business concerns that Concord can show. Operations were begun nearly seventy years ago, being inaugurated in 1823 by Mr. Amos Wood, who was succeeded by Capt. Ebenezer Symmes, for whom Mr. James S. Norris b-gan work as a salesman in 1847. In 1850 Mr. Norris purchased the business and successfully continued it for nine years without interruption, when the fire in 1859, that swept away the old South church at the corner of Main and Pleasant streets, also devoured all his buildings except the house in which he lived, with a total loss on business, buildings and stock of about $10,000 ; with characteristic energy and faith in the future he rebuilt during the summer and again established his business successfully. The war soon following he obtained contracts for supplying the military camps near the city with bread, delivering as high as two tons in a single day. In 1866 Mr. G. W. Crockett was admitted to partnership under the firm-name of J. S. Norris & Co. In 1875 Mr. Crockett sold his interest and Mr. James C. Norris became identified with the business as a member of the firm under the name of James S. Norris & Son. Again in 1878 the firm was changed to Norris & Crockett, Mr. Norris, senior, retiring, and Mr. Norris, Jr., becoming senior partner. Ten years later in 1888, Mr. Norris became associated with Mr. David D. Taylor under the present firm-name. Both partners are natives of New Hampshire, Mr. James C. Norris having been born in this city and Mr. Taylor in Sanbornton. They are familiarly known in business and social circles, and give constant personal attention to their extensive business. They manufacture crackers, biscuit, bread, cake, pastry and confectionery in great variety. The *daily* consumption of material being about twenty barrels of flour, 400 pounds of lard and three to four barrels of sugar. They have a very extensive wholesale business as well as a large local retail trade. They also handle peanuts extensively, last year over 2000 bushels were roasted and sold by them; they obtain them direct from Virginia and are of excellent quality. They possess every facility for filling the largest orders promptly, their premises are spacious and convenient and comprise two stories and a basement 40 × 90 feet and located at No. 18 South Main street, where is also a finely equipped office. They have a retail store also at No. 17 North Main street. Employment is given to thirty assistants. They are in a position to meet any honorable competition in any line of the business. They also do a large jobbing business in cigars and will furnish superior goods at the very lowest market rates. They keep three salesmen on the road for out-of-town trade, and two in the city.

Silsby & Son, Printers and Binders, and dealers in Stationery and Fancy Goods, Counting Room and Office Supplies. The manufacture of Blank Books a Specialty. No. 93 North Main Street, Concord, N. H.—The business conducted by Messrs. Silsby & Son, was founded half a century ago by Messrs. Morrill & Silsby, and for many years has been regarded as a leading and representative undertaking. The existing firm was formed in 1880 and is constituted of Messrs. G. H. H. and Geo. H. Silsby, both of whom are natives of this State. A general printing and binding business is done, particular attention being paid to the manufacture of blank books, these being made in standard sizes and styles and carried in stock, and also being manufactured to order, at short notice, after any pattern desired. Stationery and fancy goods, counting-room and office supplies are largely dealt in, spacious premises being occupied at 93 North Main street, as office and salesroom, with main factory elsewhere, a heavy and exceptionally complete stock being carried, consisting in part, of account books of all kinds, fine memorandums, pass books, order books, lawyers' and sheriffs' dockets, inventories and other books and blanks used by towns, receipt books, etc., legal blanks, draughtsmen's supplies, gold and steel pens, inks of every grade, rubber bands, albums, jewel cases, brushes, hand mirrors, dressing cases, wallets and other fine leather goods, etc. Commercial and general job printing will be done in a thoroughly workmanlike and artistic manner, and paper ruling to any pattern desired is made a leading specialty. Messrs. Silsby & Son have unusually complete facilities for the carrying on of every department of their business, and despite the many orders received are in a position to execute all commissions, both large and small, at very short notice.

C. B. Lawrence, dealer in Choice Groceries, Teas, Coffees, Spices, Flour and Grain. Also Meats, Provisions, etc. 80 South State Street, Concord, N. H.—Despite the many grocery and provision stores to be found in Concord and vicinity, there are none too many establishments of this kind where the goods furnished and the service rendered are uniformly satisfactory, and that conducted by Mr. C. B. Lawrence at No. 80 South State street, is worthy of prominent mention among those of which this can be truthfully said, for Mr. Lawrence has both the facilities and the disposition to fully satisfy every reasonable customer, and the extent of his business shows that this fact is generally appreciated by the purchasing public. The undertaking carried on by him was founded a number of years ago and at one time was conducted by Mr. C. F. Hillsgrove, who was succeeded by Messrs. Hillsgrove & Lawrence, Mr. Lawrence becoming sole proprietor in 1892. He was born in Concord, and is too generally known here to render extended personal mention necessary. A heavy and complete stock is carried, comprising choice groceries, teas, coffees and spices, flour and grain, etc., together with a full assortment of fresh, salted, smoked and canned meats, canned goods, vegetables and provisions in general. Employment is given to two assistants, and callers are assured prompt and polite attention, the lowest market rates being quoted on all the many commodities dealt in.

Chas. E. Junkins, Jr., dealer in Watches, Diamonds and Jewelry, for cash or instalments, 28 North Main Street, Room 7.—The man who has once carried a really accurate watch, will never be satisfied afterwards with a time-keeper that is not to be entirely depended upon. There is a peculiar satisfaction in owning a watch that you can "swear by," known only to those who have experienced it, and if any of our readers should be about to purchase a watch we would most certainly advise them to pay a fair price and get a reliable article. Those living in Concord or vicinity can do no better than to place their orders with Mr. Charles E. Junkins, Jr., doing business at No. 28 North Main street, Room 7, Bailey's block, for this gentleman is in a position to offer unsurpassed inducements to purchasers. He was born in Boston, Mass., and since opening his present store here in Concord in 1889 has built up a large business by close attention to his patrons and fair dealing with all. Mr. Junkins warrants the articles he sells to give entire satisfaction. He carries a fine stock of watches, diamonds and jewelry, which he sells for cash or on installments, and offers these goods at most reasonable prices. Weekly or monthly payments may be made, the goods being delivered on receipt of first payment. This establishment is open from 9 a. m. to 9 p. m., one assistant is employed and callers are assured prompt and courteous attention as well as fair dealing, and desirable goods at low prices. He has a novel method of buying a watch by the "watch club" scheme, for particulars apply for circular or in person.

M. Bateman, Practical Plumber and dealer in Plumbers' Supplies, Water Closets, Bath Tubs, Bowls, Lead and Iron Pipe, etc. All Orders Personally Attended to. 150 North Main Street, Concord.—The importance of the work done by the plumber is so evident that even the least observing cannot fail to appreciate it, partially at all events; and it is on account of its importance that we feel sure that our readers will be interested in learning of a plumbing establishment which stands second to none in the character of the work done and the fair treatment extended to every customer. We refer to that conducted by Mr. M. Bateman at No. 150 North Main street, Concord. We feel confident that the closest investigation and most careful trial will only serve to confirm the good opinion which we hold of the enterprise. It was established in 1882 by its present able proprietor, who is a practical plumber, and also deals in plumbers' supplies, water closets, bath tubs, bowls, lead and iron pipe, etc. Mr. Bateman is most excellently prepared to fill all orders with the least possible delay, for he gives employment to from six to eight skilled and experienced assistants, as occasion requires, and has every facility to aid him in turning out the best of work. He gives close personal attention to the many details of his business, being a practical plumber himself, and the result of his endeavors to please his customers is to be seen in the trade carried on, which is already extensive and is steadily increasing.

Perkins & Berry, Grocers and dealers in Flour, Corn and Meal, Masonic Temple, Concord, N. H.—The advantages derived from buying of specialists are doubtless often exaggerated, and indeed it is probable that in the case of some commodities a general trader is able to offer inducements fully equal to those extended by a dealer who handles the articles in question exclusively, but among these commodities groceries, flour, corn and meal cannot properly be included, for practical experience teaches that one who confines himself to this branch of trade is really in a position to give better value for money received than would otherwise be possible. One need not go outside of Concord to find convincing example of the truth of this statement, and as satisfactory an example as could be wished for is that afforded by the advantages offered in connection with the enterprise conducted by Messrs Perkins & Berry, and located in Masonic Temple. These gentlemen are among the most experienced dealers in groceries, flour, corn and meal to be found in this vicinity, for they succeeded Mr. J. Frank Hoit in 1876, who had been in the business for about thirty years. Messrs. Perkins and Berry are both natives of Pittsfield, and are well known throughout Concord and vicinity, Mr. Perkins having held the office of councilman. A well appointed establishment covering an area of 2100 feet is utilized and a very heavy and complete stock is carried. Four competent assistants are employed and an extensive retail business is done. Messrs. Perkins & Berry have occupied their present premises since 1889, and are ever ready to fill the most extensive orders at short notice. The lowest market rates are quoted on all the commodities dealt in, and as the firm gives especial attention to the handling of goods particularly adapted for family use, those in need of such will find it well worth while to place a trial order with them.

W. K. Day, Musical Goods, No. 25 North Main Street, Concord, N. H.—It would be a good thing for this community if more of its business men had the enterprise and energy that mark the operations of Mr. W. K. Day, doing business at 25 North Main street, for it has been remarked that some of our merchants apparently expect customers to hunt them up and insist on buying, instead of themselves taking the trouble to meet the public half way and showing them what they have to sell. Mr. W. K. Day is a native of Newmarket, N. H., and has conducted his business since 1869. Mr. Day deals in musical instruments of all kinds as well as sheet music, and a full line of musical goods. Mr. Day deals in several "makes" of pianos, his leading piano being the celebrated Ivers & Pond. He gives a full guarantee with every piano and warrants that his customers will have no reason to regret dealing with him. Mr. Day has built up a prosperous retail business which is constantly and rapidly increasing. We therefore advise all interested readers to inspect his goods and prices before purchasing elsewhere. Mr. Day is not only an experienced dealer in musical goods but has an established reputation as a teacher on the piano and organ and has a good number of pupils. As an organist he has had an experience that is a sufficient compliment to his ability, for he has presided at the organ at the South Church, Concord, for nine years and then ten years at the Unitarian church, and at the present time is organist at the Unitarian church at Manchester. Mr. Day is also identified with the New Hampshire Music Teacher's Association as its treasurer.

Globe Stable, Livery, Boarding and Hack. Colton, George & Co. 133 North Main Street, Concord, N. H.—Many people are prevented from keeping a horse by fear of the trouble and expense which they think must necessarily accompany the maintenance of such an animal in a city, but this fear is groundless to a certain extent at least, the fact being that the amount of trouble and expense incurred is directly dependent upon the discrimination exercised in attending to the matter. Of course it costs money to keep a horse, but there is no need of paying fancy prices, and we have no hesitation in asserting that although the rates charged for board at the stable of Messrs. Colton, George & Co., at No. 133 North Main street, are uniformly moderate, animals are assured as comfortable quarters, as suitable and abundant food and as kind and intelligent care as at any stable in this section of the State. The proprietors of the Globe livery, boarding and back stable, are Mr. W. E. Colton, H. S. George and A. Colton, all of whom are natives of Concord, and well known throughout the city. They give close personal attention and employ sufficient assistance to ensure prompt and efficient service in every department of their business. There are fourteen stalls on the premises and some very desirable teams are available for livery purposes, turnouts being furnished at very short notice and the prices quoted being low enough to suit even the most economically disposed.

George Main, Florist and Seedsman, also dealer in Fruit Trees, Flowering Shrubs, etc. Greenhouses Nos. 3 and 5 Merrimack Street, also Nos. 3 and 5 Orchard Street, Store in Odd Fellows Block, Pleasant Street, Concord, N. H.—The enterprise conducted by Mr. George Main was established about a quarter of a century ago, and has become one of the most extensive and popular undertakings of the kind in this section of the country. Mr. Main is a native of Rochester, N. H., and is as skillful a florist and as reliable a seedsman as can be found in this State. He has unsurpassed facilities for the cultivation of flowers, flowering shrubs, etc., and is in a position to fill the most extensive orders at short notice and at the lowest market rates. The greenhouses are at Nos. 3 and 5 Merrimack street and Nos. 3 and 5 Orchard street, and are fitted up in the most approved manner, while their extent is shown by the fact that the area under glass is about three quarters of an acre. Mr. Main deals largely, both at wholesale and retail, in flowers, seeds, flowering shrubs, fruit trees, etc., and makes a specialty of roses, handling all the popular varieties and being prepared to furnish any desired quantity at very short notice. He has a store in Odd Fellows' Block, Pleasant street, where a full assortment of plants and cut flowers may be found, together with floral designs in great variety. Appropriate emblems and decorations for weddings, funerals, etc., will be made to order at very short notice, customers having a long list of designs, ranging from the most simple to the most elaborate, to choose from. Foremost among Mr. Main's assistants is Mr. John Patterson, who has proved himself to be one of the most artistic and practical landscape gardeners in the country, having met with great success in adapting means to ends, or in other words in obtaining the best possible effects from existing conditions. Orders for landscape gardening in all its branches will receive prompt attention and we have no hesitation in guaranteeing complete satisfaction to all who may avail themselves of the service offered.

Benj. Bilsborough, House Painter and Paper Hanger, rear of Masonic Block, Concord N. H.—There are many advantages connected with owning the house you occupy but there are also some disadvantages, and among these must be classed the necessity of keeping the premises in repair. Of course one who hires a house actually pays the cost of all repairing indirectly, but he at least is spared the bother of making arrangements to have such work done, and that is considered no little trouble by many real estate owners. Still, like everything else, it depends entirely on how the task is undertaken, whether it will prove disagreeable or not, for if some little pains is taken to place orders with the right parties, repairing can be readily and properly done at moderate expense. In this connection we may fittingly call attention to the establishment of Mr. Benj. Bilsborough, located at the rear of Masonic Block, Concord, for this gentleman makes a specialty of house painting, decorating and paper hanging, and is prepared to do strictly first-class work at short notice, and at moderate rates. A sufficiently large force of experienced workmen is employed to enable all commissions to be executed without annoying delay, and no trouble is spared to accomplish results that will prove satisfactory to the most fastidious, while the proprietor, Mr. Bilsborough is well and favorably known among the enterprising business men of Concord and vicinity.

F. W. Landon & Co., Electricians, No. 26 School Street, Concord, N. H.—That electricity is coming into more general and varied use every day, is a fact too evident to require further demonstration. So rapid and continuous is the progress made in its utilization, that an exhaustive list of its applications compiled to day, would probably be incomplete before a month had elapsed. Electricity secures our safety, ministers to our comfort, and promotes our health, for, independent of its virtues as a direct remedial agent, it supplies an illuminant which consumes no air, and may therefore safely be used under conditions that make the use of gas or oil dangerous and even deadly. F. W. Landon & Co. are doing much to introduce electrical appliances in this section. This is regarded as a leading firm in Concord, in its special line of business, for it has unequalled facilities for the putting in of electric bells, fire alarms, hotel and house annunciators, gas lighting, also speaking tubes, etc. Telephone and telegraph supplies of all descriptions may be bought here to advantage. Gas-lighting by electricity reduces the liability of accidental fire to a minimum as it renders the use of matches altogether unnecessary. F. W. Landon & Co. guarantee the successful working of all electrical apparatus supplied and put up by them. Orders are promptly and thoroughly executed in all branches of this business.

W. J. Fernald, dealer in Furniture, Carpets and Draperies, corner Main and Pleasant Streets, Concord, N. H.—Everybody must have furniture, everybody must have carpets, and everybody should have spring beds, mattresses or feather beds, for these are very powerful aids in resting a tired body, and the body that works to earn the money to buy them should be made as comfortable as possible. The average individual spends one third of his life in bed, and therefore it is important that the latter be made as healthful and easy as is consistent with circumstances. When any of our readers have occasion to purchase any of the articles mentioned above, to say nothing of baby carriages, oil cloths, straw matting, feathers, etc., we recommend them before purchasing to call and examine the fine stock of goods to be found at the corner of Main and Pleasant streets, for this establishment is conducted by Mr. W. J. Fernald, a native of Dover, Maine, but who for over a score of years has conducted this enterprise successfully, until now the business occupies the entire block, comprising three floors which are used as show and salesrooms, besides a well-equipped workshop on Freight street. Six competent assistants are employed. Mr. Fernald's long experience in the business is sufficient guarantee that he knows how to buy and sell goods to the best advantage. His prices are very moderate and his representations can be confidently relied on. Mr. Fernald has been active in the affairs of the city, having served as selectman of his ward and two terms in the common council and is at present president of that body.

Miss H. E. Robinson, Teacher of Instrumental Music, 40 North Main Street, Concord, N. H.—Without for a moment disputing the self-evident fact that rapid and assured progress in the art of music is largely a matter of temperament and other natural attributes of character, it may still be maintained that the services of a competent, conscientious and enthusiastic teacher are of inestimable value in guiding pupils along the oft-times difficult path that leads to success. Many a prominent musician has testified that his or her early progress was seriously hindered by what the event proved to be incompetent instruction, and it cannot be too strongly insisted upon that careful discrimination should be exercised in the choice of instructors, especially at the beginning when improper methods will inevitably result in the formation of bad habits (from a musical point of view) which it may take years of effort to eradicate. Therefore we earnestly say to all seeking musical tuition for themselves or for others, begin right : choose a teacher of established reputation and then follow instructions implicitly. Without the least disparagement of others it may be said that Miss H. E. Robinson has gained a leading position among the teachers of instrumental music during the eighteen years that she has practised her profession in this city (of which she is a native), and we take pleasure in recommending her to our readers, being assured they will have reason to thank us should they avail themselves of her services. Her rooms are conveniently located at No. 40 North Main street, and detailed information as to terms, etc., will cheerfully be given on application. Miss Robinson has many pupils in Concord and vicinity and takes a personal and helpful interest in the advancement of each of her scholars.

The Fire Underwriters Association, Home Office, State Capital Bank Building, Concord, N. H.　It required no great amount of foresight to predict the entire success of the Fire Underwriters Association at the time of its incorporation in 1887, for as the name implies, those most prominently identified with the company are also prominent in insurance matters in general, and hence have both the experience and the ability to enable them to carry on operations to the best advantage.　By the third annual statement issued January 1, 1890, it appears that the paid up capital stock amounts to $10,000, and the net surplus to $1,273.08; while the rapid and steady growth of the company is graphically shown by the following figures: Assets, January 1, 1887, $10,868 42; January 1, 1888, $26,351.93; January 1, 1889, $38,247.61; January 1, 1890, $43,481.88.　The income from interest on investments has earned more than 18 per cent on the capital stock; and the confidence reposed in the management by the stockholders is most significantly indicated by the fact that not one share has been placed on the market for sale.　A company that has quadrupled its assets in three years and at the same time has been conducted on sound conservative principles, is certainly prosperous in the full sense of the word, and the management have excellent reason to be gratified by the result of their efforts.　The president is Captain Lyman Jackman, the vice-president, Hon. A. B. Thompson, also secretary of state; the treasurer, Mr. James Minot, also cashier of Mechanicks National Bank; the secretary, Mr. Thomas M. Lang, and the assistant secretary, Mr. C. F. Sherburne.

Chas. G. Blanchard, wholesale and retail dealer in Dry and Fancy Goods, Centennial Block, Concord, N. H.— Taking everything into consideration it may be truthfully said that there is not a dealer in dry and fancy goods, etc., located in this section of the city who is in a position to offer more genuine advantages to his customers than Mr. Charles G. Blanchard, and indeed we might go farther and say with equal truth it would be difficult to find one prepared to equal the service offered by the gentleman in question.　Mr. Blanchard began operations here in 1875 under the firm name of Blanchard & Crapo, and in 1883 Mr. Blanchard assumed entire control of the business, since which date the business has developed wonderfully. He is a native of Canterbury, N. H., and has a very large circle of friends hereabouts.　His store comprises one floor and a basement, each 20x75 feet in dimensions, and contains a large stock of dry and fancy goods, cloaks, etc. There are five efficient assistants employed, so that orders can be filled very promptly, notwithstanding the large wholesale and retail business that is done.　Perhaps the most noteworthy advantage gained by dealing with Mr. Blanchard, is the surety given that every article will prove just as represented.　The various goods composing the stock are all carefully selected from the most reputable sources, and while the prices are put away down to the "lowest notch" the quality of the articles furnished is sure to suit the most fastidious.

A. M. Follett, dealer in Staple and Fancy Groceries, No. 65 Main Street, Nashua, and No. 9 Jackson Street, Concord.—Mr. A. M. Follett is a native of Fremont, N. H., and has carried on business in this city since 1878. He is an extensive retail dealer in staple groceries and his operations are not confined to Concord alone as he has a store at No. 65 Main street, Nashua, N. H.　Both these stores are well stocked with such goods as are required by a first-class patronage and are sold at prices consistent with quality of goods.　An ample force of assistants is employed and immediate and polite attention is secured to every caller.　In 1886 Mr. Follett commenced the manufacture of fine flavoring extracts, his productions in this line are very favorably known to consumers and the trade, and are recognized by honest competitors as being first-class in every respect.　We wish him success in his business and trust that his preparations may in time become as famous as those of other Concord manufacturers whose goods now have a national reputation.

A. McArthur & Co., wholesale and retail dealers in Furniture, Bedding, Carpets, Stoves, Baby Carriages and Refrigerators, 12 Warren Street, Concord, N. H.—The sale of goods on installments may be either a blessing or a curse to a community, according to the system adopted and the spirit in which it is carried out, and we are sure that such of our readers as are conversant with the methods followed by Messrs. Arthur McArthur & Co., will agree that the accommodations this representative firm offer, are a decided and genuine benefit to the public.　This is a leading Boston house, the main store being at No. 18 Cornhill in that city, but a branch has been maintained at Concord for some years, customers here enjoying the same advantages as Boston patrons.　The Concord store is located at No. 12 Warren street, and is under the direct management of Mr. Frank D. Hugar, who is a native of New York State, but is widely and favorably known in this city, having been in business here some six or seven years.　Employment is given to three assistants, and under his efficient management, prompt and courteous attention is assured to every caller.　A large and varied stock of house furnishing goods, including furniture, bedding, carpets, stoves, baby carriages and refrigerators, is on hand to choose from at prices as low as the lowest, both for cash and on instalments.　The assortment is continually being added to, it embraces the latest novelties, and is made up without exception of honest goods that can be and are guaranteed to prove precisely as represented.　Messrs. Arthur McArthur & Co., have built up their present immense trade by keeping faith with their customers, and there is no firm in the business, in New England or indeed throughout the Union that has made a better record in this most important respect.

Kendall & Lane, Undertakers and Embalmers.　Night Bell; Telephone Connected.　Rooms No. 14 Pleasant Street, Concord, N. H.—The firm of Kendall & Lane was not formed until 1889, but as the enterprise carried on was founded a long time ago, and as the gentlemen identified with it are widely and favorably known throughout this vicinity, the concern at once took a high rank among other houses in the same line of business, and is fairly entitled to be classed with the representative firms of this section.　Operations were begun by Mr. John Brown, who was succeeded by Mr. Charles Crow, he giving place in 1883 to Mr. George L. Lovejoy, who was succeeded by the present proprietors.　Mr. H. A. Kendall is a native of Derby, Vt., and Mr. Joseph H. Lane of Sanbornton, N. H., the latter gentleman being particularly well-known in this city, as he has served as councilman, as alderman and as representative.　Messrs. Kendall & Lane are undertakers and embalmers, and utilize rooms at No. 14 Pleasant street, where they have all necessary facilities at hand to carry on operations in accordance with the most approved methods. They carry a large and very carefully chosen stock of coffins, caskets, robes and funeral goods in general, and quote very low prices on articles of standard merit.　The entire charge of funerals will be undertaken if desired, and we need hardly say that nothing will be wanting to maintain the dignity and decorum so essential on such occasions.　Orders will be given immediate attention at all hours, the office having a night bell and telephone connection, or orders may be left at Mr. Kendall's residence, No. 15 North State street or at Mr. Lane's, No. 7 Laurel street.

W. S. Baker, Fine Tailoring, Mechanicks Bank Building, Corner Main and School Streets, Concord, N. H.—The establishment conducted by Mr. W. S. Baker in the Mechanicks Bank Building, corner of Main and School streets, is well entitled to prominent mention among the representative commercial enterprises of this city, for it is the largest establishment of the kind in New Hampshire, and as regards the quality of the work turned out has no reason to fear comparison with any house in New England, Boston not excepted.　This perhaps may seem a rather extreme statement to those not familiar with the merits of Mr. Baker's productions, but it is fully justified by the facts, and an indication of its truth is afforded by the circumstance that among his customers are gentlemen who have frequent occasion to visit Boston, and who certainly would not be deterred by the higher cost of artistic tailoring in that city from placing their orders there were it possible thereby to secure better results. Mr. Baker has had long and varied experience in the business, he has the most improved facilities, employs skilled assistants, and, in short, there is no possible reason why he should not be in a position to cater satisfactorily to the most fastidious taste. He is a native of Wellfleet, Mass., and has been established in his present location since 1883. The premises comprise a salesroom of the dimensions of 30×40 feet, and two workrooms, each measuring 30×50 feet, and as employment is given to some thirty-five assistants, orders can be filled at short notice even in the busy season. A fine assortment of foreign and domestic fabrics is constantly to be found here, the very latest of fashionable novelties being fully represented. Moderate prices are quoted, and every garment is honestly made and trimmed throughout.

Scribner & Britton, Hardware, Stoves, Agricultural Implements, etc., 12 North Main Street, Concord, N. H.— This house was established about twenty-five years since by the firm of Carroll & Stone and after one or two other changes in the management we find that it was carried on in 1881 by Scribner & Blood. But since 1886, the present firm of Scribner & Britton have had sole control. Mr. Scribner is a native of Andover, N. H., and Mr. Britton of Walpole, N. H. They have been successful in building up quite a large patronage. They deal in hardware, stoves, agricultural implements, etc., and carry a large number of these articles of the latest improved makes and from the inception of their operations have made it a rule to keep faith with their customers, making no representations not fully justified by the facts. The result is that th s firm have a reputation second to none, and as their business is built on so sure a foundation, it is bound to endure and to increase steadily and permanently. Both members of the firm give close personal attention to the details of the business, thus assuring that all orders shall receive immediate and accurate attention. The various articles dealt in, are offered at as low rates as can well be named on articles of equal merit. Their large and extensive business requires the utilizing of two floors and a basement each 20×90 feet in dimensions, together with a storehouse. Employment is given to four capable and obliging assistants, and prompt attention is given to all callers.

H. B. Foster, Druggist and Apothecary, 35 North Main Street, Concord, N. H.—There are very few business enterprises in Concord or in any other city that can trace their origin back more than half a century, and for this if for no other reason the undertaking conducted by Mr. H. B. Foster is deserving of prominent and honorable mention, for it was founded in 1837 by Mr. John McDaniels, who was succeeded by Mr. Foster in 1841, the store at that time being the only one of the kind in Concord. In 1842 the firm of Foster & French was formed, Mr. Foster resuming sole control in 1843, and being succeeded by Mr. George McDaniels in 1845. In 1847 Mr. Foster again took possession, and in 1855 he was succeeded by Mr. John C. Pillsbury, who gave place to Mr. Foster in 1857. Since the latter date the present proprietor has had undisturbed possession. He is a native of Canterbury, N. H., and among all our local merchants not one can be found more highly respected throughout this community. Mr. Foster was the inventor of "Sticky Fly Paper," and still manufactures it; also manufacturing soda water and preparing various proprietary medicines which are well and favorably known in the market. He deals quite extensively in tea, and those who find difficulty in getting a tea to suit them would do well to favor him with a trial order, for he handles choice goods and quotes very reasonable prices.

It is, however, as a druggist and apothecary that he is best known, and his store at No. 35 North Main street is a favorite resort with those wishing to have physician's prescriptions compounded, for a complete stock of pure drugs, medicines and chemicals is constantly carried, and every precaution is taken to ensure absolute accuracy in even the most trivial details. Sufficient assistance is employed to enable orders to be promptly filled, and moderate charges are made in every instance.

P. H. Larkin, dealer in W. I. Goods, Groceries, Provisions, Flour, Grain, Crockery, Glassware and Fancy Goods, 256, 262 North Main Street, Concord, N. H.—The business carried on by Mr. P. H. Larkin at Nos 256, 262 North Main street, was founded some thirty five years ago by Mr. F. A. Fiske, and the present proprietor has been identified with it for about sixteen years, having commenced his experience in this store twenty-seven years ago as clerk. Commencing in 1874 as a member of the firm of Currier & Larkin, and assuming sole control in 1880, Mr. Larkin has resided in Concord nearly all his life, and is very generally and favorably known throughout this city and vicinity, both in business and social circles. He is naturally proud of the enviable reputation for enterprise and fair dealing so long associated with his establishment, and spares no pains to assure its continuance by the simple process of continuing to deserve it. Employment is given to six competent assistants, but the proprietor gives personal attention to the more important details of the business, and keeps thoroughly well-informed concerning the nature of the service rendered. A double store of the dimensions of 50 × 50 feet is utilized, together with a basement of the same size, and a cellar also of similar dimensions. A very heavy and varied stock is carried, comprising West India goods, groceries, provisions, flour, grain, crockery, glassware and fancy goods; it being exceptionally complete in every department, and made up of goods that are especially suited to family trade, and can confidently be guaranteed to prove just as represented. We need hardly say that Mr. Larkin is in a position to quote the lowest market rates on the many commodities in which he deals, and that the superior facilities enjoyed enable prompt and courteous attention to be given to every caller. This store is entitled to the credit of being the oldest grocery store in the city.

Ranlet & Marsh, dealers in Coal, Wood and Ice, No. 4 Freight Street, Concord, N. H.—The undertaking conducted by Messrs. Ranlet & Marsh is worthy of especially prominent mention, by reason of the fact that it was the pioneer in its special line in this city, this being the oldest established ice and coal business in town; but even if such were not the case the standing of the firm now carrying it on, and the magnitude of their operations would demand that favorable reference be made to the enterprise in this review of Concord's commerce and manufactures. The original proprietor was Mr. William Webster, who was succeeded by Mr. Horace Langley, he giving place in 1856 to Messrs. H W. Ranlet & Co., who were succeeded by Messrs. Ranlet & Prescott in 1874, and the existing firm being formed in 1882. The partners are Messrs. H. W. Ranlet and H. O Marsh, the former being a native of Gilmanton and the latter of Barnstead, N. H. Mr. Marsh has served as councilman and as representative, and both members of the firm rank with the best known of our resident business men, not only in trade but also in social circles. A very large business is done, and an extremely heavy stock is generally carried, there being sufficient storage capacity available to accommodate 7,000 tons of coal and 3,000 tons of ice. About 1,500 cords of wood are sold annually. Employment is given to from ten to fifteen assistants, and all orders left in person or sent by mail or messenger to No. 4 Freight street are assured immediate and painstaking attention, it being hardly necessary to add that the firm are prepared to quote bottom prices at all times.

E. N. Spencer, dealer in Fish, Oysters, Clams and Lobsters. Also, Vegetables of every kind in their season. No. 6 Pleasant Street, Concord, N. H.—Some very marked changes in the methods of doing business have occurred of late years, and in no line of trade perhaps has more change been brought about than in the handling of fish, oysters and sea food in general ; for a few years ago a fish-store was hardly supposed to be kept even neat in appearance, whereas at the present time a first class establishment of this kind is supposed to be not only neat, but even handsome in its appointments As an example of what we mean let us call attention to the store conducted by Mr. E. N. Spencer at No. 6 Pleasant street This is 22×50 feet in dimensions and so nicely fitted up and admirably kept as to be one of the most attractive in this vicinity. Mr. Spencer is a native of Barton, Vt He succeeded Mr. L. N Farley in business in 1884, under the firm name of Spencer & Abbott, which was changed in 1885 to Spencer & Nason, and since 1889 has been under the entire management of Mr. E. N. Spencer. He is a wholesale dealer in fish, oysters, clams, lobsters, and also handles vegetables of every kind in their season. His stock is always varied and tempting, his prices are invariably low, and sufficient assistance is employed to assure immediate and careful attention to every caller.

David E. Murphy, Dry Goods, Ladies', Misses' and Children's Outside Garments a Specialty, 76, 78, 80 North Main Street (opposite School Street), Concord, N. H.—One of the best known stores in Concord is that conducted by Mr. David E. Murphy, and the exceptionally high reputation it enjoys is the best proof that could be given that its management is and has been all that could be desired. Mr. Murphy is a native of Concord, and has been identified with the establishment in question since 1886. The premises occupied at the commencement of the business were located at No. 80 North Main street, but since that time the business has been greatly increased and is now three times its original size, and row occupies Nos. 76, 78 and 80 North Main street, where a very extensive stock is carried, made up of dry goods, silks, dress goods, hosiery, underwear, embroideries, laces, fringes, buttons, gloves, parasols, domestics, notions, etc., ladies', misses' and children's garments being made a specialty. Ten competent assistants are employed, and an extensive wholesale and retail business is done. The high esteem in which Mr. Murphy's store is held is easily explained, for the policy pursued by him is as simple as it is satisfactory, consisting merely of giving every customer full value for money received and offering such a variety of desirable goods that all tastes can be suited.

Sam'l C. Eastman, General Insurance Agent, 80 Main St. Rumford Block, Concord.—The benefits of insurance are so generally availed of nowadays by all classes of people, that it seems superfluous to point out the wisdom of securing such protection. The real estate owner having thousands of dollars worth of property to insure, and the mechanic having only his strength and skill for capital, both profit by the operations of the various excellent fire, life, and accident companies doing business in this country, and the work of taking out policies in these organizations is much simplified by the existence of such agencies as that conducted by Mr. Samuel C. Eastman with which many of our readers are already familiar. Among the companies represented are the Ætna of Hartford, New Hampshire of Manchester, Liverpool & London & Globe of England and Imperial of England. He is also agent for Travelers Life and Accident and American Surety Co. It will be seen from this list that Mr. Eastman is prepared to write policies of all kinds, and the facilities he offers have been very generally taken advantage of since the opening of the agency located as above. This agency was established in 1838 by Seth Eastman, followed by S & S. C. Eastman, who were succeeded by Staniels, Allison & Co , and they were succeeded by R. P. Staniels & Co., and it was

in 1890 that the present proprietor assumed sole control of the business. He is a native of Concord, and needs no introduction to most of our business men.

Commercial House, cor. N. Main and Center Sts., Concord, N. H.—People who care more for style than they do for comfort, and who judge of the desirability of the service offered at a public house entirely by the charges made in connection with the same, will not be especially interested in the Commercial house and will hardly find it worth their while to read this brief notice of the same; but the majority of our readers are not included in this class and therefore we need no apology for devoting space to a consideration of the hotel in question. The proprietors, Messrs. Sanborn & Lewis, seem to have but one object in view, and that is to make their guests feel entirely comfortable and at home. Of course they are not in the business for the fun of the thing, and they propose to make a fair profit on their investments, but they evidently believe that a liberal policy pays the best in the long run. The individual proprietors are Mr. Charles E. Sanborn and Fred G. Lewis. Mr. Sanborn will be familiarly remembered by many of the gues's of the old Eagle hotel as "Charley," who for several years served them there in various capacities and is now ready to show to any that may try the hospitality of the "Commercial house," that he is there to contribute to their pleasure and comfort. Mr. Lewis will be remembered by most everybody who has spent any time in Concord as "Fred Lewis the hackman," for he has conducted that business here for eighteen years and has hosts of friends who appreciated his promptness and reliability for always being on hand at the time appointed and giving the best of service in his line; you will find him at the depot on the arrival of trains to convey you to the Commercial house, where he will assist in looking after your best welfare. The Commercial house is very pleasantly and conveniently situated at the corner of North Main and Center streets, and has been quite extensively rebuilt and newly furnished throughout since the property came into Sanborn & Lewis' hands in 1889, twenty new rooms having been added. The house was opened about February 1, 1890, and has received such a generous patronage that they now contemplate important improvements during the summer; although the dining room will now seat about sixty persons, larger accommodations are required so that it will be enlarged to accommodate one hundred guests. It is the intention to put in hot water heating throughout the house, as also electric lighting. The house has thirty-four rooms which are comfortably furnished and neatly kept. The table is supplied at all seasons with an abundance, the bill of fare showing a good variety—the cooking and service is first class—and the prices are very moderate.

A. L. Shackford, Landscape Gardener and Florist, Cut Flowers, Plants and Seeds and Funeral Designs, 149 No. Main Street, Concord, N. H.—Mr. A. L. Shackford is the only florist in this vicinity who makes a specialty of land-scape gardening, and as he is experienced and skilled in his profession and uniformly moderate in his charges, it is not surprising that there should be a brisk and steadily in-creasing demand for his services. All orders are assured prompt and careful attention, and shade trees, fruit trees, vines and rose bushes, etc., will be pruned and otherwise cared for, and in short all the duties incidental to practical landscape gardening discharged in a faithful and satis-factory manner. Mr. Shackford deals largely in plants, cut flowers, floral emblems, etc., and has every facility at his command to enable him to fill orders without delay and at the lowest market rates. He utilizes two greenhouses, each of the dimensions of 75 × 11 feet, together with a third, used as a rose house and measuring 22 × 35 feet. A full assortment of cut flowers is constantly on hand, and wedding decorations, funeral emblems and floral designs suited to any occasion will be made to order at very short notice. Mr. Shackford showing some original and taste-ful designs, and being prepared to satisfy the most fastid-ious. He makes it a rule to deliver goods promptly at the time promised, and his customers are thus saved all annoyance and the interests of all parties are better served.

Howard L. Porter, manufacturer of Ladies' Boots and Shoes for Southern and Western trade. Concord, N. H., Boston office, 112 Summer Street.—Although the manu-facture of boots and shoes is as yet a comparatively minor industry in this city; so far as it is carried on here, it is conducted after the most approved methods, and nowhere in New Hampshire or even in Massachusetts, can there be found a more perfectly equipped factory than that utilized by Mr. Howard L. Porter. This gentleman is a native of Haverhill, Mass., and has had long experience as a shoe manufacturer; carrying on the business in Lynn, Mass., previous to his removal to Concord in 1885. He is connec-ted with the Loan and Trust Savings Bank of this city, and is very generally known in social as well as in business cir-cles. The factory he makes use of was built and equipped at an expense of some $80,000, the cost being borne by a number of prominent citizens of Concord, organized as the "Concord Shoe Factory." Mr. Porter leased the property for a term of years, and the results thus far attained have been highly satisfactory to all parties concerned. The building is five stories and a basement in height, and 166×40 feet in dimensions, and is very substantially built of brick, and most excellently lighted, the windows occupying more than half the wall surface. Power is furnished by a steam engine of the most im-proved type, and the plant of machinery is wonder-fully efficient in every respect, it being made up of the most swift, accurate and dependable machines yet devised. Mr. Porter manufactures ladies boots and shoes for the southern and western trade, and employs from 225 to 250 operatives. He has a Boston office at No. 112 Summer street, and finds no difficulty in disposing of his product as his superior facilities enable him to turn out goods that will compare very favorably with others of similar grade, and to quote the lowest market rates at all times; while all orders can be filled without undue delay.

O. H. Phelps & Co., Cash Grocery, Bridge Street, Con-cord, N. H.—The assertion is sometimes made that nothing is really gained by buying for cash, that is, except in large quantities; but we have noticed that those who do a cash business, or one that is almost entirely cash, offer greater inducements to retail buyers than those who abide by the credit system. Our readers can easily make the com-parison for themselves, and an excellent way to do it is to call at the establishment conducted by Messrs. O. H. Phelps & Co., on Bridge street, for this is a "cash grocery" and is carried on on a cash basis. Operations were begun in 1885, by Messrs Phelps & Storrs, the present firm name being adopted in 1887. Judging by the magnitude of the

business, the purchasing public are well satisfied with the methods of the management, and there is ample reason why they should be, for the firm handle strictly dependable goods, quote bottom prices and give prompt and polite attention to every caller, employment being given to three experienced assistants. A large and carefully chosen stock of fancy and staple groceries, flour, grain, etc., is constantly carried, the premises utilized having a total area of 3,200 square feet. Mr. Phelps is a native of Orford, N. H., and is widely known in Concord and vicinity. He gives close personal attention to the business, and keeps the service at the very highest standard of efficiency.

C. F. Batchelder, News Agent, Bill Poster, General Advertiser, 106 North Main Street, Concord.—All of us are apt to attach too much importance to our own affairs and to assume that we and our enterprises attract more attention than they actually do. This is a big country, and because you, being for instance a dry goods merchant, carry a large stock of desirable goods which you are pre-pared to sell cheap, it by no means follows that people will know of it unless you take the trouble to tell them of the fact. Some of our readers may laugh at the idea that extensive and persistent advertising indicates modesty, but why not? Who shows the most real vanity, the man who causes information to be spread broad-cast that he is in a certain business and makes certain offers, or the man who placidly takes it for granted that because he is doing such a thing in such a way, everyone of any account must know it without being told? Advertising is an art by it-self and no set rules can be given for the guidance of everybody for "circumstances alter cases," and a method that would pay a man in one line of business would prove unprofitable if used in another; but the next best thing to knowing a thing yourself is to know of one who knows it, and therefore we take pleasure in directing our readers to the establishment conducted by Mr. C. F. Batchelder at No. 106 North Main street, for this gentleman is a news agent, bill poster and general advertiser, and having car-ried on his present business since 1876 should, and in fact does, understand it thoroughly in every detail. He has facilities which enable him to offer the best of service to his patrons, and is always ready to give advice when de-sired as to the best method of reaching the general public or any particular class. Employment is given to nine as-sistants, and the very largest orders can be filled at short notice, while the smallest commissions are carefully exe-cuted; uniformly moderate charges being made.

Greenough & Haseltine, successors to A. G. Harris, dealers in Boots, Shoes and Rubbers, Fine Custom work a Specialty. State Capital Bank Building, Concord, N. H.—This enterprise deserves prominent mention for the methods which have characterized its past and now dis-tinguish its present management, are certainly worthy of emulation. The present proprietors, Messrs. Greenough & Hazeltine, do not find it necessary to resort to sensa-tional means to keep up and increase their trade, as they are content with the results attained, by offering strictly dependable goods at a fair margin of profit, and render such service to their patrons as shall warrant a continu-ation of their trade. Mr. H. W. Greenough who was formerly with J. C. Thorn, is a native of Canterbury, N. H., and Mr. George K. Hazeltine, who was formerly cashier of the Northern railroad, is a native of this city and needs no introduction to those familiar with business in this section. The store is 20 × 60 feet in dimensions and a complete stock of boots, shoes and rubbers is carried of a great variety of styles, sizes and widths. A specialty is made of fine custom work. A fine elegant fitting boot or shoe will be made to fit any foot to order in a manner that will not only afford ease and comfort but durability; the best of materials as well as the best skilled labor is warranted, and strict personal attention will be given all orders. The latest novelties are received constantly, keep-ing the assortment fresh and seasonable. There is no better place at which to purchase a fine boot or shoe. Remember the place—State Capital Bank Building.

The Holt Bros. Mfg. Co., successor to Holt Brothers, Turnpike and Gas Streets, Concord, N. H.—Concord wheels have a national reputation and it is not too much to say that none of the many productions of this city compare more favorably with goods of a kindred character made elsewhere. During the nearly twenty years that the firm of Holt Brothers were engaged in this line of manufacture, their wheels, wheel stock and wagon woodwork won an unsurpassed reputation for excellence of material and construction, and this reputation has been fully maintained by the Holt Brothers Manufacturing company which succeeded Messrs. Holt Brothers in 1889. The president of this company, is Mr. Charles H. Holt; the vice president, Mrs. S. A. Holt; the treasurer, Mr. Melvin L. Towle; and the superintendent, Mr. Thomas D. Avery. The company has a capital of $75,000, and operates an extensive and efficient plant located on Turnpike and Gas streets, the main building being three stories in height and 85×200 feet in dimensions; there being a two story storehouse measuring 30×100 feet, together with a saw-mill and various smaller buildings. Power is afforded by a one hundred horse engine, and the machinery is of the most improved type. Employment is given to from thirty to forty assistants, and Concord wheels are made in a number of styles, including plain wood hub, band hub and Sarven patent, wheel stock and woodwork for farm wagons, lumber wagons and carts are furnished in quantities to suit, the company doing a wholesale business, the bulk of which is confined to New England. The company have a carriage repository on South State street, and deal extensively in light carriages of both their own and Amesbury manufacture, and offer inducements not excelled elsewhere. Orders are assured prompt and careful attention, and the work turned out will prove entirely satisfactory in every respect.

Reed & Mudgett, General Dealers in Provisions, Beef, Pork, Lamb, Poultry, etc., Fresh Fruit and Vegetables of all kinds in their season, No. 131 N. Main Street, Concord, N. H.—It is more than a quarter of a century since the establishment now conducted by Messrs. Reed & Mudgett was opened as a market. It was originally established by Mr. C. W. Drake, who was succeeded in 1883 by Mr. Asa Clark, and he a few months later by the present proprietors. Mr. Reed is a native of Massachusetts and Mr. Mudgett of New Hampshire. These gentlemen are extremely well known in Concord, and indeed there are very few of our local business men more generally and favorably known, either in trade or in social circles. Messrs. Reed & Mudgett occupy premises located at No. 131 North Main street, comprising a store 20×60 feet in dimensions, and a back room 15×40 feet, which is utilized for trying out lard, etc. The stock handled includes beef, pork, lamb, poultry, etc., etc., together with fish, fruit and vegetables of all kinds in their seasons. Four competent assistants are employed, and goods are delivered promptly free of expense. There are many well-stocked and well-managed meat markets in this city, but not one can be named where the most fastidious purchaser is more sure of getting goods to suit him than at the one under consideration. A specialty is made of handling choice cuts, and the prices are always as low as can be named by any dealer in goods of equal excellence, for the proprietors enjoy the most favorable relations with producers and wholesalers, and share all benefits thus obtained with their patrons.

Mrs. Fred Pearson, Fine Millinery, 63 North Main Street, Centennial Block, Concord, N. H.—Good taste in dress is unfortunately not possessed by every one, but good judgment concerning the most advantageous establishment to patronize is a more common faculty, and can in a great measure replace the first named gift. For instance, many ladies who appreciate the help afforded by able and experienced assistance in the choosing and trimming of hats, bonnets, etc., make a practice of obtaining all their millinery goods at the establishment conducted by Mrs. Fred Pearson, and the results attained are flattering alike to that lady's good taste, and to the sound discrimination of those who avail themselves of her facilities. Mrs. Pearson deals largely in fashionable millinery of all kinds, personal attention being given to order work, and to the fitting of odd shapes and artistic blending of colors, special pains being taken to suit the individuality of the purchaser. Mrs. Pearson has a fine assortment of infants' wear, also a choice line of ladies' fine underwear, which she will take great pleasure in showing to her customers, and for which orders are solicited, commissions being executed at short notice and at reasonable rates. The premises occupied are located in the Centennial Block, and are 25×60 feet in dimensions. Employment is given to from three to ten competent assistants, according to the season. This business was formerly conducted by Mrs. Jones, who was succeeded in 1886 by Mrs. Fred Pearson, who is a native of Boston, Mass. Her energy and honorable dealings have won for her the respect of all.

Loveland & Peacock, Tailors, Chambers No. 53 North Main Street, opposite Phenix Hotel, Concord, N. H.—There are some who wear custom clothing because it fits better, is more comfortable and more durable than ready-made garments can be, while others wear it principally because it is more stylish, and they can boast of how high-priced a tailor they patronize. To the latter class we have nothing to say. They judge garments, not by their own qualities but by the reputation of the shop they come from; and therefore if a tailor be not fashionable and high priced they dismiss him as unworthy of consideration. But those who appreciate good work wherever found will be interested to learn of the inducements offered by Messrs. Loveland & Peacock, whose tailoring chambers are located at No. 53 North Main Street, opposite the Phenix Hotel, for these gentlemen are tailors of experience and skill, and turn out work equal to the best at very reasonable rates. Mr. O. H. Loveland is a native of Massachusetts and Mr. E. L. Peacock of Concord, N. H., and have carried on their present business here in Concord since 1889. They offer a fine assortment of foreign and domestic fabrics to select from, and are prepared to make up suits or single garments in a thoroughly artistic and durable manner, and at very low prices. Particular attention is given to the fitting of every garment made at this establishment, and all orders are assured immediate and painstaking attention, employment being given to from ten to twenty-five assistants.

David Webster, dealer in Choice Family Groceries, 40 Centre Street, Concord, N. H.—In one sense of the word the enterprise now conducted by Mr. David Webster may be said to have had its origin more than half a century ago, for the founder of it, Mr. A. Webster, began operations as a butcher in 1838. In 1845 he bought out the only meat market in town, and after a time added the sale of groceries. He sold out this business, and some seven years later began again as a member of the firm of A. & C. C. Webster, the undertaking started by this firm being continued by A. Webster, then by Webster & Hoyt, then by Webster & Colby, and then by Webster & Renick, the latter concern assuming control in 1863. Two years later Mr. Webster disposed of the grocery business and began to handle flour, grain, etc.; giving this up in 1868 and remaining out of business until 1873, when he resumed the sale of groceries. In 1876 the business was established in its present location, and in 1883 the firm name became A. Webster & Co., so remaining until 1886, when the present proprietor assumed sole control. Mr. David Webster is a native of Plymouth, N. H., and is very widely known both in business and social circles. He utilizes well equipped premises, located at No. 40 Centre street, and 24×55 feet in dimensions, they accommodating a large and carefully chosen stock, comprising choice staple and fancy groceries, and exceptionally complete in every department. Flour and grain are also largely dealt in, and Mr. Webster has a well earned reputation for supplying strictly dependable goods at the lowest market rates.

H. C. Sturtevant & Son, dealers in Choice Family Groceries, Fine Tea, Coffee, Sugar, Flour, Meal, Pork, Lard, Hams, Butter, Cheese, Eggs, Salt, Dried Fruit, Stone and Earthenware, etc., for Cash, McShane's Block, 17 Warren Street, Concord, N. H.—Mr. H. C. Sturtevant founded this business in 1873 and was sole proprietor until 1887, when his son, Mr. A. F. Sturtevant, became associated with him. The business has since then been conducted under the name of H. C. Sturtevant & Son. There are few of our local merchants engaged in this line of goods who are better known than these gentlemen. The assortment of choice family groceries and provisions is as complete as could be desired, for Mr. Sturtevant's long experience has made him perfectly familiar with the requirements of city trade, and prepared him to cater to it with the best possible advantage. Fine tea, coffee, sugar, flour, meal, pork, lard, hams, butter, cheese, eggs, salt, dried fruit, stone and earthenware are also to be found here, and the goods are sold as low as the lowest, as the terms are "for cash." Sturtevant & Son offer liberal inducements to purchasers, and they have every facility at hand to enable orders to be promptly filled. Goods are delivered in any part of the city free of charge. Mr. Sturtevant, who is a native of Hartford, Vt., served in the army during the late Rebellion, and he has also been a member of the legislature. Mr. A. F. Sturtevant is a native of Springfield, Mass.

Heath & Chesley, dealer in Furniture and Draperies. Hair Mattresses, made to order, a specialty. Opera House Block, 109 North Main Street, Concord, N. H.—The furnishing of a house may be a difficult or an easy matter, according to the manner in which it is undertaken, and if any of our readers have such a task to perform we can give them no better advice than to go directly to the establishment conducted by Messrs. Heath & Chesley at 109 North Main street, and choose from the extensive and varied stock there offered. By so doing, they are assured first, that they will have a full assortment, including the very latest and most desirable novelties, to select from; second that the goods will prove precisely as represented in every instance, and third that the prices paid will be as low as are quoted by any dealer on articles of equal merit. There are minor advantages such as courteous attention, prompt service, etc., which we will not mention in detail. Mr. Heath began business in 1887, and in 1889 associated himself with Mr. Chesley, under the present style of Heath & Chesley, and considering the inducements we have briefly touched upon, it is not surprising that a large trade has since been built up. Mr. Frank E. Heath, is a native of Somerville, Mass., and Mr. W. C. Chesley of Concord, both partners being too well known hereabouts to render extended personal mention necessary. The premises occupied comprise a store 20×90 feet in dimensions, and a workshop, and affords room for the carrying of a heavy stock embracing upholstered furniture, draperies, desks and parlor tables, etc. Mattresses are made to order, and repairing of all kinds is neatly and promptly done. Every article is sold strictly on its merits, and callers are assured prompt and polite attention at all times.

William O. Fraser, Monuments, Tablets, etc., Concord. —You can't get something for nothing, and you can't get first-class cemetery work without paying for it, but nevertheless there is no reason why one should pay fancy prices for first-class stone-work any more than for anything else that is first-class, and one way to avoid having to do so is to place your order with Mr. William Fraser, for while the work turned out at his shop is equal to the best, the prices are uniformly moderate. Mr. Fraser has carried on his present enterprise since 1884, at which date he began operations as a member of the firm of Fraser & McKelpin. In 1886 he assumed sole control, which he has since retained. Cemetery work of all kinds will be done in a uniformly superior manner at short notice, many beautiful and appropriate designs for monuments, tablets, headstones, etc., being constantly on hand to choose from. Estimates will cheerfully and promptly be made on appli-

cation, and those contemplating the placing of orders for anything in Mr. Fraser's line will best serve their own interests by communicating with him at their earliest convenience.

Nutting & Hayden, manufacturers of Granite Cutters' and Quarry Tools. Office and Factory, Ferry Street, Concord, N. H.—It will readily be believed that the tools used in working so hard and intractable a material as granite, must be skillfully made of excellent material if they are to do good service, and as the productions of Messrs. Nutting & Hayden are in active and increasing demand among granite cutters, the natural presumption is that they are equal to the best in both these important respects. Operations were begun in 1881 by Messrs. L. M. Nutting & Co., who were succeeded by the present firm in 1888. Mr. Nutting is a native of Danbury, Vt., while Mr. H. W. Hayden was born in Quincy, Mass., a town whose name is so associated with granite that it is almost impossible to think of one without calling to mind the other. Mr. Hayden has been in business in Concord since 1880, he carrying on a shop in the Union Steam Mill where polishing is done for granite companies and others. The premises utilized by Messrs. Nutting and Hayden are located on Ferry street, and comprise two floors of the dimensions of 50×90 feet, and a blacksmith shop measuring 30×24 feet. A specialty is made of manufacturing bush hammers, and both a wholesale and retail business is done, employment being given to from six to eight assistants, and all orders being promptly filled at the lowest market rates.

Wm. S. Davis & Son, manufacturers of Express and Hose Wagons, Open and Top Carriages and Sleighs on hand and built to order—Concord has a wide reputation in connection with the production of wagons, carriages and other vehicles, and by no means the least important among the houses which have contributed to this reputation is the firm of William S. Davis & Son, whose factory is located at the corner of South Main and Chandler streets, where an entire building comprising two stories and a basement and measuring 40×75 feet is occupied, together with a one and one-half story wood-working shop of the dimensions of 30×75 feet. The firm manufacture express and hose wagons. The latter takes first rank in the points of finish, durability and weight, being lighter and stronger than other wagons of the same capacity. They also make open and top carriages and sleighs, building the latter to order and also carrying a varied assortment in stock at all times. They have every facility at hand to enable them to turn out first class work at moderate cost, and as they employ skilled help, are well prepared to fill orders for new work and for repairing at very short notice. Carefully selected materials are used and every precaution is taken to maintain the enviable reputation their productions have long held for strength and durability. The partners are Messrs. William S. and Charles A. Davis, the former being a native of Boston, Mass., and the latter of this city. Mr. William S. Davis served three years in the army during the Rebellion, and became identified with his present enterprise in 1873. He has a very large circle of friends throughout this vicinity, as has also his son, who holds the responsible position of chief engineer of the fire department. Both members of the firm give close personal attention to the details of the business and spare no pains to improve the efficiency of the service rendered.

The Abbot-Downing Company, Manufacturers of Coaches, Wagons and Carriages.—It would be practically impossible, outside the limits of a special volume of its own, to do anything like real justice to the Abbot-Downing Co., which is one of the largest and most complete establishments of the kind in the United States. Neither would any account of the varied industries of Concord be complete without containing at least some allusion to this enterprise, and for this reason the following brief statement of a few facts concerning the company's history and present facilities may be taken in place of what we should prefer to make, a complete description and review of the business. The limited scale on which these works were originally established is matter for astonishment in view of the present magnitude of the establishment. The foundation of the business was laid in 1813, by Mr. Lewis Downing, making at the present time 77 years of continuous business, with some slight variation in the firm name, at different times. The first "Concord Wagon" was built for Benjamin Kimball of Concord, November 4, 1813, since which, thousands of them have been made and sent to all parts of the world. In 1828 the firm of Downing & Abbot was organized, who continued the business until 1847, when they dissolved partnership and established two separate houses, viz.: Lewis Downing & Sons, and J. S. & E. A. Abbot. The junior partner of the first named firm was Lewis Downing, Jr., who had been connected with the business since 1837, and who is now the honored president of the Abbot-Downing Co. In 1865 the firm of Abbot, Downing & Co. was organized, consisting of Messrs. Lewis Downing, Jr., J. S. Abbot, E. A. Abbot, Alonzo Downing, and Mr. J. H. Abbot. The Abbot-Downing Co. was incorporated in 1873, with a capital of $100,000, and is officered as follows: President, Lewis Downing, Jr.; vice-president, Joseph H. Abbot; treasurer, Edward A. Abbot; secretary, Francis L. Abbot; superintendent, R. M. Morgan. The works at the present time cover six acres, and the buildings comprise all of the most approved appointments calculated to facilitate economical manufacture, and the machinery requires a 90-horse power Corliss engine and three boilers of 150-horse power to effect the necessary action. This company is the oldest carriage company in the United States, and are the originators of the "Concord Wagons," "Concord Coaches," "Concord Wheels," and "Concord Axles." As manufacturers of coaches, wagons, carriages and trucks they are known the world over. Heavy goods are made a specialty, and in this department of manufacture they stand without a successful rival. As all parts of the vehicle, including axles, springs and wheels, are made within the works, they are enabled to furnish their customers with an article that they know to be reliable, and of the best quality obtainable. Their express wagons and trucks are the perfection of durability and fine workmanship, and are unequalled for strength, lightness, and general excellence by those of any other first class house in the world. The first stage coach was built at these works 1825. In 1865 they built thirty-four stages for Wells, Fargo & Co., to be used by them in mountain work while building the Union Pacific railroad. For the last three years they have built about fifty large stage coaches, to be drawn by twelve horses, and used in the mountainous regions of South Africa, carrying freight and passengers to the Transvaal gold fields in that vicinity. They use 400 tons of iron and steel, and 500,000 feet of lumber per year, and manufacture annually from 1,800 to 2,000 wagons. Their pay-roll is $12,000 to $15,000 per month, constituting a powerful element in promoting the industrial thrift of this community. They employ two hundred and fifty hands in Concord, forty at their repair shop in New York City, and fifteen in the lumber regions of Vermont. Their principal branches are at No. 52 Oliver street, Boston; No. 142 Prince street, New York; and at Melbourne and Sydney, Australia. Their trade is co-extensive with the globe. Wagons of various styles, and trucks, are kept in stock at all times, and orders are filled with promptness and care. This company is undoubtedly the institution which, more than any other, makes Concord famous the world over. Its officers are known as among the most patriotic, philanthrophic and public-spirited citizens of the city and State, and their names are familiar in every quarter. The president, Mr. Lewis Downing, Jr., was born and reared on the very grounds where the works of the company have stood for the past seventy-five years. On the completion of fifty years of continuous service in this industry, May 4, 1887, he presented the employes of the company with a beautifully printed and engraved souvenir, accompanied by a photograph of himself, extending his congratulations and best wishes, and referring, among other things, to the fact that thirteen of the employes had an average service of forty-two years—The longest fifty-one and the shortest thirty seven years—a wonderful record, which he justly considers unparalleled. Mr. Downing is the president of the National State Capital Bank, a director in the Stark Mills at Manchester, and takes an active interest in everything that is likely to prove advantageous to the city, county and State. The vice-president, Mr. Joseph H. Abbot, is also a native of the city, as is the treasurer, Mr. Edward A. Abbot, and the secretary, Mr. Francis L. Abbot, all are earnestly engaged in maintaining the prestige of the establishment, and thereby meeting every demand of their immense trade. We doubt if the citizens of Concord fully appreciate the great benefit it has derived from this establishment, the homes it has helped to build, and the families it has found employment for. Could the amount of money it has paid its employes, for the last fifty years alone, be correctly ascertained, it would probably astonish all, by the number of its thousands of dollars. Nearly all has been collected from parties residing out of the State, and distributed by the employes almost wholly in Concord. We hope, for the benefit of all concerned, the establishment will continue to grow and prosper, and by the sons and grandsons be carried through the balance of the century, and so make up the record of 100 years.

Porter Blanchard's Sons, Established 1818, Concord, N. H.—It is very seldom in these days of hurry and change, that a manufacturing firm can date its establishment over seventy years ago. The making of churns and dairy implements was begun in the town of Concord by the founders of this firm in 1818. The manufacture has

been continuous ever since, and from having only a local sale and reputation, their goods are now sent to every part of the world where butter is made. The high standard of excellence has been scrupulously maintained, and the uniform merit of the goods has been the reason of the large increase of sales, as the firm has never employed a travelling salesman. The goods have done their own talking wherever they have been introduced. From a very modest beginning the business now requires and occupies a four story brick factory, two hundred feet long, and it is safe to say that there does not exist a more conveniently arranged factory for the quick and economical manufacture of goods. The machinery is all of the latest patterns, and the workmen are the best that can be obtained. The cardinal points of excellence of stock and workmanship are never forgotten. It is a fact that all goods bearing the name of this firm may be safely considered "the best" in their line. They have recently greatly enlarged their line of goods, and now make or can furnish at manufacturers' prices, everything needed in a butter factory or private dairy. Their latest important invention is called a *Self Skimming Milk Can,* and is a most ingenious as well as simple device by which the cream, after it has passed to the top of the milk in a deep can, is retained by a valve and lifted off with the greatest ease and economy. It is deservedly attracting a great

deal of attention from practical dairymen who want the "latest and best." Their factory churns and other factory implements are in demand all over the world, a good number being sent to foreign countries. Their well-known family churns are conceded by intelligent and unprejudiced judges to combine more desirable qualities than any other make or kind. They have never been beaten in any fair competitive trial either in quantity or quality of butter made. In their anxiety to get something to beat the "old and reliable *Blanchard,*" manufacturers have made churns of all sorts of queer shapes, hung them at every variety of angle, and then made convenient theories to match them. But they have failed in their efforts. The *Blanchard* remains at the head of all butter-making utensils. More than one hundred thousand persons can testify to the truth of this statement. They are making the best and handsomest cheap butter box in the market. They hold from one to ten pounds, and are largely used. Their print butter carrier is just what the dairyman needs to get his butter to his customer in the very best condition. It may be made into tasteful blocks in a Blanchard butter mold, and from the cool, clean carrier, delivered to the consumer in tempting shape. The wise dairyman knows how important this is. They have a new family butter worker now ready for sale, which combines the important and desirable merits of several other kinds. It is very neat and cheap, and bound to win. The new parchment dairy paper is a great success, and every way better and cheaper than cloth for all dairy purposes. They have it for sale in any shape or quantity. All dairymen, or parties interested, are invited to send for circulars which give description, sizes and prices. Everything bearing the name of this firm as makers is guaranteed to be in every way just as represented, and made "'pon honor."

Thompson & Hoague (business established in 1855, by Gust Walker), Hardware, Iron, Steel, Agricultural and Mechanics' Tools, Mill Supplies, Cordage, Akron Sewer Pipe, Fertilizers, etc., Hardware store, 42 North Main street, "The Depot Iron store," Railroad square, Concord, N. H.—There is naturally a very brisk and continuous demand for hardware, iron, steel, mechanics' tools, etc., in so important a manufacturing and railroad centre as Concord, and among the houses engaged in this line of business are some which are well and favorably known throughout the State, notably that conducted by Messrs. Thompson & Hoague (formerly Willis D. Thompson). The main store of this firm is in Phenix block where the business was founded by Mr Gust Walker in 1855. The premises devoted to the iron and heavy hardware business (previously carried on by Messrs. Walker & Co.) are known as the "Depot Iron store," and are located in the substantial brick structure in Railroad square, opposite the passenger station. This building which was built for the purpose, has a main door which measures 50x70 feet, while the two upper floors are used for storage purposes and for the display of farming implements. Messrs Thompson & Hoague are the manufacturers' agents for the sale in this vicinity of the world renowned Buckeye mowers, of which a large number are sold each year—in fact so many are now in use as to create a large demand for the sections and extra parts of the machines for repairs. Of these the firm carry a full supply. The latest and most approved makes and patterns of sulky plows, disk harrows, corn planters, horse hoes and all other tools and machines as well as fertilizers needed by the farmer are constantly in stock. It has been said, and with truth, that the lawn mower has been one of the greatest factors in beautifying the thousand of cities and villages of our land. This house has the best—the "New Model." Blacksmiths, carriage makers and machinists being in want of too's or supplies, do well to order of this firm because they have a stock selected with special reference to their wants. New and elegant styles of bronze builders' hardware and fine locks are constantly being added to the stock of this house, which taken in connection with the plainer styles of lower price, enable this house to trim expensive residences and public buildings as well as the cheaper dwellings.

is given to four competent assistants, and all orders are dispatched in a prompt and methodical manner that all mistakes may be avoided.

Thomas Nawn, manufacturer of and dealer in Granite, near State prison, Concord.—The business conducted by Mr. Thomas Nawn has steadily and rapidly developed since operations were begun in 1881, and present indications are that it will continue to increase in the future, for Mr. Nawn gives it close personal supervision and spares no pains to maintain the high reputation he has won for filling orders in a superior manner, at short notice and at the lowest market rates. Since 1881 Mr. Nawn has been sole proprietor. He is a manufacturer of and dealer in granite and granite cemetery work of all descriptions, and has an extensive polishing mill at Penacook, besides his well appointed works near the State prison in this city. Employment is given to from twenty to thirty assistants, the number varying with the season, but at any time Mr. Nawn is prepared to fill the most extensive orders at short notice, and to turn out work that will compare favorably with any produced in this State. He caters to all tastes and all purses, for the designs he offers comprise a full assortment, from the most simple to the most elaborate, while in every case the workmanship is equal to the best. Estimates will be promptly made on application, and all communications by mail or otherwise are assured immediate and careful attention.

These five Gettysburg memorials bear Mr. Nawn's card : Second N. H. Regt. Vol ; General Berdan's Sharpshooters ; Twelfth N. H. Vol.; Eighth N. H. Vol.; Brigadier-General Lewis A. Armistead, C.S.A., erected and paid for by the National Association of the battle field of Gettysburg.

Schiller, the great musician's monument, to be erected in Columbus, Ohio, and to be one of the largest stone monuments ever built in New Hampshire, is now being built by Mr. Nawn.

G. W. Dudley, Provisions and Groceries, 5 Masonic Temple, Concord, N. H.—There are so many excellent reasons which might be given for the success attained by this house that all of our available space could be taken up in presenting them, but after all the only satisfactory way to gain an adequate idea of why a certain establishment is popular is to visit it in person and leave a trial order there, so we will not bother our readers with reasons but will simply earnestly advise them to call at No. 5 North Main street and see for themselves. The time so spent will by no means be thrown away, for the firm carry a heavy and varied stock of family provisions and groceries, and no fancy prices are charged for anything, only a fair living profit will be added to the cost. The grocery business has been carried on here in this spot for over fifteen years, and in 1875 it was conducted by Perkins, Dudley & Co., but in 1888 the present proprietor assumed entire control. The store, which is 25×70 feet in dimensions, is thoroughly fitted up in every respect, enabling customers to be conveniently and promptly served and affording accommodations for the large stock which is carried at all seasons. Mr. G. W. Dudley is a native of Barnstead, N. H., and he is familiar with all the many details of his business, to which he gives his close personal attention. Employment

R. H. Ayer, dealer in Fine Watches, Jewelry, Silverware, Engraving and Fine Repairing a Specialty. Phenix Hotel Block, Concord, N. H.— Probably watches, jewelry and silverware were never so cheap before as at the present time, but it is also true that never before was there such a quantity of "bogus" goods on the market, so that purchasers cannot be too careful in making their selections. As a matter of fact the only sure way of "getting your money's worth" is to patronize a dealer who not only knows his business but has an established reputation for looking out for the interests of his customers, and as Mr. R. H. Ayer can certainly be depended upon in both respects, it naturally follows that he is a good man to call on when anything in the line of watches or jewelry is wanted. This business was originated by Stanley & Ayer, but in 1885 Mr. Ayer became sole proprietor. This store is located in Phenix Hotel Block, North Main street, and contains a well chosen and varied stock of watches, jewelry, silverware, diamonds, pearls, gold pens, gold headed canes, spectacles and eye-glasses. He also makes a specialty of engraving and repairing watches, and everything in the line of jewelry, will be put in order at short notice, and in a thoroughly satisfactory manner at moderate rates. Three competent assistants are employed, and prompt and accurate attention is assured to all. Mr. Ayer is a native of Concord, N. H., and by his honorable business dealings has built up a high reputation in this city. He has introduced a very novel method of selling watches on the "club plan" and brings a good gold watch within the reach of most any lady or gentleman. For particulars see his circular.

W. F. Danforth & Son, Wholesale Confectioners, Agents for the All colored Unexcelled Fireworks, 10 North Main Street, Concord, N. H.—The firm of W. F. Danforth & Son are best known perhaps as wholesale confectioners, and yet the manufacture and sale of confectionery form but one department of their business, which also includes the jobbing and retailing of fireworks, toys, notions and novelties of almost every description. The firm have carried on operations since 1875, the partners being Messrs. W. F. & R. W Danforth, both of whom were born in Nashua, N. H. The premises utilized are located at No. 10 North Main street, and are 22×80 feet in size, every necessary facility being at hand to enable operations to be carried on to the best possible advantage. A competent force of experienced assistants is employed, and the heaviest orders are filled at short notice, while the smallest commissions are carefully and promptly executed. Messrs. W. F. Danforth & Son are the sole manufacturers of the genuine soft lozenge, and all their confections are made from selected material and are pure and healthful in every respect. The firm are agents for the all colored unexcelled fireworks, and deal largely in firecrackers, torpedoes, paper caps, tin horns, Japanese lanterns, flags, balloons, nickeled clocks, jewelry, umbrellas, masks, etc., together with school goods, base-ball goods, hammocks, sleds, Paris carts and wagons, walking sticks, croquet and other games, and a host of other articles too numerous to mention. Any of these goods will be supplied in quantities to suit and at positively bottom prices.

J. Hazelton & Son, dealers in Dry Goods, Millinery, Hair Goods, Laces, Edgings, Mourning Goods, etc., 73 State Block, North Main Street, Concord, N. H.—It is not to be wondered at if this is one of the best known stores in the city, for it claims to be the oldest of the kind in Concord, if not the oldest in the State. It was in 1842 that Mr. J. Hazelton established this house, and successfully conducted it until in 1885, when his son, Mr. Frank R. Hazelton, was admitted to the business and the above name was adopted. These gentlemen deal largely in millinery and fancy dry goods, of which they carry a large variety of all the novelties and new and fashionable goods which the market affords. As they are careful buyers and have from their long experience become familiar with the demands of their customers, they are always ready to supply them with all the new styles for each season, and they are also well able to show a full line of those substantial articles that do not depend upon the seasons or fashions for their sale. They have a fine display of laces, edgings, mourning goods, and also a choice line of hair goods. Mr. F. R. Hazelton has some inventions and patents which he has successfully put upon the market. The first is an umbrella displayer, and the second is hat pendants for displaying hats and bonnets, also a fire extinguisher which will be upon the market soon. The premises occupied comprise two floors each 22×75 feet in dimensions, and a basement. Employment is given to from six to ten polite and competent assistants. The fire extinguisher referred to above has recently been invented by Mr. Frank R. Hazelton, and consists of a glass keg with bale, height 17 inches, diameter, 6 inches. The keg is charged under heavy pressure by machinery with carbonic acid gas and water and hermetically sealed. Previous to charging powerful chemicals are placed in the keg and act as a reinforcement to the first volume of gas by generating a second volume of fire extinguishing gas, caused by heat of the fire. Heat is not required to generate the first volume of gas, as it is always ready under heavy pressure. In a partition fire it is inhalable on account of the *two volumes of gas.* The liquid forms a fireproof coating. There can be no waste of gas in transit, as there is when hose and nozzle are used. They cannot freeze, evaporate, rust, or be tampered with although contents are in view. The keg is amber color and handsomely lettered "Hazelton's High Pressure Chemical Fire Keg." It is splendidly adapted for use in buildings, railroad cars, steamships, and to attach to fire department or police patrol wagons. The keg weighs about ten pounds.

Lewis B. Hoit, Groceries and Provisions, No. 105 South Main Street, Concord, N. H.—The business conducted by Mr. Lewis B. Hoit may be said to have had its origin many years ago, and it changed hands a number of times before coming into the possession of the present proprietor in 1882, succeeding Mr. George B. Whittredge. Mr. Hoit has had twenty-five years' experience in the grocery business in this city, was sixteen years in the employ of Mr. Frank Hoit before he came into possession of his present store, since which time he has built up a large and increasing trade, and has become one of the most important enterprises of its kind in the city. Mr. Hoit is a native of Ware, N. H , and is generally and favorably known in Concord and vicinity. The premises made use of are located at No. 105 South Main street, and measure 100×25 feet, exclusive of two spacious storehouses, so that ample accommodations are provided for an exceptionally heavy and complete stock, comprising groceries and provisions of all kinds. Mr. Hoit caters to all classes of trade, and all tastes as well as all purses can certainly be suited at this popular store. The assortment of staple and fancy groceries includes a full line of canned goods, table delicacies, pure teas, coffees and spices, together with the leading brands of flour for family use. Choice fresh, salted and smoked meats and fresh vegetables and fruits are extensively dealt in, and as employment is given to four competent assistants callers are assured prompt and courteous attention.

George F. Clark, manufacturer of and dealer in Granite, Concord, N. H.—If anybody wants convincing proof that good taste is more general to-day than ever before in this country, let him visit an old cemetery and compare the monuments and tablets of a few generations ago with those of recent erection. He would notice not only a change in design but also in material, for granite is now the favorite monumental stone and is displacing marble as completely as that displaced slate. The cost of granite work is not nearly so high as was once the case, and if orders be placed in the proper

hands it is possible to obtain handsome granite cemetery work at very reasonable rates In this connection we may very fittingly call attention to the facilities possessed by Mr. George F. Clark, for he is a manufacturer of and dealer in granite and makes a specialty of cemetery work of all kinds, showing many appropriate and uncommon designs and quoting the lowest market rates on first-class work. He is a native of Burlington, Vt , and founded his present enterprise in 1884, as a member of the firm of Clark & Blodgett, assuming sole control in 1887. His works are located near the State prison, and every facility is at hand to enable orders to be promptly and satisfactorily filled, employment being given to from ten to fifteen assistants. Both a wholesale and retail business is done, and estimates will be cheerfully furnished on application.

T. W. & J. H. Stewart, Merchant Tailors, 82 North Main Street, Concord.—This establishment so long and favorably known as one of the most reliable in the State was established in January, 1849, by Mr. T. W. Stewart. In 1883 Mr. J. H Stewart was admitted as an equal partner, the business being carried on since that time under the present firm name, at No. 82 North Main street, occupying a modernly fitted up store, 18×90 feet, with basement same size, giving employment to from fifteen to twenty hands. They have now associated with them Mr. Charles H. Stewart, son of Mr. J. H. Stewart, who has been thoroughly instructed in the art of cutting and has already earned an enviable position among the fraternity as a first-class cutter. His business will especially be to look after the interests of the younger portion of our customers, making the firm well adapted to meet the wants of all classes. Their motto will be in the future, as in the past, honest dealing with all, prompt to meet all engagements, buy the best goods the market affords at their lowest cash value, manufacturing them into garments of the most approved style consistent with skilled workmanship and first-class trimmings. All who contemplate replenishing their wardrobe will find it to their advantage to make a thorough examination of their large stock of very desirable suitings, and everything, in fact, that is usually found in a first class tailoring establishment, before making their purchase. The Messrs Stewart would take this opportunity to extend to their customers and the public generally, their grateful thanks for their long continued and very generous patronage, promising on their part that in the future, as in the past, no pains shall be spared to meet a continuance of the same.

Prescott Piano and Organ Co., D. B. Prescott, Treasurer. Office and Factory, 71 South Main Street, Concord, N. H.—From the New York *Music Trade Review* : The Prescott upright pianos' brilliant and successful venture into the piano making field by the Prescott Piano and Organ Company of Concord, N. H., an unblemished commercial reputation of fifty-five years.

"Away up in the ancient city of Concord, N. H., honored and respected by a vast constituency of customers throughout the United States, are located the works of the Prescott Piano and Organ Company. They are the successors of the Prescott Organ Company, the grand old concern that has withstood the shocks and vicissitudes of five decades triumphantly, and made a better showing every year of its existence than it did the year before. The Prescotts are, and almost from time immemorial have been, shrewd observers of the music market and of the changes in the musical taste of the public. Some three years ago they decided to abandon the manufacture of organs, assigning as their reason for that step that the demand for those instruments had decreased and was decreasing. During these three years they have been steadily developing a piano making business, and at the present moment, thanks to their New England pluck, patience and clear headedness, the Prescott upright pianos have already acquired considerable renown. Cheered by this gratifying result of their studious application in the new field, they have put their shoulder to the wheel with renewed zest and earnestness, and stand prepared to meet every demand for their strictly first class pianos with promptitude and upon a scale of prices that cannot fail to satisfy every reasonable customer. In the construction of these Prescott uprights no labor or expense is spared. The materials of which they are made are the best to be obtained in the market. The firm's new scale is drawn with exceeding care, while the designs and finish of the case work are graceful, rich and attractive. They have also in progress a new scale of larger size. After all, the spotless repute of the Prescott Company during no less a period than fifty-three years is the best assurance that can be given that only first class work will be allowed to leave their factory. The proud and honorable position which has been maintained by them for more than half a century will not be allowed to become a thing of the past so long as a drop of the old Prescott blood remains in the firm, and as yet there is no sign of any diminution in the supply of that fine New Hampshire fluid. For all of which rea-

sons dealers and others are strongly recommended to investigate the Prescott upright pianos, and correspondents will find it to their signal advantage to arrange for new local agencies. The factory and office address is No. 71 South Main street, that of the warerooms No. 92 North Main street, Concord, N. H."

A. W. Davis, dealer in Ladies' and Children's Tailor-made Garments to Order, No. 7 Capitol Street, Concord.—This business was founded in 1875 by Patterson & Davis, who were succeeded in 1876 by Weeks, Patterson & Davis. In 1879 there was another change,—the new firm consisting of Patterson & Davis. In 1884 the present proprietor, Mr. A. W. Davis, who is a native of Warner, N. H., assumed full control and possession of the premises. His principal trade is in making ladies' and children's garments to order. He also sells some cloths and trimmings. Mr. Davis has extensive facilities and a practical knowledge for conducting this business. His experience has been large, and his long connection with this house has enabled him to secure a class of trade that is reliable, and can be depended upon, so long as garments for ladies and children are made in the elegant and tasteful style for which this establishment is noted. These "tailor-made garments" are of superior make and finish, while the style and fit are unequalled by any similar concern. Mr. Davis has in his employ ten skillful assistants, who can be depended upon for finishing garments in the most satisfactory manner. Every effort is made to please each customer in their individual taste, as all garments are custom made. Orders will be fil'ed in the shortest time possible, with good work

Lee Brothers, Practical Plumbers, Steam, Hot Water and Gas Fitting. No. 12 Pleasant Street, Concord, N. H.—These gentlemen are natives of this city and established this business in 1888. The premises utilized are about 1100 square feet in dimensions, and in addition they have a basement. They are practical plumbers, steam and hot water fitters, and may be relied upon as thorough workmen, in every detail of their business, which at the present day, with the extensive use of steam and hot water pipes, requires the knowledge of skilled engineers and a conscientious fulfilment of contracts. Orders for plumbing, steam, hot water and gas fitting will be given prompt and skillful attention, satisfaction being guaranteed both as regards the results attained and the reasonableness of the charges made. Lee Brothers have the facilities, the ability and the disposition to satisfy their customers and that they do so, is shown by the steady increase of their business. As a sanitary measure for the promotion of health the plumbing trade occupies a position in the front ranks of improvements, and has become a necessity in this age of progress. Their business requires the services of from fifteen to twenty skillful employees, according to the season. They carry in stock a full line of steam and plumbing goods. They are also agents of the "Gurney Hot Water Heater." Messrs. Lee Bros. are the originators of a steam boiler, a sample of which is at this store, which is undoubtedly the best in the market at the present time.

to sell at the lowest market rates, it would be strange if Mr. Willard were not able to offer exceptional inducements to those who appreciate strictly reliable goods, and that as a matter of fact he does so, must be known to all our readers. Trustworthy articles, fair prices—this is the combination which builds up trade, and this is the combination familiar to all the patrons of this popular store

W. P. Underhill & Co., Prescription Druggists, 132 North Main Street, Concord, N. H.—To say that the pharmacy conducted by Messrs. W. P. Underhill & Co. is worthy of the utmost confidence may seem a superfluous statement to those who are already conversant with that firm's methods, but as not a few of our readers even among those residing in Concord have not had an opportunity to learn the relative merits of our more prominent druggists, we feel that such information as we can give will prove acceptable especially as we propose to confine our statement within bounds, that their truth can be easily demonstrated. The establishment alluded to was opened by E. H. Rollins & Co. over fifty years ago, and has been under the control of the present firm since 1874, the individual members of which are W. P. Underhill and L. H. Piper. The premises utilized are located at No. 132 North Main street, and are 20 × 65 feet in dimensions. The stock carried is of itself such as to enable the firm the ability to fill all orders without delay, for it is very complete in every department and is made up of pure drugs, medicines and chemicals, carefully selected, and obtained from the most reputable manufacturers and wholesalers. Toilet articles, perfumery, etc., are dealt in to some extent, but not enough to cause the more important branches of the business to be neglected, for the proprietors recognize the fact that the true province of the druggist is to render the best possible service in the filling of physician's prescriptions, etc., and indeed we know of no other pharmacy in this section where such orders are given more conscientious attention. Messrs. W. P. Underhill & Co. are assisted by two clerks, and as the best materials are dealt in, and no exorbitant prices charged, it is but natural that a large business should be done. Messrs. Underhill & Co. have perhaps the finest and most costly soda fountain in the State, and it certainly is a beauty. The fact is well established in this vicinity that this is headquarters for the best soda, summer or winter. They keep a full line of foreign and domestic cigars and are agents for "Huyler's confectionery" of New York.

E. W. Willard & Co. have the finest and best equipped dry goods store in the State and probably in New England outside of the large cities. Entrance to the store is gained through the southeast corner which opens into a commodious vestibule. Inside the main store one is at once struck with its beauty. Its fittings are not elegant in the true sense of the word, but they are handsome and the whole effect is very pleasing. The arrangements of the main store are such as to allow of counters on all four sides, with commodious shelving. The center of the room is taken up with counters, Boston style, the whole giving ample room for the display of goods and allowing their classification. At the centre the main feature is the glove department with a cabinet of eighty small drawers for the reception of the goods and special arrangements of counters for fitting the gloves to the purchaser with ease and comfort. Three young ladies connected with the store have taken lessons from a New York fitter, and Mr. Willard has made this department a success. The main show window is 30 feet long and seven feet deep, and is handsomely decorated. Messrs. E. W. Willard & Co., in Opera House Block, are among the best known dry goods concerns in New Hampshire, having been established in 1878 by Mr. E. W. Willard who was born in Orford, N. H. During the twelve years that Mr. Willard has been connected with the management of the undertaking in question, he has become so well and favorably known throughout this State that extended personal mention is quite uncalled for, so we will simply state that he ranks with the representative business men, the establishment under his control being truly representative in the best sense of the word. The premises utilized comprise what was originally built for three stores and is the largest dry goods store in Concord, and the heavy stock on hand is made up of dry goods, small wares, and an extremely large line of cloaks, kid gloves, and gents' furnishing goods, in which an extensive business, both wholesale and retail in character, is done. Employment is given to a good force of courteous and efficient assistants, and the prompt and polite attention assured to customers is not to be forgotten when estimating the causes of this establishment's great popularity among all classes in the community. Enjoying the most favorable relations with producers and making it a point

Henry Ivey, manufacturer of and dealer in Concord Granite Monuments, Building Stone, etc., Concord — Many an otherwise fine monument has been spoiled in its effects by being constructed of inferior stone, and many a fine piece of stone has been ruined by incompetent and careless workmanship, so it is obvious that in placing orders for cemetery work of any kind it is of the first importance to use discrimination so that both material and workmanship will be all that could be desired. One sure and easy way to bring about this gratifying result is to place the order with Mr. Henry Ivey, for he is a leading manufacturer of Concord granite monuments, headstones, tablets, etc., and both the design and execution of his work will bear the most critical comparison, while the stone is carefully chosen with special reference to the effects desired. Mr. Ivey began business here in 1880, and the magnitude of the trade he has built up during the past decade affords convincing evidence that the advantages he offers are appreciated. He deals largely in building stone, and every order, large or small, is assured prompt and painstaking attention.

The First National Bank, of Concord, N. H.—"Credit to whom credit is due," is a most excellent rule to be guided by, and the business men of Concord and vicinity appear as a class to carry out its precept, for they are outspoken in their commendation of the work done by the First National bank and freely admit that this institution has proved and is still proving to be a most potent factor in the development of the material interests of the city. With the growth of the credit system there has been a corresponding growth in the possible usefulness of financial institutions, and as this system has come to stay, (being in fact essential to the extensive transactions of business) it is sound public policy to encourage and support in all legitimate ways the banking service of the country. During the quarter of a century that the First National bank has been in existence, manufacturing and commercial methods have been materially changed and in some instances completely revolutionized, and it is largely owing to the readiness with which the management has foreseen and accommodated its methods to these changes that the bank has attained its present leading position and preserved its credit unimpaired through all the panics and periods of business depression that have occurred since its incorporation in 1864. It has never been content to follow in the footsteps of others but has pursued an independent, aggressive and consistent policy, sharply discriminating between speculation and investment and adhering steadfastly to legitimate methods. By this course it has gained an enviable reputation in the financial world, has proved a source of profit to its stockholders and has attained a financial condition which can be matched by but few banks in New England, the present surplus fund and undivided profits amounting to more than $200,000 on a capital stock of $150,000. A general banking business is done, a prominent feature being the handling of investment securities The deposits of individuals, firms and corporations are solicited and will be received on the most favorable terms, and safe deposit boxes are rented at moderate rates. The gentlemen identified with the management of this representative bank certainly need no introduction to our Concord readers for they are very generally known throughout the State, as will be seen from the following list:

President,
WILLIAM F. THAYER.

Cashier,
CHARLES G. REMICK.

Assistant Cashier,
WILLIAM A. STONE, JR.

Directors,

THOMAS STUART,	WILLIAM M. CHASE,
SOLON A. CARTER,	WILLIAM F. THAYER,
WILLIAM P. FISKE,	C. H. ROBERTS.

STATEMENT OF THE

FIRST NATIONAL BANK OF CONCORD, N. H.

May 19th, 1890.

RESOURCES.

Loans and discounts.........................	$656,153.31
U. S. bonds..............................	200,000.00
Other stocks and bonds...................	272,337.50
Due from reserve agent and other national banks........................	317,433.90
Banking house............................	10,000.00
Legal tender notes, specie, and cash items....	58,222.31
Premiums and current expenses.............	7,978.15
	$1,522,125.17

LIABILITIES.

Capital stock...........................	$150,000.00
Surplus fund and undivided profits........	208,963.95
Dividends unpaid........................	780.00
National bank notes outstanding..........	45,000.00
Deposits................................	1,117,381.22
	$1,522,125.17

John Swenson, manufacturer of and dealer in Concord Granite Monuments, and cemetery work of all kinds. Producer of Blue Concord Granite. West Concord.—The facilities enjoyed by Mr. John Swenson as a manufacturer of and dealer in Concord granite monuments and cemetery work, enable him to offer particular inducements to customers and have had the effect of building up a large and steadily growing business. He has been identified with his present enterprise since 1883, being a member of the firm of Swenson & Downing up to 1888, when he assumed sole control. Employment is afforded to from ten to twenty assistants, and no trouble is spared to assure the prompt, accurate and satisfactory filling of every order. Mr. Swenson is a producer of the celebrated blue Concord granite, and that coming from his quarry is unsurpassed for fineness of grain and beauty and uniformity of coloring. He is prepared to furnish this stone in quantities to suit, and quotes prices in strict accordance with the lowest market rates. Cemetery work of all kinds is also done in a superior manner at moderate figures, and customers are given an opportunity to choose from an almost endless variety of designs, varying from the most simple to the most elaborate.

S. Wallace & Son, Stair Builders. Stair Building in all its Branches. 17 Pearl Street, Concord, N. H.—Stair building is a distinct and very important branch of the carpenter's trade, and requires long experience and a high degree of skill to carry it on successfully, for although some stairways are easy enough to build, there are others which necessitate careful calculation and very accurate work, and of course the practical stair-builder has to "take things as they come," and be competent to fill orders for anything and everything in his line promptly and satisfactorily. Many residents of Concord will involuntarily associate stair building and the firm of S. Wallace & Son, for this concern have been prominent in this line of industry ever since 1865, continuing a business which was founded by Mr. Samuel Wallace twenty years before. Since 1887 Mr. W. D. Wallace has been sole proprietor, but the old firm name is still retained. He is a native of Syracuse, N. Y., and served a year in the army during the Rebellion. Mr. Wallace is very widely and favorably known throughout this section, and fully maintains the high reputation so long associated with the enterprise he carries on. Stair building in all its branches will be done in a superior manner at short notice, and estimates will be promptly furnished on application. The shop is located at No. 17 Pearl street, and communications to that address are assured immediate and careful attention.

W. S. Wilson, Florist; dealer in Cut Flowers, Bouquets, Funeral Designs, Bulbs, etc., 49 South Street, Concord, N. H.—People have become so accustomed to having an abundant supply of flowers the year round, that they seldom stop to consider the means by which this most desirable result is brought about, but the subject is an interesting one and a visit to a well-appointed greenhouse will repay every thinking person. There is an immense amount of labor involved in the raising of flowers for the market, and a constant care and watchfulness which we believe has no parallel in any other line of business. Considering the difficulties met with and the cost of the necessary apparatus, it is surprising that flowers can be sold at the prices quoted on them, but competition will do wonders, and it has certainly resulted in the discovery of improved methods of flower culture. One of the most popular florists in this city is Mr. W. S. Wilson, and there is most excellent reason for his popularity, as Mr. Wilson offers unsurpassed inducements to his customers and is noted for the taste displayed in the designing of wedding and funeral emblems, the arranging of bouquets, etc. He deals extensively in cut flowers, bulbs, rose bushes, etc., and maintains a greenhouse on South street. It is heated by hot water and is exceptionally well equipped throughout. He does both a wholesale and retail business, and orders sent by mail or otherwise, will receive early and careful attention.

The Union Guaranty Savings Bank, Concord, N. H.—
All honestly conducted and ably managed savings banks
are admirable institutions, insomuch as they promote frugal and prudent habits and tend in every way to advance
the welfare of the community in general, but there are
degrees of merit even in such institutions and the Union
Guaranty Savings bank is clearly entitled to a position in
the first class. It was incorporated in 1887, and its charter requires that depositors must be paid a rate of interest
not less than four per cent. per annum and there can be no
passing of dividends. The sum of $50,000 was deposited
by the trustees and other members of the corporation, to
be forever held as a guaranty fund against all loss to
depositors and to insure them both their principal and
interest. Many of those identified with this enterprise are
also identified with the First National bank, which shares
its office with the savings bank, and as the latter is managed in connection with this (widely known as one of
the soundest and most successful banks in New England)
depositors are afforded even greater security and other
advantages than the guaranty plan would indicate. The
patronage of all classes of citizens is solicited, and deposits
of one dollar and upwards will be received. The first day
of January in each year there will be declared to general
depositors, on all sums then on deposit, dividends at the
rate of four per cent. per annum on all sums which have
been held for a less time than one year, and four and one-
half per cent. on all sums which have been on deposit for
one year next preceding, reckoning from the first day in
each month; provided, that in case deposits are made
immediately before the first day of April, or are with-
drawn soon after the first day of April, so as to cause the
bank to bear an undue proportion of the taxes, the officers
reserve the right to deduct an equitable amount from the
interest on account of such taxes. Every year it is becoming more difficult to invest small sums safely and profitably in the ordinary channels of trade, and the usefulness
of such an institution as this is consequently sure to
steadily increase with the progress of time. Depositors
have the great advantage of knowing positively what
their annual income from any given sum will be, and
there is certainly not the least question as to the entire
security of the principal. The facilities offered have been
generally availed of, as is shown by the statement
appended to this article, while excellent management is
indicated by the financial exhibit of the same. That the
conduct of affairs is in experienced and reliable hands is
even more forcibly demonstrated by the following list of
officers: President, Solon A. Carter; treasurer, William
F. Thayer; trustees, Thomas Stuart, William M. Chase,
Solon A. Carter, Edward B. Woodworth, William F.
Thayer, Charles H. Roberts, Henry A. Emerson,
Alvah W. Sulloway, Edmund E. Truesdell, Charles
C. Danforth, John E. Robertson, Edson J. Hill, John
Whitaker, Timothy P. Sullivan, George P. Little, James
H. Rowell, Edwin H. Carroll.

UNION GUARANTY SAVINGS BANK, CONCORD, N. H.
Statement May 19, 1890.

Resources—Loans, $341,050.77; Stocks and Bonds,
$117,025.00; Bank balances and other cash items, $13,-
729.03; total, $471,804.80.
Liabilities—Guaranty fund, $50,000.00; Deposits, $406,-
454.53; Discount and interest, $15,350.27; total, $471,-
804.80.

Martin H. Spain, Granite Quarry, Concord. We have
not the figures at hand showing the amount of capital invested in the granite business in Concord, and the annual
production of this stone, but those who are at all familiar
with the city need not have figures quoted to them to make
them realize that this is a leading representative industry,
and is developing at a rate that is as gratifying as it is phe-
nomenal. Everybody has heard of "Concord granite," and
although there is an almost endless variety of kinds of
granite, few of them can compare in merit and popularity
with those coming under that general head. We know of
no better example of Concord granite than that taken from

the quarry of Mr. Martin H. Spain, and we are not alone in
this belief, for in the judgment of experts the stone quar-
ried by Mr. Spain has no superior in its special line. He
has all necessary facilities at hand to enable him to fill
orders without undue delay, and he is in a position to
quote the lowest market rates and to furnish stone in
quantities to suit.

H. O. Matthews, Carriage and Sleigh Painter, Hall's
Court, Concord, N. H.—No practical man needs to be told
that it pays to keep a carriage, sleigh or other vehicle well
painted, for experience has taught him that the gain in
durability more than compensates for the cost, leaving
appearances out of the question altogether. Of course,
good workmanship and the use of good stock are essential
to a satisfactory and durable job, but there is no difficulty
in securing these, and one sure way to do it is to place the
order with Mr. H. O. Matthews, who utilizes a well-
equipped shop comprising two floors of the dimensions of
40 × 50 feet, located in Hall's Court, employs from three
to five assistants, and is prepared to do first-class work at
short notice and moderate rates. Mr. Matthews is a native
of Canterbury, N. H., and began operations in 1875. He
is very generally known, not only in this vicinity but
throughout New England, for he is the most extensive
breeder of thoroughbred swine in New Hampshire and has
stock for sale at all times, orders being received from every
State in New England, not only for swine but also for
fancy poultry in which he deals very largely, handling ten
varieties. The "Pine Grove Breeding Farm," is one of
the most celebrated establishments of the kind in the
country, and to those interested in thoroughbred stock is
well worth travelling many miles to visit, for from 150 to
250 swine are to be seen there at all times, including such
famous varieties as Poland, China, Yorkshire, Chester
White and English Berkshire. They are of registered
pedigree, and the buyer knows just what he is getting for
his money and may depend upon having bottom prices
quoted, for Mr. Matthews' facilities are such that he is prepared to easily meet all honorable competition. At the
late New Hampshire State Fair, held at Manchester, he
took all the first and second stock premiums, his exhibit
attracting much favorable attention from the public and
the press. All orders, large or small will be carefully filled
at short notice, and all communications are assured
prompt and painstaking attention, any desired information
being cheerfully given.

John H. Mead, Wood Turning, Union Steam Mill.
Concord, N. H.—There are few if any better equipped
establishments of the kind in this city, than that carried on
by Mr. John H. Mead, and popularly known as the Union
Steam Mill. The reputation that Mr. Mead, holds for
the doing of uniformly satisfactory and accurate work,
shows that the facilities under his control, are taken full
advantage of and improved to their utmost limit. At the
Union Steam Mill, every preparation is made for the doing
of wood turning, sawing, etc., of all descriptions. Mr.
Mead's business is a large and growing one, for builders and
others have discovered that he adheres closely to agree-
ments, and may be depended upon to finish a piece of
work at the time promised. To those familiar with the
principal causes of the annoying and expensive delays so
associated with building operations, this fact will explain
the popularity of the establishment under notice, and this
popularity has been greatly aided by the moderate prices
at which Mr. Mead fills the orders entrusted to him.
His work is always reliable, and his mill one of the best
known of the kind in this vicinity. Mr. Mead makes a
specialty of stair balusters, newel posts of all kinds,
bridge pins, carriage seat sticks, etc. He has recently
secured the service of a professional pattern maker from
Boston, and is prepared to execute any work in this line,
from plans or specifications, or for inventors' experimental
machinery, jobbing, cabinet work and saw filing. All
orders executed with promptness and despatch and at
reasonable prices.

Clapp & Co., Brass and Iron Founders, all kinds of Foundry Work, Railroad Castings, etc. Prompt attention given to orders by Mail or Express. Correspondence solicited. No. 8 Chandler Street, Concord, N. H.—There is probably no more thoroughly equipped brass and iron foundry in the State than that carried on by Messrs. Clapp & Co., at No. 8 Chandler street, and the work turned out is worthy of the facilities provided, for it has no superior in its special line, and, indeed, some of the concern's productions are conceded by practical men to be unrivalled for efficiency of design and excellence of workmanship. The firm is constituted of Messrs. S. F. Prescott, H. W. Ranlet, W. T. McLam and F. L. Badger, all of whom are old residents of Concord and are very generally known in social as well as in business circles. Employment is given to about thirty assistants, and the facilities are such that all orders can be filled at short notice. A general brass and iron founding business is done, all kinds of foundry work being furnished at moderate rates, and estimates will be cheerfully and promptly given on application. Patterns will be made to order, railroad castings of all kinds will be supplied with the least possible delay, and especial attention is given to locomotive cylinders and other dry sand work. Builders' materials are largely dealt in, including columns, crestings, chimney caps, sash weights, ash mouths and boiler doors with double flanges, girders, plates, sidewalk gratings, manhole coverings, coal holes and other standard builders' supplies. Clapp & Co.'s

Improved Chimney Caps are very popular among architects and builders, as they are ornamental and durable, increase the draft and afford perfect protection to the chimney. They are made in plain and ornamental styles and in a sufficient variety of sizes to suit all cases. Stable fittings of all kinds are kept in stock or made to order at short notice, among these goods being mangers, hay racks, watering troughs, drain spouts and gutters, hitch weights, hitch posts, etc. Machinists' supplies are also extensively handled, the lowest market rates being quoted on pulleys, hangers, gears, boxes, shafting, washers of all kinds, couplings, bushings, brackets, etc., etc. Other prominent productions are carriage supplies, polishing rings for granite,

clothes jigger heads, sled shoes and blacksmith's tuyere irons. Clapp & Co.'s New Combination Drinking Fountain is a leading specialty and the demand for it is very large and steadily increasing. These fountains are made in the best manner, the pipes are all brass and consequently cannot rust out, and a sufficient variety of styles are made to suit all circumstances and conditions. But little water is used and that is so admitted as to keep the contents of the bowl in a circular motion which absolutely prevents freezing. It

is so arranged that separate pipes furnish the supply for horse, dog and man. The firm also manufacture H. W. Clapp & Co.'s Patent Sewer Inlet Gratings, Traps, etc., and solicit correspondence concerning anything in their line, giving immediate and careful attention to all mail and express orders.

Mead, Mason & Co., Contractors, Builders and Manufacturers, Builders' Supplies, etc. Proprietors of the Union Steam Mills, Concord, N. H.—This firm have for very many years held a very prominent position among the large contractors and builders of New England. The business was first founded in 1847 by C. E. Mead and W. G. Mason and thus continued until 1857 when N. J. Mead became a partner but under the old firm name. In 1884 Mr. N. J. Mead retired from the firm, and E. C. Mead and W. M. Mason were admitted to partnership. The plant of the firm in this city is a three-story building 80×100 feet in dimensions and is supplied with all the modern improved machinery demanded for the business and run by a 100-horse power engine. The productions of the firm comprise a great variety, but the leading specialty has been church and public building furniture and furnishings, having seated more churches than any other firm in New England. They have executed very fine work in this city in the State House, the new government building and the Unitarian Church, also in the Congregational churches in Manchester, N. H., Newton, Mass., Arlington, Mass., Somerville, Mass., the M. E. Church, at Manchester, N. H., the Boylston street Church, Boston, and very many others that might be named but perhaps the most prominent and extensive piece of work this firm has performed may be found in the Central Park flat building, Valencia, on Fifty-ninth street and Seventh avenue, New York—a most elegant structure and having 2000 rooms under one roof. The business of the firm extends throughout New England, New York and adjoining States. Offices, Concord, N. H., Manchester, N. H., and 10 Canal street, Boston, Mass.

Frank H. George, successor to W. C. Elkins & Co., Stoves, Furnaces, Ranges and Kitchen Furnishing Goods. Job Work a Specialty. 142 North Main Street, Concord, N. H.—The undertaking carried on by Mr. Frank H. George is doubtless familiar to many of our readers, for it has been in operation for about sixteen years, and has been conducted by its present proprietor since 1879, he having succeeded W. C. Elkins & Co. Mr George is a native of Plymouth, N. H., and is thoroughly familiar with every detail of the business with which he is identified, as may easily be seen by the character of the service he offers the public, for there is not a dealer in stoves, furnaces, ranges, etc., in this vicinity, that is prepared to hold out more genuine inducements to customers. The premises occupied comprise one floor and basement, each 20×65 feet in size, which are well arranged and fitted up with the most improved facilities for the doing of job work, at short notice and in first class style, and those who appreciate the importance of having work of this kind done in an honest and painstaking manner, can do no better than to place their orders with Mr George. He employs three competent assistants and guarantees satisfaction to every customer. The store is located at No. 142 North Main street, and the leading makes of stoves, furnaces and ranges are carried in stock as well as a full line of kitchen furnishing goods, and offered in great variety at the lowest market rates. "Honest goods at honest prices" is a very attractive motto, and its spirit is certainly thoroughly carried into effect at this representative establishment. This is also headquarters for first class refrigerators.

Mrs. H. N. Newell, Fashionable Millinery, 75 State Block, Main Street, Concord, N. H.—There is no business in which that indispensable quality, "style," exerts a more powerful and controlling influence, than is that of the dealer in millinery goods, and it is owing to this fact that some people fail, while others succeed, under apparently precisely similar circumstances. A successful milliner must have good taste, and must be able to distinguish between that which is attractive; no two ladies look precisely the same in the same bonnet, or to put it more clearly, the same arrangement of trimming etc., is not equally becoming to two ladies, even though they be of similar complexion, and alike in general appearance. This fact is well known, but still it is too often disregarded, and insufficient allowance made for the influence of individuality. Mrs. Newell was formerly a resident of Meredith, N. H., and was engaged in the millinery business for twelve years previous to her coming here in 1878, when she established business in this city. That she has been successful her numerous customers can prove. In 1890 she made an addition to her business by engaging in the variety business, and she has now two connecting stores, the one occupied as a variety store is 18×76 feet in dimensions, while the other used for millinery purposes is 22×76 feet in size. Employment is given to from three to twelve assistants, according to the season. In the variety store she has a large collection of 5 and 10 cent goods. Also crockery, glassware and toys, etc. Mrs. Newell has gained a good position in the rank of honorable dealers in this city.

Gay Brothers, producers of Fine Concord Granite, Concord.—The consumption of Concord granite has become very large and gives every indication of continuing to rapidly increase for an indefinite period, for despite the the many kinds of granite on the market, there is none which combines all the valuable characteristics to be found in the Concord stone. Of course, all Concord granite is alike, some varieties of it excelling in one respect and some in another, but the product of certain quarries is remarkably high and uniform in quality, and none is more noteworthy in this connection than that of which Messrs. Gay Brothers are proprietors. This quarry yields a fine Concord granite that is sure to satisfy the most exacting taste; and those who wish to obtain stone admirably suited for the highest grade of ornamental or monumental work can do no better than to place their orders with Gay Brothers, for not only is the material they furnish unsurpassed, but their prices are low and all commissions are carefully and promptly executed. The firm is constituted of Messrs. A. L. and J. E. Gay, both of whom are natives of New Hampshire, and are generally and favorably known throughout Concord and vicinity.

P. W. Webster, Carpenter and Builder, Main Street, Concord, N. H.—Among the various carpenters and builders doing business in this city, mention should be made of Mr. P. W. Webster, who utilizes a two story shop on Main street, for he has a well deserved reputation for turning out good work and the business done is not only large but steadily increasing. The premises are fitted up with all necessary facilities and a sufficient force of assistants is employed to enable all orders to be filled at short notice, the number, of course, varying with the time of year, etc. Jobbing orders are assured special attention, and it is safe to assert that all who may favor Mr. Webster with their patronage in this department will have no reason to regret having done so. Contracting for buildings is an important portion of the business, and estimates will cheerfully be furnished for the erection or remodelling of dwelling houses or stores. Repairing of all kinds will be done in first-class style at short notice, and the work will prove durable as well as neatly finished, for good materials are used and no trouble is spared to ensure satisfactory results. Mr. Webster is prepared to figure very closely on contract work, and those contemplating building will best serve their own interests by giving him an opportunity to put in a bid

W. A. Thompson, dealer in Fine boots, shoes and rubbers. Lowest prices in the city. Bailey's Block, Concord.—Those who have had long experience in the shoe business say that no two persons wear their shoes out exactly alike, as each individual has his distinctive style of walk, as he has of speech, of penmanship or of general manner. Now granting this to be true, it is not surprising that a dealer finds it necessary to carry a large and varied stock, in order to satisfy all his patrons, for as each has his own style of walk, so each would naturally have peculiar ideas as to the qualities he wants combined in a shoe. It is by no means every dealer who appreciates this fact, but evidently Mr. W. A. Thompson is one of them, for his assortment of footwear is so extensive and so skillfully chosen that all tastes and all purses can be suited from it. This business was founded in 1880, under the name of Thompson & Co., and was located in Statesman Block, but in 1882, Mr. W. A. Thompson became sole proprietor and in 1885 he removed to his present location, Bailey's Block. The premises will measure 20½ × 65 feet, affording ample opportunity for the carrying of a large stock of ladies' and gentlemen's fine boots, shoes and rubbers. The magnitude and character of his patronage show that his methods are appreciated by the purchasing public. Mr. Thompson's prices are the lowest in the city, and the services of five courteous and competent assistants are required to attend to the large number of customers.

John A. White, manufacturer of Wood working Machinery, No. 31 South Main Street, Concord, N. H.—The business of which Mr. John A. White is proprietor was founded just about a quarter of a century ago, operations having been begun by Messrs. Kimball, Ford, Dunklee & Co., in 1865. The following year Mr. D. F. Dunklee assumed sole control, but before the year was out became a member of the firm of Dunklee & Tilton. This concern gave place to Messrs. Dunklee & Allen in 1869, and in 1876 Mr. F. N. Stevens became sole owner; he being succeeded by the present proprietor in 1877. Mr. White is a native of this city, and served in the army during the Rebellion. He is almost universally known in manufacturing and general business circles, and his enterprising methods have had the natural effect of materially developing the business since it passed under his control. He manufactures a great variety of wood working machinery and holds numerous valuable patents, many of his productions not being obtainable elsewhere. The premises utilized are located at No. 31 South Main street, and contain a very complete plant of improved machinery, enabling operations to be carried on to the best possible advantage. The main shop measures 40×150 feet, and there is a wing of the dimensions of 32×62 feet. Employment is given to from thirty to fifty assistants, and no trouble is spared to maintain the high reputation so long held for promptness and accuracy in the filling of orders. The high favor in which Mr. White's productions are held by practical wood workers is due in a great measure to their excellence of design, but the excellence of material and perfection of workmanship should by no means be left out of the reckoning, for they secure durability under the most trying conditions and reduce the liability to get out of order to a minimum.

Phenix Livery, Boarding and Hack Stable, Dodge & Bickford, Concord, N. H.—The Phenix Livery and Hack Stable has been carried on for many years, and has long ranked among the best managed and most popular establishments of the kind in this section of the State. Among the proprietors have been Messrs. James Rowell, William K. Norton, and George Foster, the latter gentleman being succeeded by Messrs. Dodge & Bickford, the present owners, in 1885. Mr. C. W. Dodge is a native of Claremont, N. H., and Mr. M. F. Bickford of East Canaan, N. H., both these gentlemen being too well known in this vicinity to require extended personal mention. Under their skillful and liberal management the Phenix Stable has become more popular than ever, and we have no hesitation in guaranteeing satisfaction to all who may make use of the facilities there provided. It is located in the rear of the Phenix House, and contains sixty comfortable stalls besides ample carriage room, etc. A livery, hacking, boarding, feed and sale business is done, employment being given to six competent assistants and all orders being assured immediate and careful attention. First-class teams will be furnished at very short notice and at uniformly moderate rates, and hacks will be supplied for weddings, funerals, parties, etc., any number desired being furnished, together with experienced and careful drivers. Messrs. Dodge & Bickford keep their turnouts in the best of condition and are thereby enabled to cater successfully to the most fastidious trade.

John McGuire, Granite Quarry, Concord.—The granite quarries of Concord and vicinity have been a very important source of wealth to that section, but present indications are that their importance is to steadily and very largely increase in the future, for granite is becoming more popular every year, particularly for monumental and ornamental purposes for which Concord granite is peculiarly adapted. Among the many quarries now successfully worked in this vicinity, that controlled by Mr. John McGuire should be given prominent and favorable mention, for the quality of the stone taken from it is strictly first-class, and the proprietor has facilities which put him in a position to fill the most extensive orders at short notice, while his policy is to execute the smallest commissions carefully and promptly. Employment is generally given to six or eight assistants, and this force can be largely added to at very short notice should occasion require. Mr. McGuire quotes the lowest market rates at all times, and those placing orders with him may rely upon being treated squarely in every respect.

Lee & Kenna, dealers in Groceries, Flour, Grain, Teas, Coffees, Spices, Tobacco, Fruit, etc., 5 South Main Street, Concord, N. H.—Those who have had extended dealings with this house do not need to be told of the advantages of placing orders here, but the many who are in search of a well equipped and thoroughly reliable grocery store, will thank us for calling their attention to that conducted by Messrs. Lee & Kenna, for it will be found to "fill the bill" in every particular, and both as regards the completeness of the stock, and the efficiency of the service, merits far more extended mention than our space enables us to give it. This business was established in 1877 by Lee & Kelleher, but in 1880, the present firm of Lee & Kenna was formed, and they have made their store a prime favorite in the vicinity in which it is located. The premises will measure 23 × 70 feet and contain a carefully chosen stock of groceries, flour, grain, teas, coffees, spices, tobacco, fruit, meat, etc. These goods are especially adapted to family use and guaranteed to prove as represented in every respect. These gentlemen are both natives of Concord, N. H., and have many friends in social as well as in business relations. They are careful buyers and are in a position to quote low market rates on all commodities handled, and to furnish goods satisfactory to the most fastidious. Sufficient help is employed to assure prompt service to all, and all orders will be accurately delivered at short notice.

Sullivan's Drug Store, 9 North Main Street, Concord, N. H.—One generally feels considerable hesitation in giving advice as to what physician shall be consulted, or at what pharmacy prescriptions shall be compounded, for the consequence of advising wrongly in either case are too grave to be lightly assumed. Still we feel perfectly sure that all who may patronize the establishment conducted by Mr. D. W. Sullivan, at No. 9 North Main street, will have no reason to regret having done so, for we know that the stock of drugs, medicines and chemicals there carried is full and complete and we also know that Mr. Sullivan may be depended upon to compound every prescription with which he is entrusted with care. He is a New Hampshire man by birth, and opened his present store in 1888. The premises occupied comprise a store 20×50 feet in dimensions, in addition to a large storeroom. The store is well arranged and fitted up for the purposes for which it is used. Mr. Sullivan endeavors to handle only pure and fresh drugs, etc., and secures that end as far as possible by procuring his supplies from the most reputable sources. He is very moderate in his charges, and employs three efficient assistants, who enable him to fill all orders without undue delay.

Boston One-Price Clothing Co., John G. McQuilken & Co., Proprietors. Dealers in Ready-Made Clothing, Hats and Caps, Gents' Furnishing Goods. "Blue Front," opposite the Clock, Concord, N. H.—In every community, whether it be large or small, there are certain houses which are recognized as the leaders in their particular line, and there is no branch of business but what this rule applies to, for as sure as a particular industry or branch of trade is represented at all, just so sure must some one concern lead, other houses following more or less successfully as the case may be. Of course in so important a trade center as Concord is there are numerous examples of this truth, and one of the most striking of them, is that afforded by the position held by the "Boston One-Price Clothing Company," John G. McQuilken & Co., proprietors. This store is known as the "Blue Front," opposite the clock. Business in this line has been conducted in this location for several years, and by three or four different firms, but in 1888 the above named company assumed control and have attained a good position as a leader in ready-made clothing, hats and caps, also as dealers in gents' furnishing goods. The premises occupied will measure 20×80 feet, and a heavy stock of imported and domestic goods is carried, which always includes the very latest novelties and is complete in every department. Employment is given to two assistants who are competent to give courteous and prompt attention to every caller, while the prices will be found reasonable for the fine quality of goods exhibited.

F. H. Upton, dealer in Provisions, Canned Goods, Fruits, etc., 41 Washington Street, Concord, N. H.—It is comparatively easy to get first-class groceries in Concord and vicinity but first-class meats are by no means so common, it being notorious indeed that many who pay for such products are in fact supplied with second rate articles. There are some dealers however, who appreciate the large demand for choice meats and are excellently well prepared to cater to it, and among these a leading position is held by Mr. F. H. Upton, who carries on a well-equipped meat market at No. 41 Washington street, and does a first-class retail business. Mr. Upton established the grocery and provision business in Concord in 1872. In 1889 he removed to his present location, and now deals in meats, canned goods, fruits, etc. The store occupied is 22×40 feet in dimensions and contains a heavy stock of the above named food supplies, while no trouble is spared to keep it so complete in every department that all tastes and purses can be suited. Efficient assistants are employed and much of the popularity of this establishment is due to the prompt and courteous attention assured to every caller. Mr. Upton is a native of Bow, N. H., and is well known throughout Concord, having held the office of councilman.

I. M. Savage & Son, dealers in Dry Goods, Groceries, Flour, Corn, Meal, Oats and Shorts, No. 6 South Main Street, Concord. N. H.—The business carried on by Messrs. I. M. Savage & Son is an old-established one having been founded by Mr. Franklin Evans in 1863, who was succeeded by Mr. I. M. Savage in 1883, the present firm of I. M. Savage & Son having been formed in 1888. Mr I. M. Savage is a native of Kingfield, Me., and his son, Mr. G. R. Savage, of Hillsboro, N. H., and both members of the firm are so extensively known hereabout as to render further personal mention quite unnecessary. The premises utilized are 20 × 70 feet in dimensions, and located at No. 6 South Main street, and contains a heavy and varied stock made up of dry goods in general together with a full assortment of groceries, corn, meal, oats and shorts. All these goods are offered at the lowest market rates, and as they are thoroughly dependable in character and as guaranteed in every instance to prove precisely as represented, it is not surprising that this store should be a great favorite among discriminating purchasers. The facilities enjoyed are so extensive that all orders can be filled at short notice. Despite the uniform superiority of the results attained, the charges are very reasonable, being as low as is consistent with the handling of a first-class stock of fresh and reliable goods.

W. H. Perry, manufacturer and dealer in Granite. Rattlesnake Mountain Crystal Granite for Rockfaced Monuments a specialty. Designs made to order. Concord, N. H.—The time has long since gone by when custom demanded that houses, churches, dress, and mortuary emblems should all be reduced to the same dull level of uniformity, and the spirit of the present age is to give reasonable expression to individuality and allow personal characteristics to express themselves in every legitimate way. A modern cemetery is relieved of that cold formalism which characterizes old burying grounds, by the tasteful variety of the monuments no less than by the work of the landscape gardener, and this variety is due in a great measure to the use of granite in the construction of mortuary emblems. What are technically known as rockfaced monuments are now very popular among people of refined taste and it is natural that such should be the case, for effects attained are not all conventional and are capable of almost endless variation. Of course the grain and quality of the stone used are of the first importance, and it is generally conceded by expert judges that the Rattlesnake Mountain crystal granite is most admirably adapted for such monuments, being in fact unsurpassed by any stone in the market. Mr. W. H. Perry is prepared to show some beautiful monuments made from this material, for he makes a specialty of handling and working it, and furnishes it rough or finished in any desired quantity. He is a native of England, and has been connected with his present enterprise for a number of years. Up to 1880 he was associated with others, but since that date he has been sole proprietor. Employment is given to from thirty-five to fifty assistants, and cemetery work will be done in a superior manner at a short notice and at moderate rates. Original designs will be made to order in thoroughly artistic style and estimates will cheerfully be furnished on application.

Morrison & Searles, dealers in Beef, Pork, Lard, Ham, Poultry, Sausage, etc., Vegetables of every kind in their season. No. 8 Pleasant Street. Concord, N. H.—The policy pursued by these gentlemen of handling none but dependable goods, and of quoting the very lowest prices that can be named on such articles has had the natural result of gaining great popularity for this establishment since Messrs. Morrison & Searles assumed control in 1886, for the public are quick to appreciate liberal and honorable methods, and may be depended upon to patronize any enterprise conducted in accordance with such principles. They employ two efficient assistants, and as they also give close personal attention to the various details of their business, are enabled to insure prompt and polite attention to every caller. The beef, pork, lard, ham, poultry, sausage, etc., offered at this house are selected from the most reliable resources, and are hard to equal for their freshness and superior qualities, and as they are careful buyers and have become familiar with the tastes of their regular customers they have no left-over stock to accumulate, which they are obliged to force upon those who patronize them. They also have all kinds of vegetables in their season which are kept in a fine and inviting condition. The premises occupied are located at No. 8 Pleasant street, and are 25 × 60 feet in dimensions. Every effort is made to make this store a favorite with the most economically disposed as well as with the most fastidious.

Munns & Paige, practical Steam and Gas Fitters; also dealers in Plain, Galvanized and Brass Pipe and Fittings of all descriptions; office in the Old Post-office, School Street, Concord, N. H.—The business carried on by Messrs. Munns & Paige was established in 1864, and has never been more worthy of rapid and steady development than since it passed under the control of the present firm, made up of Messrs. James Munns and E. F. Paige, the former a native of England and the latter of this State. The enterprise may be divided into two departments,—plumbing, and steam and gas fitting, etc. The concern carry a full stock of plumbers' supplies, including sheet lead and lead pipe, water closets and wash bowls, copper baths and sinks, brass works and plated faucets, etc., which they offer at the lowest market rates, and which with the aid of from eight to twelve assistants, enables them to fill all jobbing orders, etc., at very short notice. A full assortment of plain, galvanized and brass pipe and fittings of all descriptions, and other steam and gas-fitting supplies is also carried, together with a nice line of gas-fixtures comprising the latest fashionable novelties, as well as plain styles for business use. Messrs. Munns & Paige are agents for Gold's Low Pressure, Self regulating Steam Apparatus, which is absolutely safe in the most inexperienced or careless hands, is very economical in the use of fuel, and for these and other reasons is particularly adapted for the heating of dwellings, schools, hotels, etc. The firm are prepared to set this apparatus up at short notice, and to guarantee it to do all that is claimed if used as directed. They are also agents for the Imperial gas machine, which is thoroughly practical and will give permanent satisfaction.

Norman G. Carr, Watchmaker and Jeweler, and dealer in Watches, Clocks, Jewelry and Spectacles, 34 North Main Street, Concord, N. H.—Perhaps there are few among the business men or residents of this city, who realize that this is the oldest established house conducting business continually without change in the firm or interruption to business in the city. That such is the fact is claimed by the proprietor, Mr. Carr. Business in this line was founded here in 1852, by Mr. Chas. Pearson, who was succeeded in 1856 by Mr. Norman G. Carr, who has continued in the trade until the present time, and as the residents of Concord have a well deserved reputation for patronizing home establishments, the wisdom of this course is well indicated by the general high standing of the local retail business enterprises. There is little encouragement for a dealer to endeavor to offer unusual inducements, when he knows that all having important purchases to make will visit some adjoining city, but when the contrary is the case, the result is soon perceptible. Take the store conducted by Mr. Carr, for example, and the truth of the principles we have hinted at, will be made manifest. Mr. Carr carries as fine a stock of watches, jewelry, etc., as can be found in the city, and his prices cannot be discounted by any retailer of whom we have any knowledge. Mr. Carr is a practical watchmaker and jeweler, and his long experience in this business is a guarantee that his advice and judgment in purchasing anything in this line is exceeded by none.

George H. Moore, dealer in Boots, Shoes and Rubbers, 13 North Main Street, Concord, N. H.—It is well worth while to take some little pains in the selection of footwear, for not only is one's appearance dependent in a great measure on the character of the boots or shoes worn, but one's comfort and ease may be seriously interfered with by prolonged use of badly-shaped or ill fitting foot coverings. Right here is one of the principal reasons why selection should always be made from a large and varied stock, for it is hard to find two people whose feet are shaped precisely alike, and the only way to provide for the special requirements of all classes is to carry an extensive assortment of styles, sizes and grades, so that not only all tastes but all purses also can be suited. Such has been the policy pursued by Mr. George H. Moore since operations were begun by him in 1877, and it is therefore not at all surprising that a large retail business should have been built up, particularly as the prices quoted will compare favorably with the lowest named elsewhere on goods of equal merit. The proprietor, Mr. George H. Moore, is a native of Concord, and well known among the most enterprising business men. The premises used are located at No. 13 North Main street, and are of the dimensions of 18×70 feet, the extensive stock being displayed to excellent advantage. Mr. Clark carries a superior stock of the finest and best class of goods in all widths, sizes, and one-half sizes. Employment is given to two competent and courteous assistants, and callers are assured immediate and careful attention.

Crawford & Stockbridge, Book Binders, Paper Rulers, and Blank Book manufacturers, 18 North Main Street, Concord, N. H.—For forty years has the business now conducted by Messrs. Crawford & Stockbridge, been successfully carried on, so it is not surprising that it should rank with the best-known and most truly representative undertakings of the kind in the State. Operations were begun by Mr. F. S. Crawford, in 1850, and various changes have since occurred in the ownership, although Mr. Crawford has been identified with it from the first. He was succeeded by Crawford & Chick, they by Crawford & Danforth, they by F. S. Crawford, and he by the present firm in 1883. The senior partner is a native of New York city, and Mr. E. A. Stockbridge was born in the state of Maine. Four commodious rooms are occupied, at No. 18 North Main street, and every facility is at hand for the filling of orders for book binding, paper ruling and blank book manufacturing. Special attention given to numbering checks, drafts, coupon tickets, etc., all work done at short notice and in first-class style. Employment is given to eight efficient assistants, and no trouble is spared to maintain the enviable reputation long enjoyed for filling orders promptly at the time and exactly in the manner promised. Blank books of any size, kind or pattern will be furnished in quantities to suit, and the firm are prepared to quote bottom prices on all the goods they handle.

J. B. Merrill, Meat and Vegetables, 226 North Main Street, Concord, N. H.—It is said that the average American family demands the best grades of meats, and will not be satisfied with anything inferior, even at a much less price. Although this may be an exaggeration, still it is undeniable that many families find it very difficult to get satisfactory meat, even when they are prepared to pay the regular market rates for it. The trouble is, they do not look for it in the right place. Some dealers do not trade in first-quality meats at all, although they are not likely to say so when questioned about it. On the other hand there are establishments where a specialty is made of such meats. Prominent among these is the store kept by Mr. J. B. Merrill, at No. 226 North Main street, this being an old stand and having more than a local reputation for furnishing strictly high-grade goods at fair prices. All kinds of meats and fresh vegetables are largely dealt in, efforts being made to supply goods that will prove entirely

satisfactory to the most fastidious. Mr. Merrill gives his close personal attention to the business, and with his competent assistants, is prepared to fill orders promptly, assuring immediate service to every customer. This business was founded several years ago. It was in 1889 that Mr. Merrill succeeded Mr. W. A. Crowley. Mr. Merrill is a native of New Hampshire, he has been a representative and also a councilman. Formerly he was a woollen manufacturer in Barnstead, N. H., continuing that business for about twelve years. Was at one time colonel in the State militia, and has been deputy sheriff and served seven years as sheriff.

Thurston & Emmons, retailers in Dry Goods and Small Wares, Dress Goods and Garments a specialty, 64 North Main Street, Concord, N. H.—Among the leading dry goods houses in this section of the State, prominent mention must be made of Messrs. Thurston & Emmons, for although this firm is of comparatively recent origin, having been organized in 1889, the undertaking carried on was founded in 1865 and has for years ranked with the representative enterprises of the kind in this vicinity. The original proprietors were Messrs. F. B. Underhill & Co., who were succeeded by Messrs. Stearns, Winphier & Co., and they by Messrs Thurston & Downing, the latter change taking place in 1885. The present proprietors are both New Hampshire men by birth, Mr. C E Thurston being a native of Lyme, and Mr G. B. Emmons of Bristol. Mr. Emmons has served as alderman, and both he and Mr. Thurston are too well and favorably known in Concord and vicinity to render extended personal mention necessary. Mr. Emmons is actively engaged in other enterprises in the city, and while he keeps thoroughly conversant with the business of the firm, he is actively represented by his son, Mr. Harry G. Emmons who gives constant and personal attention to the business. He is a native of Concord and educated in Concord schools. The firm utilizes spacious premises, at No. 64 North Main street, comprising one floor and a basement, having an area of 5,000 square feet, together with a side room forty feet square. An extremely heavy stock of dry goods and small wares is carried, and as the firm makes a specialty of dress goods and garments they offer particular inducements in these lines, their store being in fact looked upon as the headquarters for them so far as Concord is concerned. Employment is given to ten competent and courteous assistants, and prompt and careful attention is the rule to all. Messrs Thurston & Emmons quote bottom prices, and every article sold is guaranteed to prove as represented in every respect.

Dooning & Fellows, Grocers, Corner Broadway and South Streets, Concord.—When Daniel Webster was asked, if there was any opening for a young man in the legal profession, he replied, "There is always room at the top," and this principle holds good in trade as well as in the professions. There are many grocery stores in Concord, but there are also a good many people, and as there is a constant demand for dependable groceries, prompt service and generally fair dealing, we feel confident of the permanent success of the enterprise of Messrs. Dooning & Fellows, which was commenced during the current year, for they deal in groceries of all kinds and spare no pains to satisfy every customer. Their progressive and reliable methods have already built up quite an extensive business, and at its present rate of increase it will soon double in magnitude, for those who place a trial order with this firm find it for their interest to call again when anything further in the grocery line is wanted. Their store is located at the corner of Broadway and South streets, and contains a carefully chosen stock of staple and fancy groceries, especially adapted to family use, "Full value for money received," is the motto of this establishment and an examination of the goods and prices will show that it is carried out to the letter.

Cummings Brothers, Monumental Works, Cummings' New Block, South Main Street, Concord, N. H. Branch Houses at Franklin and Pittsfield, N. H.—It is generally rather difficult for one to decide where to leave an order for monumental work, for the most of us are not very well posted on such a matter and hence do not know how to intelligently discriminate between good and bad work. Under these circumstances, it is evident that much depend- ·ence must be placed upon the commercial standing of the various houses engaged in this industry, and taking this for a basis we find that the firm of Cummings Brothers makes as good a showing as any of our marble workers. The business of which they are now the proprietors was founded by O. and G. A. Cummings in 1853 at Franklin, and in 1861 they established their business in Concord, and in 1864 Mr. G. A. Cummings assumed full control of affairs, and so conducted the business until 1868, when the present firm of Cummings Brothers was established. These gentlemen are both natives of Acworth, N. H., and have a most intimate acquaintance with their business in every detail. The firm as now constituted is made up of Messrs. George A. and Milou D. Cummings; they give ·close personal attention to all orders and spare no efforts to satisfy their customers even beyond their expectation if possible. They are both very well known and highly esteemed throughout Concord and vicinity, Mr. G. A. Cummings having been connected with the city govern- ment as mayor, alderman and councilman. Messrs. Cum- mings Brothers have branch houses at Franklin and Pitts- field, N. H., and give employment to about fifty competent workmen. The premises occupied in Concord are located in Cummings' New Block on South Main street, and com- prise one floor and a basement each 22 × 70 feet in dimen- sions. Cummings Brothers conduct one of the largest enterprises of the kind in the State, and order work is done at the shortest possible notice, and in a thoroughly com- petent and artistic manner, the firm putting their prices down to the lowest possible figure.

H. W. Brickett, dealer in Fine Groceries, Flour, Grain, ·etc., 158 North Main Street, Concord, N. H.—The advan- tage of dealing with a house that carries a large and varied stock, guarantees the quality of its goods, gives prompt and polite attention to customers, and sells at the lowest market rates are too evident to require explanation and when we say that the enterprise carried on by Mr. H. W. Brickett at No. 158 North Main street, is so managed as to combine all these good points, we need not persuade our Concord readers to give it their patronage, for their ·own self interest will dictate that they do so. Mr. Brickett succeeded the firm of C. C. Webster & Co. in 1881, and for the reasons given above, has built up a large and grow- ing retail trade. Mr. Brickett is a native of Hampstead, N. H., and is a gentleman well acquainted with the line of business he has chosen and gives his close personal atten- tion to every detail of the establishment. Employment is afforded to two efficient and courteous assistants, and although the extent of the trade carried on renders the serving of many customers necessary, still, every patron is assured prompt and polite attention. Fine groceries, flour and grain of all grades are extensively handled, and the prices quoted on these goods are such as will bear the severest examination.

A. C. Ferrin, Contractor for Mason Work and Builder. and dealer in Lime, Brick, Cement, Calcined Plaster. Sand and Hair. Office, 12 School Street, Concord.—One of Concord's best known business men is Mr. A. C. Ferrin, who was born in Hebron, N. H., served in the navy dur- ing the Rebellion, and began operations in this city nearly a score of years ago, as a member of the firm of Ordway & Ferrin, becoming sole proprietor in 1888. He is a con- tractor and builder, and dealer in lime, brick, cement, cal- ·cined plaster, sand and hair, being prepared to furnish those commodities in any desired quantity at short notice and at the lowest market rates. Employment is given to

from forty to fifty assistants, and the most extensive con- tracts for mason work can be filled very promptly and in an entirely satisfactory manner. Mr. Ferrin is prepared to figure very closely on all kinds of masonry, brick work, plastering, stucco work, etc., and will cheerfully furnish estimates on application, or quote exact figures on receipt of plans and specifications. Whitewashing, whitening and coloring will be done in workmanlike style at low rates, and cellars will be cemented at short notice, the best of material being used, thereby assuring durability and the entire exclusion of all dampness from below. His office is located at No. 12 School street, all communications to that address being assured immediate and painstaking atten- tion. Mr. Ferrin built the Odd Fellows Block and the new High School building in this city.

G. W. Wadleigh, wholesale and retail dealer in Milli- nery and Hair Goods. Also manufacturer of Human Hair Switches, Wigs, etc., Wigs, Ventilated Seams, Puffs, Curls, Coquettes, Perfections, Water Waves, Frizzes, Weft, etc. Workmanship not excelled. Ordered Work of all kinds a Specialty. 140 North Main Street, opposite Opera House, Concord, N. H.—It would be difficult, and probably an impossible task to give an adequate idea of the stock car- ried at the establishment of G. W. Wadleigh, No. 140 North Main street, by any verbal description, and so, even did our space permit, we would not attempt to do so. Suffice it to say that those who wish to see the latest nov- elties in millinery and hair goods or who wish to purchase anything in that line for cash at the lowest market rates, or who desire to be assured of prompt attention and hon- orable dealing, can do no better than to visit the establish- ment mentioned. They will not be disappointed at the result, for this house has long held the reputation of carry- ing on one of the most skillfully and liberally managed establishments in Concord. The premises occupied meas- ure 20×65 feet. The millinery business was established by Mr. Wadleigh in 1850, and in 1880 the manufacture of hair goods was added, and the business has steadily increased until it has reached its present large proportions. The fine stock on hand is displayed to excellent advantage and comprises millinery goods, also human hair switches, wigs, puffs, curls, etc., etc. Employment is given to ten efficient assistants, and courteous attention is assured to all, and every article dealt in is strictly guaranteed to prove as represented in every respect. Mr. Wadleigh is a native of Sutton, N. H., and it is by long continued appli- cation to his business that he has gained his present high reputation, having been in business here for forty years.

E. McQuesten & Co, General Store, 47 South Street, Concord.—The business conducted by Messrs. E. McQues- ten & Co., at No. 47 South street, was founded many years ago and has long been looked upon as one of the most truly representative enterprises of the kind in Con- cord. Since passing under the control of the present firm, in 1888, it has become more popular than ever, for not only has the old reputation for square dealing been fully maintained but increased pains have been taken to keep the stock complete in every department, to handle none but reliable goods and to quote prices as low as the lowest, while it is generally conceded that at no store of the kind in this city is the service more prompt, courteous and gen- erally efficient. The premises comprise two floors and a basement, each of which is 30 × 75 feet in dimensions, and no space is wasted either for a heavy stock is carried, comprising full lines of staple and fancy groceries, teas, coffees and spices, canned goods, meats, fish, and all kinds of seasonable fruits and vegetables, together with a care- fully chosen assortment of dry and fancy goods. Mr. McQuesten is a native of Northfield, N. H., and is thor- oughly familiar with the handling of general merchandise. He gives close personal attention to the many details of the business and takes especial care to see that orders are promptly and accurately delivered. The goods are sold strictly on their merits, every article being fully guaran- teed to prove precisely as represented.

C. E. STANIELS, Dist. Supt.,

CONNECTICUT ∴ MUTUAL ∴ LIFE.

| ASSETS, | $37,874,971 71 |
| SURPLUS, | 5,530,000.00 |

MOTTO: *Nec mora, nec requies*

STATE CAPITAL BANK BUILDING,

CONCORD, N. H.

Concord Beef Co., Receivers and Commission Merchants in Swift's Chicago Dressed Beef, Mutton, Lamb and Veal, Railroad Square, near Stratton, Merrill & Co., Concord, N. H.—It is safe to say that a man who never heard of "Swift's Chicago Dressed Beef," must have been "brought up in the woods," and pretty far back in the woods at that, for although this product has been on the the eastern market for not more that twelve or fifteen years, it is now known practically everywhere and is accepted as the standard wherever known. The wholesale distributing house for this section of the State, is carried on by the Concord Beef Company, which was organized in 1885, and of which M. W. Nims, has been manager from the beginning. Mr. Nims is a New Hampshire man by birth, and is too widely known hereabouts to require extended personal mention. He is very popular among the customers of the company and there is every reason why he should be, for he keeps the service at a high standard of efficiency and fills both large and small orders without delay. The company are not only receivers of and commission merchants in Swift's Chicago Dressed Beef, but also handle mutton, lamb and veal very extensively; utilizing a refrigerator which will hold thirty tons of ice and two carloads of meat. The premises occupied are located in Railroad square, near Stratton, Merrill & Co., and are spacious and conveniently arranged. Pork, sausages, tripe, hams, etc., are constantly in stock, and the prompt and accurate filling of orders is assured by the employment of three competent assistants.

Oliver Ballou, dealer in Portrait and Picture Frames, Swiss Carvings, Artists' Materials, etc., No. 92 North Main Street, Concord, N. H.—In a volume such as this, which treats of the manifold interests of Concord, it is evident that those branches of trade and manufacture which are dependent on the work of the artist, must necessarily occupy a prominent place. Of these not the least important is the dealing in artists' materials, and to obtain those of the best quality is an important point for the artist to consider, to the end that his work shall be properly executed and finished. Mr. Oliver Ballou, who is engaged in the above named business, was associated with Mr. Robinson in 1884, but in 1888, he became sole proprietor of these premises, which measure about 1200 feet, besides a basement which he utilizes. He deals largely in portrait and picture frames, Swiss carvings, artists' materials, etc., and this house has become known to the trade as a prominent, substantial and trustworthy establishment for the sale of fine art goods. Mr. Ballou is a native of Alexandria, N. H., and we may say that he is in a position to offer to the trade as fine a quality of the goods dealt in, as can be found in this vicinity, and in all departments of his business he has inducements to offer not elsewhere to be duplicated. The "Fine Art Store," has become a favorite resort for all lovers of fine workmanship, and goods are cheerfully shown and all callers are cordially and politely attended to.

N. C. Nelson, Watchmaker, Engraver, and dealer in fine Watches, Clocks, etc., repairing fine watches a specialty, No. 5 School Street, Concord, N. H.—It would be foolish to deny that modern methods of watchmaking have been beneficial to the general public, but it would be equally foolish to deny that one of their effects has been to diminish the number of really competent watch repairers. Under former conditions, every practical watchmaker was of necessity competent to do repairing; under present conditions a man may work at watchmaking—that is, at making one part of a watch—for ten years, and then be no more able to do repairing than when he first begun. Yet everybody carries a watch, and there is a great and increasing demand for thoroughly expert repairers. We feel that we are doing our readers a genuine service in calling to their attention the nature of the service rendered by Mr. N. C. Nelson, doing business at No. 5 School street, for he has carried on the trade of watchmaking, repairing and engraving ever since 1865 and there is no man in New Hampshire better qualified to succeed with the most difficult and delicate jobs. For a long time Mr. Nelson confined himself to doing repairing and engraving, etc., for the trade, but for the past eight years he has filled orders for the general public, and also handled watches, clocks and jewelry at retail. He was born in Exeter, N. H., and is very widely known throughout Concord and vicinity. Employment is given to from two to three assistants, and all orders are assured prompt and careful attention; moderate charges being made in every instance and watches, etc., being furnished at the lowest market rates.

Andrew Bunker, manufacturer of Sash, Doors and Blinds, at Union Steam Mill, Concord, N. H.—The manufacture of doors, sash and blinds has attained immense proportions of late years and is still steadily increasing, some of the establishments engaged in it turning out goods enough in a day to furnish a good-sized village. The factory carried on by Mr. Andrew Bunker does not cover acres of space and its productions are not numbered by the hundred thousand, but so far as quality is concerned no factory in the country can make a better showing. The proprietor is a native of Barnstead, N. H., and certainly ought to be able to produce a superior article, if experience goes for anything, for he has been engaged in his present line of business ever since 1855, beginning operations as a member of the firm of Rexford & Bunker and having had sole control for nearly thirty years. His factory is at the Union Steam Mill, and is equipped with the most improved machinery, special attention being given to order work and all commissions being executed in a superior manner at short notice and at moderate rates. The premises measure 30 × 100 feet, exclusive of the storeroom, lumber-room and dry-house. Mr. Bunker uses well-seasoned stock, employs experienced assistants, and spares no pains to fully maintain the enviable reputation his products have long held among practical men throughout this section.

P. H. Coleman, Carriage and sign painter, Concord, N. H.—Not only the appearance but the durability of a vehicle is dependent upon the manner in which it is painted, and those who think to save money by letting carriages or signs go uncared for in this respect, make a great mistake. Carriage and sign painting, is a business by itself, and in order to be sure of attaining the best results, it is necessary to place orders with one who makes a specialty of such work and has both the facilities and the experience to enable him to guarantee satisfaction to the most critical. Such a man is Mr. P. H. Coleman, doing business in Concord, N. H., and we take pleasure in recommending him to our readers, for those who have had dealings with him speak in the highest terms of his skill and reliability. Mr. Coleman was connected in this enterprise with Mr. Bickford in 1876, but he became sole proprietor in 1877, and his business as carriage and sign painter has steadily increased; the premises which he now occupies, comprise two floors each 30×70 feet in dimensions beside an elevator and storeroom. He employs two efficient assistants, thus being in a position to fill all orders at short notice. Carriage painting, sign painting and lettering, will be done in a thoroughly workmanlike manner, carefully selected materials being used, and the durability as well as the beauty of the work being given due consideration. Repainting and varnishing done with neatness and dispatch, and at reasonable rates Mr. Coleman has gained the highest respect of all who are acquainted with him, and is a member of the common council.

Rogers & Mandigo, dealers in Stoves, Furnaces, Tin and Wooden Ware, etc., 9 Warren Street, Concord, N. H.—The business conducted by Messrs. Rogers & Mandigo was founded in 1886, by Mr. Geo. D. Richardson, who was succeeded by Messrs. Richardson & Bean, this firm giving place to Mr. A. W. Bean, and he to the present proprietors in 1889. The original premises were located on Main street, but since 1887 the present commodious quarters at No. 9 Warren street, have been utilized. They comprise one floor and a basement of the dimensions of 25×50 feet, and contain a large and complete stock of stoves, furnaces, tin and wooden ware, kitchen furnishings, etc., including the latest novelties as well as a full line of those staple goods that are always in demand. Some radical improvements have been made in cooking and heating stoves of late years, not only adding to their efficiency but reducing the consumption of fuel, and Messrs. Rogers & Mandigo are prepared to furnish the most convenient and economical styles at the very lowest market rates, so it is well worth while to give them a call when anything in this line is wanted. Jobbing orders are given prompt and careful attention, and tin roofing will be done in a neat and durable manner at moderate rates. Mr. A. E. Rogers is a native of Massachusetts, while Mr. D. L. Mandigo, was born in New York State, and both are thoroughly familiar with the practical details of their business and give personal attention to the filling of every order.

P. A. Clifford, Sanitary Plumber, Gas Fitter, and dealer in Plumbers' supplies, Water Closets, Bath Tubs, Bowls, Lead and Iron Pipe, etc., fine Plumbing a specialty, 14 School Street, Concord, N. H.—Everybody knows that "an ounce of prevention is worth a pound of cure," but everybody does not take advantage of this knowledge, and the result is that much serious sickness occurs that is entirely unnecessary, as it is plainly the consequence of carelessness. Some of the most common and deadly diseases are caused by defective plumbing, for sewer gas is as much a poison as arsenic, and the only way to keep it out of a house is to have the drainage system scientifically arranged and thoroughly constructed. In this connection we take pleasure in calling attention to the facilities possessed by Mr. P. A. Clifford, for the doing of sanitary plumbing, as he makes a specialty of such work and is thoroughly competent and reliable. His place of business is at No. 14 School street, and here may be found a complete line of plumbers' supplies, water closets, bath tubs, bowls, lead and iron pipe and fittings, etc., these articles being of the most improved type, and being offered at the lowest market rates. Mr. Clifford employs from six to twelve assistants, and is in a position to give immediate and careful attention to every order. Gas fitting will be done in a superior manner at short notice, but a specialty is made of fine plumbing, and no house in the State does better work in this line or quotes more moderate prices.

James H. Rowell & Co., Concrete Paving, etc., Residence, School Street, Concord, N. H.—The perfect pavement has yet to be discovered, but in many respects a well-made concrete pavement leaves but little to be desired. Of course it is not so durable as stone, when exposed to all kinds of traffic, but it is well to bear in mind that wear and tear are inseparable from friction, and that as a matter of fact the question is whether the most of the wear shall come on the road or on the vehicles, horses, goods and drivers. In Washington and in some other cities, asphalt pavement, or other form of concreting, is extensively used and gives the best of satisfaction, and although the severe frosts in the more northern States necessitate especial care in the laying of such pavement, it can be used to excellent advantage if put down as it should be, and as Messrs. James H. Rowell & Co. are prepared to do, and have done for eighteen years past. The business carried on by this concern has been practically managed by the present proprietors since 1873. Mr. Rowell is a native of Concord, and has served the city for eight years as road commissioner and superintendent of streets, and in the discharge of the duties of those positions has made a study of roads and road making with so long and varied a practical experience as to be thoroughly familiar with the subject in every detail. He is in a position to fill orders in a most satisfactory manner, and at the lowest possible cost. Concrete walks for private grounds, public parks, sidewalks, etc., will be put down in a neat and durable manner at moderate rates, and estimates on any work of this kind will be cheerfully furnished on application.

J. R. Hosking, dealer in Concord and other Granite Monuments, Headstones and Tablets, Concord, N. H.—The comparatively high cost of marble, granite and other ornamental stones, as well as the difficulty of working such materials combine to make monuments, headstones, etc., quite expensive even under the most favorable circumstances, and when an order is placed with a dealer who charges extra for his "name," and quotes a high scale of prices throughout, the result is enough to frighten a man of ordinary income. Now we do not want to convey the idea that Mr. J. R. Hosking, is prepared to give "something for nothing," for that would be absurd, but we would like to impress upon our readers the fact, that he is satisfied with a fair profit and is in a position to save money for those who wish anything in his line of business. Mr. Hosking, is a native of England and has been identified with his business here in Concord since 1880. He deals in Concord and other granite, and is prepared to furnish monuments, headstones, tablets, etc., at short notice and at prices that are exceptionally low when the quality of the work is considered. He makes a specialty of all drapery carved work, figures and statuary, the workmanship being of high order. The premises occupied are located on Peacock street, near the ice house. Employment is given to ten skilled workmen, thus enabling all commissions to be promptly and carefully executed. Communications addressed to Mr. J. R. Hosking, will be given immediate attention, while all transactions entered into, are sure to be as intelligently carried out, as the work is artistic. Some very fine specimens of his work can usually be seen at his place of business.

E. A. Moulton, House Painter, Paper Hanging, Concord.—If Mr. E. A. Moulton is not thoroughly acquainted with his business in every detail it is certainly not from lack of experience, for he has carried on his present enterprise since 1856, when he succeeded his father, Mr. James Moulton, Jr., who had founded it a score of years before, so that the undertaking has been carried on by the same family ever since 1836. Judging from the reputation and the character and extent of the patronage enjoyed by the present proprietor, it is safe to assume that he is one of the most skillful and reliable house painters in the State, and that he makes it an invariable rule to employ experienced assistants only. Mr. Moulton utilizes a two-story shop and has every facility at hand to enable him to fill orders at short notice and in a thoroughly workmanlike manner. He uses carefully selected stock and his work is therefore durable as well as ornamental, while his charges are reasonable in every instance. Jobbing is promptly and skillfully attended to and as Mr. Moulton is prepared to figure closely on contracts for painting new houses, factories, etc., builders would do well to give him a chance to put in a bid. Paper hanging in all its branches is also done in first-class style and orders by mail will receive immediate and painstaking attention.

Michael Casey, Granite dealer and manufacturer of Monuments, in Concord, Sunapee, Souhegan and Barre Granites, also Statuary, Urns, Tablets. Address Box 344, Concord, N. H.—Most people find it very difficult to make choice of a monument or headstone when occasion requires the purchase of anything in this line, for of course few have much experience in the selection of such articles, and it is hard to choose things with which one is not familiar. Therefore we feel that we are doing our readers a service in calling attention to the facilities offered by Mr. Michael Casey, for this gentleman has had an extended experience in connection with dealing in granite and the manufacture of monuments, statuary, urns, tablets and cemetery work of all kinds. Mr. Casey also deals in Concord, Sunapee, Souhegan and Barre granites, rough stock being furnished on application. Mr. Casey founded his present business in 1884, under the firm style of Kelliher & Casey. In 1888 he assumed the entire control, and has gained the reputation of filling orders at short notice. Correspondence is solicited and estimates given promptly at the lowest rates. Ten competent workmen are constantly employed and an extensive wholesale and retail trade is transacted. Orders for granite or any kind of cemetery work addressed to P. O. Box 344, will receive immediate and intelligent attention, and all agreement entered into will be honorably kept, while all branches of the work will be performed in a strictly first-class manner.

Darius Philbrick, Livery, Sale and Boarding Stable, Boarding and Transient a Specialty. The old American House Stable, Formerly "Gass's." Rear of White's Opera House, Concord —Mr. Philbrick has been engaged in this business since 1874 but it was in 1887 when he became proprietor of the stable located at the rear of White's Opera House, since that time he has gained a leading position among such enterprises in this section. Those conversant with Mr. Philbrick's methods, will agree with us that this is only what was naturally to be expected, for the majority of the public are sure to appreciate liberal and intelligent service, and it would be difficult to find more thoroughly satisfactory accommodations than those furnished at this well-managed establishment. The premises are kept in the best condition and every facility is at hand for the proper care of horses, as special attention is given transient and boarding horses, having thirty-seven stalls, and every accommodation for feeding with good care and kind treatment. Several teams are at hand for livery purposes, and orders can be filled at short notice. As Mr. Philbrick gives his personal attention to his business those leaving their orders here may be assured of prompt and satisfactory attention being given them in every respect. He is a native of Epsom, N. H., and by his honorable dealings has won the respect of all.

John A. Fraser, Monuments, Tablets, etc.; Residence 31 Franklin Street, Concord.—In some lines of work imperfection of material, deficiencies of workmanship, or inappropriateness of design may be pardonable under some circumstances and perhaps may not materially injure the effect desired, but this is never the case with monumental or cemetery work of any kind, and hence it is better to have no tablet, headstone or monument at all than to have one defective in design, material or construction. But happily the residents of Concord and vicinity are not reduced to this alternative, for orders for cemetery work may be placed with some of the various manufacturers in this city in the full assurance that they will be filled in a manner to which no reasonable exceptions can be taken. Mr. John A. Fraser holds a leading position among such manufacturers, and both as regards quality of work turned out and prices quoted on the same he has no reason to fear comparison with anyone in the State in a similar line of business. He employs from four to nine assistants, and can fill orders at very short notice,—sparing no pains to deliver work promptly at the time promised. Mr. Fraser resides at No. 31 Franklin street, and all communications to that address are assured immediate and careful attention.

Daniel Parker, Steam Carpet Beating Works. Carpets thoroughly cleaned without injury. Special attention given to Renovating Feathers, Hair Mattresses, etc. Orders left at 63 South Street, or at Ayers' Carpet Store. Works at Union Steam Mill, Concord, N. H.—Of course there is no law (except the law of common sense) to make people take advantage of improved methods, but when the improvement is so decided and so easy to see as is the case when carpet beating by machinery is compared with that done by hand, it seems very strange that everybody should not appreciate it and act accordingly. The residents of Concord and vicinity are given an excellent opportunity to avail themselves of the advantages of steam carpet beating, for since Mr. Daniel Parker began the renovating business in 1882, he has turned out work equal to the best, while his prices have been within the means of all. Very careful handling is assured all goods entrusted to Mr. Parker's Steam Beating Works, who, by no means confines himself to beating carpets, but also successfully undertakes feather and hair mattress renovating, etc. Carpets are thoroughly cleaned without injury, and orders left at No. 63 South street or at Ayers' carpet store, will receive prompt attention. Mr. Parker is a native of Canada, and has every facility in the way of improved machinery, for the proper conduct of his several departments of business. A sufficient force of workmen is employed, and large or small orders are assured immediate and intelligent attention.

John H. Fagan, Dining and Lunch Room, 121 North Main Street, Concord, N. H. - Whether we "eat to live," or "live to eat." the fact still remains that on the quality and amount of the food consumed our health and enjoyment are largely dependent, therefore it is of the first importance to know where appetizing and nutritious meals may be obtained at prices within the means of all. As good a place as we know of is the establishment conducted by Mr. John H. Fagan at No. 121 North Main street, for these dining rooms are most liberally and intelligently managed, the bill of fare being skillfully made up, the food being excellently cooked, and the prices remarkably low considering the accommodations offered. This business was started about ten years ago, and has been carried on by its present able proprietor since 1889. Mr. Fagan is a native of Concord and the growing popularity of his establishment is chiefly due to the careful personal attention he gives to the endless details of its management. The premises utilized are neat and attractive in appearance and have a seating capacity for forty guests. Competent assistants are employed and all patrons may depend upon receiving immediate and courteous attention, and the quality of the food furnished is sure to satisfy the most fastidious.

Charles L. Worthen, Contractor and Builder. Cabinet Work, Furniture Repairing and Job Work of all kinds. All Orders will receive Prompt Attention. 28 School Street, Concord, N. H.—Most every man has a desire to have a house of his own that will not be precisely the same as a dozen others, or, in other words, that has some individuality. When the supply of money is unlimited, such a house is very easily obtained, but as the majority have to calculate closely when about to build, considerable difficulty is met with. We would recommend all who think of building in this vicinity to consult with Mr. Charles L. Worthen, who is a contractor and builder. He makes a specialty of building private residences, and is prepared to construct them in a thoroughly satisfactory manner, and furnish materials which are properly seasoned, that there shall be no shrinkage in doors or floors. He is prepared to make contracts for large or small jobs in building. He also gives particular care to cabinet work, furniture repairing and job work of all kinds. All orders will receive prompt attention. His terms are cash, and all who have dealings with him may feel satisfied that honest work will be performed.

A. C. Sanborn, dealer in Staple and Fancy Groceries. Also wholesale agent for Oriental Powder Mills, and Red Beach Bone Phosphate. 160 and 164 North Main Street, Concord, N. H.—The grocery establishment now conducted by Mr. A. C. Sanborn, was originally founded by Mr. S. Butterfield, the present proprietor assuming control in 1882. In 1888 Mr. Sanborn bought out the firm of Pitman & Co. and added meats to his line of trade. He spares no pains to accommodate customers, and makes a practice of selling reliable goods at fair prices. Mr. Sanborn is a native of Gilmanton, N. H., and served in the army during our late Civil War. He is not only thoroughly acquainted with his business in every department, but also gives it his close personal supervision. The premises utilized are located at Nos. 160 and 164 North Main street, the grocery department being 25×80 feet in dimensions and the provision 18×60 feet, with a spacious basement under all. The stock of staple and fancy groceries, meats, butter, cheese, flour and canned fruit of all kinds, also grass seed, plaster and country produce carried is very large. It is carefully selected to meet the demands of a first-class family trade, and the articles composing it are in every case warranted to prove just as represented. The tea, coffee and spices handled by Mr. Sanborn will be found of uniformly superior quality, and we would especially call the attention of the more fastidious of our readers to the finer grades, as we believe these to be unsurpassed in this city at any price. Entire satisfaction is guaranteed, employment being given to eight well-informed assistants, and all orders are promptly attended to. Mr. Sanborn is also wholesale agent for the Oriental Powder Mills, and Red Beach Bone Phosphate, and also has charge of renting tenements, having over eighty now in charge.

Underhill & Kittredge, Druggists and Apothecaries. Prescriptions carefully dispensed. Corner of Main and School Streets, Concord, N. H.—Highly useful as the services rendered by the druggists are, it would be a boon to the community if all such enterprises could be conducted by thoroughly experienced men, but as such a condition of things, however desirable, is hard to find, the only way to do is to content ourselves as best we may, with the few instances in existence. A distinguished example of an establishment of this kind is that exhibited in the case of Underhill & Kittredge, whose store is located on the corner of Main and School streets This business was founded in 1863, by the firm of Fitch & Underhill, who were succeeded in 1865, by the present firm of Underhill & Kittredge, they having conducted the enterprise for twenty five years. They do both a wholesale and retail trade. The premises consist of one floor 35 × 70 feet in dimensions, and a basement, which are fully stocked with an unusually fine assortment of drugs, chemicals, medicines, and all druggists' sundries, and every facility is at hand to give customers prompt and accurate service. The prescription department is given unusual prominence and it need not be suggested that a thoroughly educated man in active practice is much less apt to make mistakes or to follow instructions blindly, than one who has no special fitness for such work. Mr. Underhill is a well-known alderman, and has been councilman. He is also commissioner of pharmacy and is president of the New Hampshire pharmaceutical association. Mr. Kittredge served in the army during the late Rebellion for three years and he has also been a member of legislature. Every article dealt in is warranted genuine and of the best quality.

Charles Barker, manufacturer and dealer in Hard and Soft Soap. Bridge Street, Concord, N. H. This business was founded in 1875, by Barker & Wise. In 1877 the name of the firm was changed to Barker & Farrar, who were succeeded in 1879 by Chas. Barker & Co. In 1884 Mr. Charles Barker, the present proprietor, who is a native of Waterford, Me., assumed full control of the establishment. He is a manufacturer, and both wholesale and retail dealer in hard and soft soap. The premises occupied comprise a shop that consists of two floors, 20 × 30 feet in dimensions, with an addition of one floor which measures 30 × 40 feet. Practical experience has proved the necessity of using only superior soap, either for the toilet or household purposes, as it is obvious that noxious articles in its manufacture must be both unhealthful and inefficient. We take pleasure in calling attention to the merits of the various soaps produced by Mr. Barker. His long established reputation for making good soap is familiar to all in this vicinity, and, as he has every facility at hand for its production, we feel convinced that the soap which be offers to day cannot be excelled. The following are some of the names given to a few of the varieties of his hard soap: "American Laundry," "Boss Soap," "Winchester Soap," "No. 1 Extra," "Cream Toilet," suitable for toilet or shaving use. He has also a fine article in soft soap, for sale, which is one of the best made. He is prepared to receive orders for any quantity of soap, which will be filled and delivered at short notice.

A. G. McAlpine & Co., manufacturers of and dealers in Marble and Granite Monuments, Headstones, Borders for Cemetery Lots, etc. Office and Yard, Penacook Street, near State, Concord, N. H.—To the cultivated eye monumental work is either good or bad, for if such work is not artistic in design and first class in workmanship it is simply bad, there being no room for such a thing as an intermediate grade in this connection. Of course some specimens of poor work are worse than others, but the main point is, is a certain monument or tablet first-class? for if not it cannot help being unsatisfactory. We take especial pleasure in calling attention to the enterprise conducted by Messrs. A. G. McAlpine & Co., from the fact that this firm are in a position to prove that it is not necessary to pay fancy prices in order to get first-class monumental work. Of course they are in the business to make money, but ideas as to money making differ, and evidently they believe in a moderate margin of profit on many orders rather than an exorbitant profit on a few. At all events, they turn out work that cannot be excelled for beauty of design and fineness of finish, and they quote uniformly reasonable rates. The business was founded by Messrs. Blanchard & McAlpine in 1875, and in 1877 passed into the hands of Mr. A. G. McAlpine, who in 1878 became associated with Mr. O. F. Swain under the present firm-name. Both partners are natives of New Hampshire, Mr. McAlpine having been born in Hopkinton and Mr. Swain in Hebron. They give close personal attention to the business and employ twelve assistants, all orders being filled at short notice. The office and yard are located on Penacook street, near State, and contain all necessary facilities for the production of marble and granite monuments, headstones, borders for cemetery lots and cemetery work of all kinds. A large assortment of designs is at hand to select from and estimates will cheerfully be furnished on application.

W. M. Colby, Florist, 25 South Street, Concord.—It is difficult to believe that the age of miracles is past when we see some of the wonderful things accomplished nowadays, for a few years ago nothing would have been deemed more miraculous than that conversation could be carried on between people many miles apart, or that lightning could be so effectually harnessed as to be used for illuminating purposes and motive power,—the same current of electricity lighting a car and driving it through the streets at the rate of twenty miles an hour. The raising of the most delicate plants and flowers in mid-winter in our bleak New England climate is another everyday miracle, and is none the less wonderful because we have become so used to it as not to give it any special thought. An elaborate, expensive and well managed plant is necessary to the attainment of the best results in the florist business, and the high reputation Mr. W. M. Colby has gained in this field of industry since beginning operations here in 1878, is in no small degree due to the enterprise he has shown in providing the most improved facilities and maintaining them at the very highest standard of efficiency. The premises utilized by him are located at No. 25 South street, and are both commodious and well arranged. The greenhouses are heated by hot water, and nothing is wanting to allow operations to be carried on to the best advantage. Plants, shrubs, cut flowers, etc., are extensively dealt in, both at wholesale and retail, and a specialty is made of floral designs, Mr. Colby showing great originality and excellent taste in their arrangement. Floral emblems and decorations suited to all occasions may be obtained here at very short notice, and the prices quoted will compare favorably with those named by any dealer in articles of equal merit. Mr. Colby is a native of Bow, N. H., and has a large circle of friends in Concord and vicinity.

Geo. Abbott, House Painter, rear 70 North Main Street, Concord, N. H.—It is a good policy to keep a house well painted, even aside from the question of appearances, for the severe climate of this section will soon rot or otherwise injure woodwork not protected by several good coats of paint, and the damage when once done is practically impossible to repair. A good job of painting will wear for several years, even in the most exposed situations, and in this as in many other things, "the best is the cheapest," for cheap painting is a delusion and a fraud. In order to secure first-class results a first class painter must be patronized, and no one in this vicinity is more deserving of being ranked as first class, than is Mr. Geo. Abbott, doing business at the rear of No. 70 North Main street. He only employs thoroughly skillful workmen, and is well prepared to fill orders for all kinds of house painting, in a prompt and thoroughly competent manner, Mr. Abbott is very moderate in his prices, his rates being as low as is consistent with the use of carefully chosen stock and the employment of skilled labor. House painting in all its branches is most thoroughly understood and artistically executed, and no one in Concord is better prepared to do a thoroughly first-class job at reasonable rates than is Mr. Abbott. He keeps a full line of painters' stock and materials for sale at prices as low as the lowest.

A. Hollis, Granite Quarry, Concord.—When we come to sum up what should be the characteristics of a perfect ornamental and monumental stone, and compare the result with the characteristics of Concord granite the difference is so slight and unimportant that it at once becomes evident why the latter stone has become so widely popular, and why the demand for it is increasing so rapidly and so constantly. The superiority of granite over marble for cemetery purposes is so pronounced that in some cemeteries,—notably one in Brookline, near Boston, Mass ,—the use of marble is positively forbidden, and all who have visited the cemetery in question will agree that the beauty of the effects thus far attained vindicates the wisdom of the prohibition. The stone produced at the quarry operated by Mr. A. Hollis, in this city, is most admirably adapted for cemetery work, and in fact for ornamental stone work of all kinds, for it is close and even in grain and its coloring is beautiful and uniform. The "Good Samaritan" group on the Ether monument in the public garden, Boston, shows what can be done with stone from this quarry. Mr. Hollis served in the army in the late war as 2d lieutenant Forty-fifth Mass. Vol., and captain in the Fifty-sixth Mass. Vol., and was brevetted major April 2, 1865. He is well known in Concord and vicinity as a reliable business man.

Kimball, Danforth & Forrest, Contractors and Builders, dealers in Lumber and Mouldings, Clough's avenue, Concord, N. H.—The firm of Kimball, Danforth & Forrest, was formed in 1889, but the enterprise with which they are identified is of much earlier origin, and ranks among the representative undertakings of the kind in this section of the State. Operations were begun in 1872, by Messrs. Whittemore & Kimball, who were succeeded in 1884 by Messrs. Kimball & Danforth, Mr. Danforth having prior to that date been foreman for Messrs. H. H. Amsden & Son. The existing firm is constituted of Messrs. Chas. Kimball, a native of Dunbarton ; S. B. Danforth, a native of Pennacook ; and George S. Forrest, a native of Belmont. The concern are extensive contractors and builders and large wholesale and retail dealers in lumber and mouldings, planing, sawing, matching and all kinds of wood work will be done to order at short notice ; the most improved facilities being at hand and employment being given from thirty to sixty assistants. The premises utilized are located on Clough's avenue, and comprise two floors of the dimensions of 50×70 feet. Special attention is given to dressing birch flooring and kiln drying, and the service offered is uniformly prompt reliable and efficient, for the members of the firm give the details of the business close personal supervision, and being experienced, practical men are fully competent to carry on operations to the best possible advantage. This firm have not been long in the field but are taking excellent rank for good work, as the Franklin school building and New Eagle hotel attests.

J. H. Toof, Concord Steam Laundry, and Bath Rooms, 22 Warren Street, Concord, N. H.—"Cleanliness is next to godliness," according to the proverb, and the facilities for cleanliness afforded by Mr. J. H. Toof, are of great benefit to the public and fully deserve the extensive patronage they receive. This gentleman is a native of Canada, and has carried on his present enterprise since 1879. The "Concord Steam Laundry Office and Bath Rooms," both of which he is proprietor, are located at No. 22 Warren street, but the laundry works are located elsewhere, the premises comprising two floors, each of the dimensions of 30×70 feet with attic. They are fitted up throughout with the latest improved machinery, and as employment is given to from twenty to thirty experienced assistants, it is obvious that a great deal of work must be turned out here every day. And so there is, for a busier establishment it would be hard to find, and it is safe to say there is not a laundry in New England where more uniformly satisfactory results are attained. Great care is taken not to injure the garments; no harmful chemicals are used, the machinery is as gentle as it is efficient in operation and in short there is no reason why the public should not be as perfectly satisfied, as in fact it is with the accommodations provided. The scale of prices is moderate and work is delivered without extra charge. The gents' bath rooms are in the building with the laundry office and are opened day and evening, except Sunday, and are very conveniently arranged, the whole having an area of 30×60 feet. You can take a hot bath, a cold bath or a medium bath, for the heat of the water can be easily and exactly regulated and if you can't bathe here in comfort, you can't do so anywhere. Everything is "neat as a pin," and the charges are very reasonable.

Chase's Art and Stationery Store, 25 North Main Street, Concord, N. H.—Mr. I. G. Chase is a native of Danbury, N. H., and considering that he has carried on business here since 1882, it is hardly necessary to add is as well-known a business man as there is in town, for Chase's Art and Stationery Store is known as the headquarters for all kinds of stationery and fancy goods. He carries a very complete line of stationery, comprising the very latest fashionable novelties, and also offers a well-chosen assortment of picture frames, mouldings, etc., as well as albums, pocket-books, artists' supplies, together with fancy goods of every description, and our readers will be glad to know that goods of standard quality may be bought here at prices below those quoted elsewhere in this vicinity, and also that the stock is exceptionally large and varied as well as desirable, and those of our readers who appreciate good articles, in the above named lines but can't afford or don't wish to pay fancy prices for their goods, would do well to test those offered at this popular store. Mr. Chase is constantly adding to his stock, and as the public are quick to appreciate progress and honorable business methods, it is not surprising that his establishment is largely patronized. The goods are dependable, the prices are low, and customers are sure of courteous and prompt attention.

Harry Phillips, Granite Monuments, Head Stones, etc., North State Street, Concord.—Of course the average man knows very little about monuments, headstones, etc., and when he has occasion to place an order for anything in this line it is natural that he should want to feel sure that he is dealing with a reliable person who will advise him to the best of his ability and give him a fair return for money expended. Now there are many responsible and reputable manufacturerers of monumental work, etc., in Concord and vicinity, but it is no discredit to any of them to say that not one is more worthy of the highest confidence than Mr. Harry Phillips, whose office and yard are located on North State street. He is a native of England and has had sole control of his present establishment since 1889, having then succeeded Messrs. Ola Anderson & Co., who had carried it on since 1887. The premises are spacious and well arranged, and employment is given to from nine to twelve assistants, so that orders can be filled at short notice. Mr. Phillips does both a wholesale and retail business and is well prepared to quote the lowest market rates in connection with strictly first class work. He shows many attractive designs for granite monuments, headstones, tablets, etc., and furnishes curbing and cemetery work of all descriptions; estimates being promptly given, and communications by mail or otherwise being assured immediate and careful attention.

The North End Fish Market, F. Battles, Proprietor, 149 North Main Street, Concord, N. H.—Prominent among the enterprising business houses of Concord is the North End Fish Market. The business which was established in 1884 by Mr. F. Battles has grown rapidly and steadily from its inception. The stock carried is large and consists of fish, oysters, etc., everything being of the best quality which can be selected by the experience and thorough knowledge of the proprietor. These goods, which comprise every variety of fish in their season, are purchased from first hands, and on such advantageous terms as to enable him to furnish his customers with good supplies at reasonable prices. Mr. Battles is a native of Boston, Mass., and he served in the army during the late Rebellion. The premises occupied are located at No. 149 North Main street, and will measure about 400 feet. Mr. Battles is highly esteemed for his industry, enterprise and sterling business qualities. Employment is given to sufficient help that all customers may be attended to with promptness, and all orders are accurately filled.

William P. Ford & Co., manufacturers of Stoves and Plows, Office, 165 North Main Street, Concord, N. H.—Many radical changes have taken place in the construction of stoves and plows during the past half century, and it speaks well for the management of the enterprise conducted by Messrs. William P. Ford & Co., that since operations were begun, in 1837, the productions have steadily maintained a leading position in the market and are to-day in active demand throughout New England. Of course their design has been modified from time to time, and improved methods of manufacture have been adopted, and with what success is best shown by the ease with which all competition is now met. The founder of this representative undertaking was Mr. William P. Ford, it subsequently being carried on by Messrs. Ford & Martin ; Ford & Pillsbury and W. P. & T. H. Ford, this latter firm assuming control in 1845, and being succeeded by the present one, twenty years later. The partners are Messrs. W. P. Ford, George H. Marston and John W. Ford, the first named gentleman being a native of Sanbornton, the second of Gilmanton, and the third of this city. The premises utilized comprise a main building measuring 175×65 feet, and various outbuildings; the works being equipped with improved machinery driven by a thirty-horse engine. Employment is given to from thirty to forty assistants, and orders are filled at short notice; the product being sold to jobbers throughout New England. The warerooms and office are located at No. 165 North Main street, and occupy two floors of the dimensions of 30×75 feet. A full line of the firm's productions is carried in stock, and an examination of it will show that the reputation for first class workmanship so long held is now as well deserved as ever.

Dickerman & Co., Wholesale Grocers and dealers in Flour, Grain, Feed, Provisions, Lime and Cement. Tobacco and Cigars a specialty ; Office and Warehouse, Bridge Street, Concord, N. H.—The firm of Dickerman & Co. was formed in 1888, succeeding Messrs. Dickerman, Leavitt & Co., who had begun operations in 1887. The partners are Messrs. G. O. Dickerman and Samuel H. Bow, the former being a native of this city and the latter of Warner, N. H. Both these gentlemen are very widely known in business circles, and the establishment with which they are now identified is one of the most extensive of the kind in the State, and is steadily growing in popularity, as the exceptionally complete facilities provided enable the firm to fill the largest orders at short notice, and to quote the very lowest market rates on dependable goods. The office and warehouse are located on Bridge street, the building containing four floors of the dimensions of 60 × 125 feet. An immense stock is carried, comprising staple and fancy groceries, flour, grain, feed, provisions, lime and cement. A specialty is made of tobacco and cigars, the most popular brands being handled and very low prices quoted. There is a grist mill connected, fitted up with improved machinery driven by a sixty-horse engine. The firm have a private track from the Northern railroad, and receive flour and grain directly from the West. Custom grinding is quite an important department of their business, and all such orders are filled at short notice. Employment is given to ten assistants, and no trouble is spared to ensure promptness and accuracy in the execution of every commission. Their rapidly increasing trade substantiates their claim that they sell goods as low as Boston, thus giving to their trade a large saving in the matter of freight.

LEADING BUSINESS MEN OF EAST CONCORD.

THE OLD WAY   THE NEW WAY

Samuel Eastman & Co., sole manufacturers of the Perfection Holder and Nozzles, Deluge Pipes, Automatic Siamese, Standard Leather Hose and Fire Supplies. Patented in United States and Foreign Countries. East Concord, N. H.—The business conducted by Messrs. Samuel Eastman & Co., was founded by Messrs. C. Robinson & Son and was removed to its present location in 1872. The firm manufacture harnesses and leather belting to some extent but they make a specialty of standard leather hose and fire supplies, including the "Deluge" hose and nozzles, "Automatic Siamese," and last, but by no means least, the "Perfection" nozzle and holder. This latter device was patented July 16, 1889, and April 8, 1890, What is thought of it by practical firemen may be judged from the fact that it is now used in more than one hundred city departments, including New York, Brooklyn, Pittsburgh, Boston, New Orleans and many corporations maintaining a system of fire protection. It is pronounced the best device for handling fire hose ever invented, and the manufacturers have received second and third orders from departments where opportunity has been given to test the merits of the appliance under the most unfavorable circumstances. The nozzle and holder is "built for business,"—it is not merely a pretty toy that is all right in theory but deficient in practice; on the contrary it will bear almost any amount of hard usage and its adjustment is practically instantaneous. By its use one fireman can hold two, three or four nozzles under the heaviest pressure, and the streams are superior in solidity and will reach farther than those thrown through the ordinary discharge pipe. That the firm have confidence in their appliance is shown by the following special offer : "We guarantee all orders for two or more Perfection nozzles and holders ; that one person can hold two nozzles of any size at the same time, one in each hand, under any pressure, or we agree to forfeit, to the department ordering, both nozzles and holders." This feat was easily accomplished at an exhibition in Hartford, Conn., on two 50-foot sections of hose, with 1¼ inch nozzles, on their new self propeller, the most powerful steam fire engine in public use in the world. This exhibition was so satisfactory that at its close an order was given for a full supply of the Perfection nozzles and holders for each company of the entire Hartford department. The holder converts any section of hose into a discharge pipe, the short nozz'e and its form reduces all friction of water to a minimum. The nozzle and holder is made of brass, highly finished and nickel-plated, being as ornamental as it is useful. Messrs. Samuel Eastman & Co. are the sole manufacturers of this valuable appliance and are prepared to fill all orders, large or small, at short notice.

Wm. A. Cowley, dealer in Meat, Provisions, Groceries, Flour, Hay and Grain. Teas and Coffees a Specialty. Terms Cash. East Concord, N. H.—Mr. William A. Cowley is a native of Norton, Mass., and is very widely and favorably known in Concord and vicinity, he being one of the most active and prominent business men of East Concord, where he maintains saw and grist mills and a spacious and well-stocked warehouse. The premises utilized for store purposes comprise two floors of the dimensions of 32×40 feet, and contain a large and very carefully chosen stock, made up of fresh and salted meats, provisions, staple and fancy groceries, flour, hay and grain, the goods being selected expressly for family trade and being obtained from the most reliable sources. Mr. Cowley quotes the lowest market rates on all the commodities he handles, and by employing four experienced assistants is enabled to easily handle his extensive patronage and to assure prompt and courteous attention to every customer. He caters to all tastes and to all purses, and offers particular inducements in the line of teas and coffees, making a specialty of these luxuries, or rather necessities, for they are now so widely used as to merit the latter title. The most fastidious can place an order at this establishment in the full assurance of receiving entire satisfaction, and the most economically disposed will find Mr. Cowley prepared to quote satisfactory prices on thoroughly dependable goods.

Lyman Knowles, Granite Cutter, East Concord, N. H. —It is almost a quarter of a century since Mr. Lyman Knowles became identified with stone cutting and cemetery work. Therefore it is not at all surprising that he should have a most thorough knowledge of the business. Mr. Knowles is a Belmont, N. H., man by birth, and began business in East Concord in the year 1867, where his reputation for turning out the best of work has long been firmly established. Mr. Knowles is one of the oldest granite cutters in town, and his facilities for doing cemetery work of all kinds at short notice are strictly first-class. His shop is centrally located and those wishing to make inquiries in regard to anything in his line will find him always ready to give all the information in his power. Estimates of the probable cost of any desired work will be cheerfully furnished, and we may say right here that Mr. Knowles' prices are sure to be as low as can be named on really first-class work. A choice variety of designs are at hand for the inspection and guidance of those wishing to erect a memorial to departed relatives or friends. Mr. Knowles gives close personal attention to every order, and guarantees that all work executed by him will be done in a neat and thoroughly satisfactory manner, both as regards prices and workmanship.

W. O. Field, Hennery, Market Gardening. etc., East Concord —There has been all manner of fun made of "scientific farming," and undoubtedly those who try to carry on a farm on knowledge gained from books alone will surely make an utter failure of it, but there is such a thing as combining scientific and practical methods in the proper proportions, and when this is done success is as certain as anything can be. The wonderful results gained by some of the market gardeners near the great cities show what can be accomplished by scientific methods and a favorable location, and in short the more the subject is looked into the more plainly it becomes evident that it pays to use brains in farming as in manufacturing or store-keeping. One of the best known market gardeners in this vicinity is Mr. W. O. Field, who is a native of Northfield, Vermont, and has been identified with his present enterprise since 1888. He utilizes spacious premises at East Concord, and finds a ready market for his products, as they are of first class quality and he offers them at the lowest prevailing rates. Mr. Field's specialty, however, is the raising of fancy fowl and no breeder in the State is more successful in this line. His hennery is one of the most commodious and most completely arranged in New Hampshire, it being two stories in height, 375×16 feet in dimensions, and heated by hot water. It has a capacity of from 5000 to 6000 fowl, and every facility is at hand to ensure cleanliness and other favorable conditions. Mr. Field makes a specialty of thoroughbred fowl, and will furnish fowl and eggs for breeding purposes in any quantity and at short notice and low prices. He manufactures an incubator which is endorsed by practical men as the most economical, efficient and reliable in use. He has had nine years experience with it, and is pre-

pared to guarantee that it will do all that is claimed for it and prove entirely satisfactory if used intelligently in accordance with instructions. The incubator is strongly made, and should be examined by every one interested in fowl and fowl raising.

John H. Robinson, manufacturer of all kinds of Brick, East Concord, N. H.—There is no building material in the market but what has some special advantages, for otherwise, of course, there would be no demand for it and consequently it would never have been placed on sale; but when we come to sum up the advantages of the many materials used for building purposes, we find that by far the greatest number are combined in brick. A brick building may be highly ornamental or severely plain, it may be adapted for a magnificent mansion, or a substantial, business-like factory, it costs much less than stone, is much more durable than wood, and may be made more perfectly fire-proof than would be possible by the use of any other material. Other advantages could easily be named but these of themselves are enough to account for the enduring and increasing popularity of brick for building purposes. Mr. John H. Robinson, of East Concord, is a manufacturer of all kinds of brick, and he is prepared to fill the heaviest orders at short notice, as he generally has a large stock on hand, and employs from twenty to thirty men in the making of brick at all times. He quotes the lowest market rates on all grades and kinds, and those wishing to place an order for brick of any description will best serve their own interests by communicating with Mr. Robinson and giving him an opportunity to state his figures

LEADING BUSINESS MEN OF WEST CONCORD.

Thomas Fox, manufacturer and dealer in Fine Granites, Monuments, Tablets, Headstones and every description of Cut and Polished Monumental Work, West Concord, N. H.—The great and steadily increasing popularity of American granites for monumental purposes is one of the significant and gratifying "signs of the times," for it shows that we have outgrown our foodness for "imported" articles to a certain extent, and it also shows a decided raising of the standard of public taste, for from an artistic point of view, granite is far superior to marble for cemetery work, no matter whether the marble be of foreign or domestic origin. Some idea of the beautiful effects attainable in American granite monuments, tablets, headstones, etc., may be gained by visiting the establishment conducted by Mr. Thomas Fox in West Concord, for he is a leading manufacturer of such work, and generally has a variety of finished monuments, etc., on hand. He deals in all kinds of fine granite and is prepared to furnish this stone in quantities to suit, at short notice and at the lowest market rates. Every description of cut and polished monumental work will be made to order in a superior manner, together with posts, curbings and all kinds of cemetery and building work. The business is both wholesale and retail. Immediate and careful attention is given to orders and correspondence, estimates being promptly furnished on application and no pains being spared to deliver work at the time agreed upon.

Eastman & Co., dealers in Dry Goods and Groceries, West Concord, N. H.—One of the oldest-established mercantile enterprises in West Concord is that carried on under the firm-name of Eastman & Co., it having been in successful operation ever since 1830. After various changes in ownership it came under the control of Eastman, Currier & Co., this firm assuming possession about a quarter of a century ago, or in 1864. Subsequently the undertaking passed into the hands of Eastman & Shepard, and in 1885 the existing firm was organized, the partners being Mrs. A. F. Eastman, Mr. O. L. Shepard and Mr. G. R. Parmenter. Mr. Shepard is a native of Gilmanton, N. H., and has had a continuous service in this same store twenty-three years, twenty-one years as a member of the firm. Mr. Parmenter is a native of Warren, Vt. Both these gentlemen give personal attention to the filling of orders, and sufficient assistance is employed to ensure immediate and careful service to every caller although an extensive business is done, spacious premises being occupied and a large and varied stock carried. Dry goods, groceries, flour and grain are among the important commodities dealt in, and it is generally understood hereabouts that at no establishment in this section can equally dependable goods be obtained at lower rates. The assortment is constantly being renewed, and as all classes of trade are catered to the patronage is as general as it is extensive.

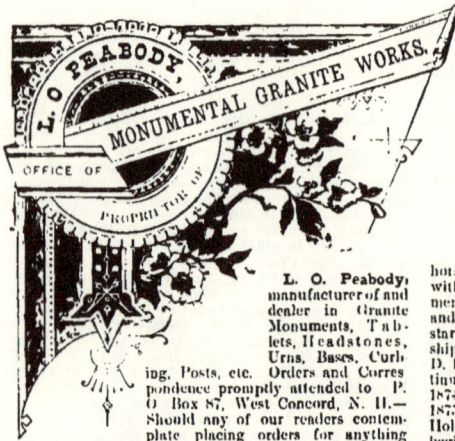

L. O. Peabody, manufacturer of and dealer in Granite Monuments, Tablets, Headstones, Urns, Bases, Curbing, Posts, etc. Orders and Correspondence promptly attended to. P. O. Box 87, West Concord, N. H.—Should any of our readers contemplate placing orders for anything in the line of cemetery work, they will best serve their own interests by communicating with Mr. L. O. Peabody, P. O. Box 87, West Concord, for he is a leading manufacturer of and dealer in granite monuments, tablets, headstones, urns, bases, curbing, posts, etc., and is prepared to suit the most exacting taste and to quote the prices that will bear the severest comparison with those named by any other producer of equally desirable work. All communications are assured immediate and painstaking attention, for Mr. Peabody solicits correspondence and is always ready to promptly forward estimates on application. His facilities for filling orders at short notice are unsurpassed, and employment is given to from five to ten assistants. There is a growing demand for unconventional designs in cemetery work and many of those shown at this establishment are as remarkable for originality as they are for tastefulness and beauty. Every detail of construction is skillfully and carefully carried out, and the fineness of finish characterizing Mr. Peabody's productions goes far to explain the high praise they receive from the most competent and unprejudiced judges.

B. T. Putney, Granite Quarry, West Concord.— Undoubtedly some very foolish things are done in the name of "fashion," but occasionally the dictates of that capricious authority have sound common sense back of them, and a prominent case in point is that afforded by the prevailing taste for granite monuments, tablets, etc. Of course the present popularity of this stone for cemetery purposes is by no means entirely the result of the vagaries of fashion, but it is unquestionable that the demand has been greatly increased by the fact that granite cemetery work is "the correct thing," from a fashionable point of view, as well as from the standpoint of utility and common sense. No matter how extensive the consumption of this stone may become there will be little if any difficulty in filling orders promptly, for the supply is practically unlimited, and there are many active and enterprising men engaged in quarrying. Mr. B. T. Putney holds a leading position among such so far as Concord is concerned, and he is ready to furnish granite for curbing and building work, in quantities to suit at bottom prices. He employs from six to eight assistants, and is prepared to fill orders promptly and accurately in the summer season. He also keeps constantly on hand and for sale dynamite (Miners' Friend) and blasting material, such as fuse, both electric and cotton or waterproof. Post office address, B. T. Putney, P. O. Box 63, Concord, N. H.

Concord Manufacturing Co., Flannel Manufacturers, West Concord, N. H.—In so important a business center as Concord, N. H., many cases can be pointed out of extensive development from comparatively small beginnings but few of them can parallel that of the enterprise now carried on by the Concord Manufacturing Company. It was inaugurated in 1843 by Mr. B. F. Holden, who came to Concord from Massachusetts and bought a small flour mill and cloth mill at West Concord. But one set of cards was operated at the beginning, but improvement followed improvement as frugal and intelligent management provided the means for extension until now it affords employment to about 125 hands, running fifty-four looms and 4020 spindles. Both steam and water power are employed, there being two engines with total capacity of 110-horse power. The premises occupied consist of two mills with a total floorage of 45,000 square feet. The gentlemen who are and have been identified with this enterprise, and its changes are as follows: in 1847—four years after starting the business Mr. B. F. Holden formed a partnership with his brother Daniel, the firm-name being B. F. & D. Holden, the development of the business steadily continued resulting in the incorporation of the company in 1874. Mr. B. F. Holden was president up to his death in 1875, the position now being filled by Mr. Edward D. Holden. Mr. Daniel Holden has been treasurer from the beginning, and very few men can look back upon an equally long and honorable business career, especially in a continuous connection with the same enterprise, for he was born in 1809 and has been prominently connected with the enterprise under notice for forty-three years. The original capital of the company was $100,000 but it has lately been increased to $150,000. The company have purchased a fine water privilege on the Contoocook river at Penacook, and have built a fine dam and prepared the foundation for a large mill—to be built as early as circumstances may determine,—a fine view of this dam may be seen in the historical part of this book. The flannel manufactured by this company is disposed of through Messrs. Parker, Wilder & Co., the selling agents in New York and Boston, and has an established reputation for strength, durability, beauty and finish. With the contemplated new mill completed there is every reason to believe that the future prosperity of this enterprise will be worthy of its exceptional past.

Frank R. Clark, dealer in all grades of Cemetery Work, Monuments, Tablets, Headstones and Curbing; also Concord, Barre, Quincy and Sunapee Granite, Concord Granite a Specialty, West Concord, N. H.—It is not a good plan to take too much for granted, and those who argue that where open and free competition is present, as is the case in the granite business, one dealer can offer as great inducements as another, would learn if they made personal investigation that this principle although plausible in theory is not borne out in practice. This is not the place to point out the reasons why some dealers can, and do offer special advantages, and indeed our readers are much more interested in learning what dealers do afford the most efficient and economical service than in ascertaining how they do it. Without further preface then, we would call attention to the establishment carried on by Mr. Frank R. Clark, in West Concord, for he announces that all in need of any work in his line will find it to their advantage to get his prices before going elsewhere, and the best of this announcement is that it is fully justified by the facts. Mr. Clark deals in all grades of cemetery work, monuments, tablets, headstones and curbing, and also in Concord, Barre, Quincy and Sunapee granite, making a specialty of Concord granite. Positively bottom prices are quoted in every department of the business and the quality of the work will in all cases compare favorably with that of similar grade produced by other manufacturers. Particular attention is given to setting work, and every order is assured prompt and careful attention.

Edwards & Dravis, dealers in American and Imported Granites, Monuments, Tablets, Headstones, Statuary, Urns, Bases and all kinds of Cemetery and Building Work, P. O. Box 21, West Concord, N. H.—Builders and others who have frequent occasion to place orders for granite, are of course well acquainted with the comparative standing of the various firms located in Concord and vicinity, and hence need little or no information as to the facilities offered by these concerns, but the large majority of our readers do not belong to this class and no doubt there are many of them who wish to place an order for a monument, tablet, headstone or something else coming under the head of cemetery work, but do not know just where it can be placed to the best advantage. Therefore we take pleasure in making mention of the enterprise conducted by Messrs. Edwards & Dravis, for they give particular attention to cemetery work, and are in a position not only to suit the most fastidious but to quote prices as low as can be named on strictly first-class work. The firm is made up of Messrs. T. D. Edwards and Geo. R. Dravis, the former a native of Vermont, and the latter of New Hampshire. Both have had extended experience in the business, and as they give personal attention to the filling of orders, the efficiency of the service is assured. Employment is afforded to from eight to twelve assistants, and the most extensive commissions can be promptly executed. American and Imported granites will be supplied in any desired quantities at the lowest market rates, and monuments, headstones, tablets, urns and cemetery and building work of all kinds are made to order in the most artistic manner, an almost endless variety of designs being offered to choose from. The works are at West Concord, and communications addressed to P. O. Box 21 are assured immediate and careful attention.

W. S. Lougee, Granite Monuments, etc., West Concord. —Even were there no difference in the quality of the work turned out by the various manufacturers of granite monuments, etc., it would still be worth while to exercise some discrimination in the placing of orders, for not only do the prices quoted on such work vary appreciably, but some manufacturers pursue a much more liberal policy than others and spare no pains to faithfully carry out every agreement and to deliver orders promptly when promised. Not one of our local monumental workers has a higher reputation in this respect than Mr. W. S. Lougee, and the extensive business he has built up since beginning operations in 1884 is the natural consequence of the methods which have given rise to such a reputation. He is a native of Concord and served more than a year in the army during the Rebellion. He has held the position of State representative, and is very widely known in social as well as in business circles. Mr. Lougee employs from four to eight assistants, and manufactures granite monuments and cemetery work of all kinds, including headstones, tablets, curbing, urns, etc. No better finished stone work is obtainable in this city than that coming from this well-managed establishment, and the designs are so many and varied that all tastes and all purses can surely be suited.

LEADING BUSINESS MEN OF PENACOOK.

Foote, Brown & Co., dealers in Dry Goods, Groceries, Hardware, Crockery, Room Paper, Paints and Oils, Grass Seeds, Farming Tools, etc., Penacook.—The premises utilized by Messrs. Foote, Brown & Co., are very commodious, they comprising two floors and a basement, but they are not a bit too large, for this firm carry the largest stock of general merchandise in the county and have use for every inch of space available. Anything like detailed mention of their assortment is entirely out of the question, for a mere catalogue of it would occupy several pages, but suffice it to say it comprises dry goods, groceries, hardware, crockery, room-paper, paints and oils, grass seeds, farming tools and other equally useful commodities. Messrs. Foote, Brown & Co. cater to all classes of trade, and their policy of furnishing dependable goods at bottom prices affords sufficient explanation of the magnitude of their business. Employment is given to four assistants, and customers are served with a promptness and courtesy which might profitably be imitated at many a much smaller establishment. This enterprise is as truly representative as any to be found in this vicinity, it having been inaugurated not far from half a century ago and having held a leading position almost from the first. The original proprietors were Messrs. H. H. & J. S. Brown, they beginning operations in 1845, and being succeeded by Messrs. Putnam & Bean, who gave place to Mr. David Putnam, he to Messrs. Putnam & Hall and they to Messrs. Hall & Foote, this latter firm assuming control in 1870. In 1875 the style was changed by David A. Brown purchasing the interest of Mr. Hall, to Brown & Foote and in 1886 Mr. D. A. Brown sold to Stewart I. Brown when the existing firm name was adopted. Mr. Charles E. Foote is a native of Salisbury, N. H., and Mr. Stewart I. Brown of Concord. Both these gentlemen are too well known throughout this section to call for extended personal mention, and we will only add that they spare no pains to maintain the high reputation so long associated with the undertaking with which they are identified.

John Whittaker, manufacturer of and dealer in Lumber, Penacook.—A review of the prominent business men of Concord and Penacook containing no mention of Mr. John Whittaker would be considered by the majority of the residents of that section as much like the play of "Hamlet" with "Hamlet's" part left out, for Mr. Whittaker is not only an active, enterprising and successful business man but is prominent in public and social life also, he being one of the best-known and most highly-esteemed citizens in the county. It is not uncommon to hear a man spoken of as having "hosts of friends," but it is seldom that the expression is so well justified by the facts as it is when used in connection with Mr. Whittaker for his genial disposition and straightforward method, make friends for him everywhere, and the official position he has held have brought him prominently before the public and so enlarged his list of acquaintances that literally "their name is legion." He is a sir knight of Mount Moreh Commandery, Concord, and has represented Penacook, ward one, in both branches of the city government, and also in the State Legislature, besides serving a number of years as chief of the Penacook Fire Department. He is a native of Hopkinton and comes of a family that has never been backward in serving the country when service counted for something, his grandfather having been a soldier in the Revolution, his father in the War of 1812, while he was in the National Civil Service during the Rebellion. Mr. Whittaker is an extensive manufacturer of and dealer in lumber, his mills being located at what is known as the "Borough." The business was founded many years ago, and in 1865 came under the control of Messrs. Whittaker, Caldwell & Amsden, they being succeeded by Messrs. Whittaker, Allen & Amsden, and Mr. John Whittaker becoming sole proprietor in 1885. The mills are equipped with a complete plant of improved machinery run by water power, and sufficient assistance is employed to enable all orders to be filled at short notice, both a wholesale and retail business being done.

WORKS OF THE CONCORD AXLE COMPANY.

Concord Axle Company, manufacturers of Original Concord Axles, Penacook, N. H.—The "Original Concord" Axles are known and prized throughout the civilized world, their reputation for strength and durability being such that even did the Concord Axle Company manufacture nothing else they would still have to maintain extensive works in order to supply the demand for these famous articles. The enviable record made by the "Original Concord" Axles is the legitimate result of the use of the very best metal and the employment of skilled labor in their production, and as similar methods are followed in the manufacture of the other axles, springs, etc., made by the company it naturally follows that they too meet with a ready sale and never fail to give the best of satisfaction. This business was established away back in 1835 by Mr. Warren Johnson, and after several changes in ownership came into the possession of Messrs. D. Arthur Brown & Co., in 1863. The existing company was incorporated in 1880, its management being substantially in the hands of those who have been identified with the enterprise since 1863. Mr. D. Arthur Brown is treasurer, the president being Mr. C. H. Amsden, and the superintendent Mr. E. H. Brown. The premises utilized cover a good deal of ground, and are equipped with an elaborate plant of improved machinery, driven by water power. The foundry is 140 × 50 feet in dimensions, and there is a forge shop, a machine shop, a finishing shop and six large store houses, besides an office building, measuring 25 × 38 feet. Employment is given to 100 men, and some 700 tons of wagon axles are made per year, together with about 300 tons of castings. The product goes to every portion of the country, and quite an extensive export business is also done. Besides the Original Concord Axles, the company manufacture "Concord Express" axles, "Vulcan," or common axles, Iron Hub Axles, Crank or Jigger Axles, Half Patent Axles, tire-benders, thorobrace irons, axle boxes, castings, etc. They are selling agents for the Archibald Patent Iron Hub wheels, Palmer's Concord Springs, Farr's Patent Sand Bands, whiffletree springs, etc. The company are the sole manufacturers of the Concord Polishing Machine, for polishing granite and other stone. It is simple, efficient, easily managed and durable and is now successfully used at Concord, N. H., Quincy, Mass., Barre, Vt., and elsewhere. All parts are interchangeable and any part may be ordered by number, thus rendering repairs convenient and inexpensive, and obviating long delay in case of accident.

E. S. Harris, Dustin Island Woolen Mills; Flannel and Dress Goods, Penacook, N. H.—Since the enterprise conducted by Mr. E. S. Harris, proprietor of the Dustin Island Woolen Mills, was inaugurated in 1848, many and pronounced changes have taken place in manufacturing methods, for forty years is a very long period in modern industrial development. During that forty years, American woolens have greatly improved in quality, and whereas in 1850 domestic competition with foreign manufacturers was regarded by many as out of the question, in 1890 unprejudiced and competent judges agree that in certain lines the productions of some American makers of woolen goods will compare very favorably with imported fabrics of the same grade. One of the chief difficulties which domestic manufacturers have had to contend with is the absurd bias in favor of things "imported," which has been a national characteristic, but our country grows wiser as it grows older and we are beginning to understand that native productions may easily be equal, and in many instances are far superior to any that can be imported. The Dustin Island Woolen Mills are equipped throughout with improved machinery for the management has always been progressive and has spared neither trouble nor expense to improve the quality, and when possible to diminish the cost of the finished product. The original proprietor was Mr. Almon Harris, he being succeeded by Messrs. Almon Harris & Sons and they by Messrs. E. S. Harris & Co. The present proprietor was born in this State, and assumed sole control of the business in 1882. He is very generally known in manufacturing and mercantile circles, and his productions have gained a high reputation among consumers and the trade, their uniformly excellent quality commending them to the most discriminating purchaser. They comprise a full line of flannels and dress goods, and in design as well as in material and construction they are well fitted to hold their own in any market. Five sets of machinery are utilized and employment is given to from sixty to seventy five operatives. The production for March, 1890, was 78,500 yards, and with such facilities we need hardly add that Mr. Harris is prepared to fill the most extensive orders at comparatively short notice and to quote the lowest market rates at all times.

H. H. Amsden & Sons, manufacturers of Pine and Ash Chamber Furniture, Penacook, N. H.—It is asserted by those who are in a position to speak with authority on the subject, that furniture was never before so cheap as it has been during the past five years, and indeed even the least observant among our readers cannot have failed to notice the lowness of the prices now quoted on furniture in general, and especially on chamber furniture. The reasons given for this reduction in price, are generally the close competition now existing in this line of industry, and the diminution of the cost of production by the use of improved labor-saving machinery. That sharp competition is now the rule is too evident to call for proof, and that the machinery now used in first class factories is wonderfully ingenious and efficient may be seen by visiting the establishment carried on under the firm-name of H. H. Amsden & Sons, for this is not only the largest furniture factory in New England but is one of the best-equipped in the whole country. The main building is five stories in height, and 84 × 200 feet in dimensions, and there are also commodious dry-houses, lumber sheds, etc., the premises being very conveniently arranged and every facility being present that will tend to reduce the cost of production to a minimum without impairment of quality. The factory is thoroughly equipped with the automatic sprinkler throughout. The elaborate plant of machinery is driven by water power, there being a 200-horse waterwheel utilized, but steam power is also available when required. Employment is given to 150 assistants, and some idea of the magnitude of the product may be gained from the fact that about 300,000 feet of lumber is consumed monthly, which is mostly obtained from Canada. The conveniences for drying lumber are complete with a capacity for 150,000 feet. The firm manufacture ash and oak chamber furniture exclusively and dispose of most of it in New England and in New York State, although they enjoy quite an extensive Southern trade and ship many orders to South America and Africa. A specialty is made of goods in knock down for export, and the heaviest orders can be filled at very short notice. The various processes incidental to manufacture are carefully and skillfully supervised, and from the selection of the stock through all the details of seasoning and working-up, no trouble is spared to assure a continuance of the enviable reputation the products of this factory have so long enjoyed among consumers and the trade. The policy of the management in a nutshell is to furnish uniformly dependable goods at the lowest possible figures, and the great magnitude of the business shows how generally this policy is appreciated. The undertaking was founded in 1851 by Mr. B. F. Caldwell, who in 1853 was succeeded by Messrs. Caldwell, Amsden & Co. Ten years later the firm of Caldwell & Amsden assumed control, and in 1868 the existing firm-name was adopted. Mr. C. H. Amsden, the present proprietor, is a native of Boscawen, N. H., and has served as alderman and as State senator, and was the Democratic candidate for governor in the last election, running ahead of his party ticket in a manner very complimentary to him personally as indicating his personal popularity throughout the State. In business circles he is also most favorably known, his enterprise occupying a leading position among the distinctively representative undertakings of this section.

D. B. Weymouth, General Store, Penacook, N. H.— Premises comprising two floors and a basement, each of which measure 20×60 feet, giving a total floor space of 3600 square feet, can accommodate a very heavy stock, and the fact that this is the capacity of the premises utilized by Mr. D. B. Weymouth, and that practically all the available space is made use of, demonstrates beyond the need of further statement that the assortment of goods he offers is very complete. It is also very varied, for he deals in general merchandise and carries full lines of groceries, flour and grain, boots and shoes in full assortment, styles, widths and sizes, and other commodities too numerous to mention. This business was founded a number of years ago and came under the control of the present proprietor in 1889. Mr. Weymouth was born in Andover, N. H. His business policy is as simple as it is popular, it being to give full value for money received. Of course careful management is necessary in order to do so but Mr. Weymouth is a close and discriminating buyer and is therefore enabled to quote the lowest market rates on goods that will prove entirely satisfactory.

Fisherville Saw Co., manufacturers of Circular, Gang and Cross Cut Saws and Whittletree Springs, Penacook, N. H.—The business conducted by the concern whose card we print above was established half a century ago and and is clearly entitled to a prominent place among the representative undertakings of this section. The circular, gang and cross cut saws made by this company have gone into general use, in many cases under the most exacting conditions, and the record they have made substantiates the claim that while quoting prices about the same as those named by other saw manufacturers, the company's policy is not to attain the limit of cheapness but the limit of goodness. Saws of all descriptions are manufactured, including ice saws, which will be made to order at short notice. Cast steel whittletree and yoke springs are also extensively manufactured, they being very popular, as they are made from the best No. 1 steel, are far superior to any others in the market and are fully warranted. The company give particular attention to the repairing of circular saws, and restore them to their original condition, as they are very careful to avoid any process which while apparently putting the saw in good order would so injure it as to greatly impair its durability. They claim to do the best job of saw repairing obtainable, and in the opinion of practical men they are prepared to make that claim good in every respect. Correspondence is solicited, and all communications are assured prompt and careful attention. The manager, Mr. G. S. Locke, is a native of London, N. H., and is widely known in manufacturing circles. He gives careful personal attention to the filling of orders, and employs a sufficient force of assistants to ensure the prompt execution of every commission.

Frank E. Bean, dealer in Cream, Vienna and White Bread, Brown Bread, Cakes, Pastry, Cream Cakes, etc., Penacook, N. H.—There are some bakers who apparently have never heard the old proverb, "You can't make a silk purse out of a sow's ear," for they insist upon using inferior materials and then wonder why the public refuse to accept their productions as first class. Extensive facilities and experience and skill will go far towards ensuring satisfactory results, but material of good quality cannot be dispensed with in the manufacture of bread, cake and pastry that is designed to suit the most fastidious taste. Evidently Mr. Frank E. Bean appreciates this fact, for he not only provides improved facilities and employs skilled assistants, but gives careful personal attention to the choice of materials, sparing no pains to get the best the market affords. As an inevitable consequence his productions stand high in the favor of the public, and while he caters to all classes of trade he finds no difficulty in perfectly satisfying the most critical. Mr. Bean was born in Salisbury, N. H., and as a member of the firm of Harlow & Bean succeeded Mr. Chas. Wiggins in the control of the enterprise to which we have reference, in 1855, assuming sole possession in 1878. He utilizes one floor and a basement, having a total area of about 1,000 square feet, and carries a large and varied stock which is constantly being renewed and is consequently always fresh and tempting. It includes cream, Vienna and white bread, cakes, pastry, etc., and orders can be filled without delay, employment being given to three assistants.

**+ DR. TOPLIFF'S +
SYRUP OF TAR
CURES COUGHS, COLDS, SPITTING
OF BLOOD AND CONSUMPTION.**

managed in the full sense of the term He is a native of Concord, and has carried on his present enterprise for ten years, succeeding in 1880 Mr. C. C. Topliff, who had been proprietor since 1865. Mr. Hoyt also succeeded Mr. Topliff as proprietor and manufacturer of "Topliff Syrup of Tar," one of the best known cough and consumption cures, and quite an extensive wholesale business is done in this valuable remedy. Mr. Hoyt is thoroughly familiar with every detail of his business, and as he gives personal attention to the filling of orders the service is as reliable as it is prompt and obliging. Premises having an area of 1,200 square feet are occupied, and a full assortment of drugs, medicines and chemicals is constantly carried, enabling physicians' prescriptions to be compounded without delay. Every facility is at hand to ensure absolute accuracy in every detail of this department of the business, and the ingredients used are obtained from the most reliable sources and may be depended upon for freshness and purity. Uniformly moderate charges are made and no trouble is spared to fully maintain the high reputation so long held in connection with this service. Mr. Hoyt deals in toilet and fancy articles, druggists' sundries and other goods usually found in a first class pharmacy, and quotes the lowest market rates on all the commodities he handles.

J. Irving Hoyt, Druggist, Penacook, N. H.— Should the various mercantile establishments located in Penacook and vicinity be mentioned in the order of their comparative usefulness, that conducted by Mr. J. Irving Hoyt would be clearly entitled to a leading position in the list, for on the whole, no retail establishment is more useful than a well managed drug store, and that of which Mr. Hoyt is proprietor is well

Harry S. Harris, Livery, Boarding, Transient and Hack Stable, Washington House, Penacook, N. H.—The stable connected with the Washington House has been carried on for many years and has changed hands many times, but it is safe to assert that the service rendered was never moreefficient and satisfactory than it has been since the present proprietor, Mr. Harry S. Harris, assumed control in 1888. He was born in Boscawen, N. H., and has had no little experience in the stable business, as might be easily guessed from the character of the accommodations he affords. There are seventeen stalls on the premises, and a general livery, boarding, baiting and hacking business is done, employment being given to three assistants, and all orders being assured immediate and painstaking attention. First class livery teams will be furnished at uniformly moderate rates, and such of our readers as enjoy driving, and have no team of their own would do well to make trial of the accommodations supplied by Mr. Harris, for we are sure that the result will be entirely satisfactory. Horses boarded here are assured comfortable quarters, kind treatment and an abundance of suitable food, and the charges made in this department are low enough to suit the most economically disposed. Hacks will be furnished at very short notice, the drivers being careful and well informed, so that strangers wishing to view the vicinity will find this a most excellent and pleasurable way in which to do it. Mr. Harris gives careful supervision to affairs and spares no pains to thoroughly satisfy every customer.

Foote & Morse, dealers in Dry Goods, Groceries, Flour, Crockery, Glass and Wooden Ware, Country Produce and Farming Tools, Concord Street, near Penacook House, Penacook, N. H.—There may be some advantages gained by the practice of dividing business up into specialties, as is the practice in the cities, as for instance one dealer handling nothing but groceries, another nothing but glassware, a third nothing but provisions, etc., but there are many disadvantages also, and that such is the case is seen in the popularity of the great city "department" stores, which are only general stores under a new name. There are many establishments in Penacook and vicinity carrying a desirable line of general merchandise, but not one which we can more heartily recommend to our readers than that conducted by Messrs. Foote & Morse. This is located on Concord street, near the Penacook House, and comprises one floor and a basement, measuring 40×60 feet. This is the oldest store in Penacook, the original part having been built in 1836, the first firm being Johnson & Gage. From time to time additions have been added to it until now it contains a large and complete stock to select from, among the more important articles contained in it being dry goods, groceries, flour, country produce, crockery, glass and wooden ware, and farming tools. These goods are obtained from the most reliable sources and are guaranteed to prove just as represented, while the prices quoted on them will prove satisfactory to the most economically disposed. Prompt and polite attention is assured to every caller, and all orders will be accurately filled at very short notice. This business was founded a good many years ago, and in 1874 came into the possession of Messrs. Foote & Gates, who succeeded Mr. Geo. M. Dudley, and were succeeded by the present firm in 1879. Mr. H. T. Foote is a native of Salisbury, N. H., and Mr. G. A. Morse of Peabody, Mass. Both these gentlemen are widely known throughout this vicinity, not only in business but also in social circles.

A. Linehan, Fruits of all kinds, Confectionery, Cigars, Tobacco, Notions, etc., Main Street, Penacook, N. H.—Generally speaking, every penny paid out for fruit is well invested, for no one article of food is more healthful, and fresh, ripe fruit used in reasonable moderation will save many a doctor's bill, as well as a good deal of discomfort and even positive suffering. But it is of the first importance that the fruit should be sound and ripe, and therefore some discrimination should be exercised in its purchase, for dealers who do not give special attention to the handling of fruit are apt to keep what they do handle so long that it becomes in some cases totally unfit to eat, although it may not appear so. Mr. A. Linehan makes a specialty of fruits of all kinds, and his assortment will always be found fresh and desirable. He quotes the lowest market rates, and those wishing anything in the fruit line would do well to call at his store on Main street, and there make their selections. Mr. Linehan was born in Danbury, N. H., and founded his present business in 1890. He does not confine himself to handling fruit by any means but also deals in confectionery, cigars and tobacco, etc. A full line of notions ranging in price from five cents to one dollar, is on hand to choose from, and a visit to the store will prove both pleasant and profitable.

Miss M. S. Peaslee, dealer in Millinery and Fancy Goods, Penacook, N. H.—We believe it has never been satisfactorily demonstrated just who or what is the "leader of fashion," the fact being that certain articles are fashionable while others are not, while apparently there is not the least reason for the distinction. Still the saying goes, "As well be out of the world as out of the fashion," and as the ladies of Penacook and vicinity are far from being "out of the world," it is not surprising that they should have strong objections to being "out of the fashion." There is certainly no reason why they should become so, as our local dealers show decided enterprise in offering the latest novelties to their patrons, and, indeed, so far as millinery and fancy goods are concerned one would have to journey a good ways to find a more desirable assortment of fashionable novelties than may be seen at the establishment conducted by Miss M. S. Peaslee. This lady is a native of Gilmanton, N. H., and has had great experience in connection with her present business, having formerly been a member of the firm of M. S. & E. V. Peaslee, who carried it on from 1873 up to the year 1886, when the present owner assumed sole control. It would be useless for us to mention the stock in detail for it is constantly changing and always comprises the leading novelties, so that a description would be "out of date" before it could reach the public. Order work is given prompt and skillful attention, and low prices are uniformly quoted in every department of the business.

J. F. Hastings, Undertaker and Funeral Director, Robes, Coffins and Caskets always in Stock. Also dealer in Harness and Saddlery, Trunks, Travelling Bags, Sleigh Robes, Blankets and Whips, Wolf and Rubber Coats, etc. Penacook, N. H.—There is such a great number of small but yet important details to be attended to in preparing for a funeral, that some of them are very apt to be forgotten by one inexperienced in such matters, and the worry caused by thinking that something may have been neglected is of itself enough to warrant the employment of a competent funeral director, for when this is done all anxiety is at once at an end, as one may rest assured that an experienced man making a specialty of undertaking and funeral directing will leave nothing undone that should have been attended to. Mr. J. F. Hastings executes many important commissions of this kind, and it is natural that his services should be largely availed of, for he has served the public for years in this capacity and has won a high reputation for reliability and general efficiency. Mr. Hastings was born in Bristol, N. H., and became identified with his present business in 1876, as a member of the firm of Crother & Hastings, who were succeeded by Thurber & Hastings the following year, Mr. Hastings becoming sole proprietor in 1879. He occupies commodious and well arranged premises, and constantly carries in stock a full assortment of robes, coffins, caskets, etc., harness and saddlery, trunks, bags, sleigh robes, blankets and whips, wolf and rubber coats, etc., are also largely dealt in, and the lowest market rates are quoted on all the articles handled, while prompt attention to every caller is assured by the employment of two efficient assistants.

W. W. Allen, Dry Goods, Room Paper and Carpeting. Ladies' Outside Garments. Country Produce taken in Exchange. Penacook, N. H.—It is safe to assert that no more truly representative mercantile enterprise is located in Penacook than that conducted by Mr. W. W. Allen, for this has been successfully carried on for more than forty years, and, indeed, has held a leading posion from the start. The original proprietors, Messrs. Dutton & Pratt, began operations in 1848, and were succeeded in 1851 by Messrs. Pratt & York, who gave place to Messrs. Pratt & Allen in 1855. In 1858 the firm of Allen & Hall assumed control, they being succeeded in 1862 by Mr. W. H. Allen, and he in 1886 by the present proprietor, who is a native of Concord and is universally known in this section of the State both in business and social circles. He has served two terms as representative, and is now a member of the board of aldermen. Mr. Allen utilizes spacious and well-arranged premises, their total area being about 2,000 square feet. He carries a large, varied and most skillfully chosen stock, and as the lowest market rates are uniformly quoted, and prompt and polite attention is assured to every caller by the employment of three competent assistants, it is not to be wondered at that no more popular establishment can be found in this vicinity. Among the more prominent articles dealt in may be mentioned dry goods, wall paper, carpeting and ladies' outer garments, and the latest novelties in these lines are always well represented. Mr. Allen takes country produce in exchange, and spares no pains to fully satisfy every customer.

Albert A. Huff, Meats and Vegetables Penacook, N. H. Mr. Albert A. Huff has carried on his present enterprise only since the beginning of the current year, but his business experience is much more extended than this fact would seem to indicate, for he was proprietor of a store from 1872 to 1886, so that for about fourteen years he had an opportunity to become familiar with the needs of the public. He was born in Smithfield, Maine, and served more than two years in the army during the Rebellion. Mr. Huff occupies premises having an area of about 1200 square feet, and carries a very extensive and carefully chosen stock, made up of fresh, salted, smoked and pickled meats, all kinds of vegetables in their season, canned goods from the most reputable packers, and other equally useful commodities. The assortment is certain, varied and complete enough to admit of all tastes and all purses being suited, and as two competent assistants are employed prompt and careful attention is assured to every caller. Mr. Huff carefully supervises all departments of the business and is ever on the lookout to improve the service rendered, as he knows what will prove beneficial to his customers cannot fail to advance his own interests also.

Fisherville Sovereign Co-operative Asso'n, dealers in Groceries, Flour, Cutlery, Clothing, Boots, Shoes, Rubbers, etc. J. C. Farrand, Agent, Rink Building, Penacook, N. H.—It is an undeniable fact that the large majority of the co-operative enterprises inaugurated in this country have failed, and this is the stock argument of those who deny that industrial and mercantile co-operation is practicable, but in every instance of failure the fault has been either in the management or in the conditions under which the experiment was tried, and the principle of co operation remains as sound to-day as ever it was. Were it so radically wrong and so visionary as its opponents would have us believe, success would be impossible, so that the fact that there are many co-operative undertakings in successful operation conclusively proves that the objections made to the principle are unfounded. The residents of Penacook need not go away from home to find a prominent example of successful co-operation, for in the enterprise conducted by the Fisherville Sovereign Co operative Association they have an undertaking which was founded fourteen years ago and has steadily gained in utility and popularity. The association was incorporated in 1876, and its officers have shown most commendable ability and zeal in administering its affairs and in avoiding the mistakes which have proved disastrous to similar enterprises. The public have learned by experience that the undertaking is worthy of hearty and permanent support, and that such is given it may be judged from the fact that four assistants are required to properly attend to the many orders received. The president is Mr. J. C. Richards, the treasurer, Mr. F. A. Abbott, and the agent, Mr. J. C. Farrand, all of whom are too well known in Penacook and vicinity to render detailed personal mention necessary. The association occupy very spacious quarters in the rink building and carry a heavy stock of general merchandise, including groceries, flour, cutlery, clothing, boots, shoes, rubbers, etc., together with a full assortment of fresh and salted meats, fresh fish and lobsters. The goods are strictly dependable in every respect, the service is prompt and obliging, and customers get unusual value in exchange for every dollar they expend at this thoroughly well managed establishment.

George N. Dutton, dealer in Dry and Fancy Goods, Millinery, etc., manufacturer of the Dutton Cuff Holder, Penacook, N H.—The popularity of the establishment conducted by Mr. George N. Dutton is by no means the result of luck, but on the contrary has been brought about by hard, intelligent and faithful work continued through a term of years. The proprietor is a native of Concord and became identified with the co erprise in 1885, as a member of the firm of Sanders & Dutton, assuming sole control in 1888. He deals in dry and fancy goods, milli-

nery, etc., and is manufacturer of and dealer in the "Dutton Cuff Holder," which is one of those little devices that once used are never willingly dispensed with. The premises utilized afford space for the accommodation of quite an extensive stock, and on the score of magnitude alone Mr. Dutton's assortment is paralleled by few if any similar stocks in this section, but its quality is even more remarkable than its quantity, and the very latest fashionable novelties are always well represented. All classes of trade are catered to, and the closest buyers agree that at no store in this section is more genuine value given for money received. Callers are assured prompt and courteous attention, goods being cheerfully shown and every opportunity given to make a deliberate and satisfactory selection.

F. B. Clough & Co., Furniture. Repairing and Upholstering. Penacook, N. H.—When purchasing articles of any description it is well to remember that the first cost is but one of a number of things that should be considered, and especially is this true in the case of furniture, for thoroughly well made furniture will last and look well for many years, while that composed of inferior material carelessly put together will become shabby and broken down in a very short time. And after all, the difference in the first cost is by no means great, and in proof of this assertion we would refer our readers to the establishment conducted by Messrs. F. B. Clough & Co., for this firm deal in thoroughly dependable goods, and yet quote prices low enough to suit the most economically disposed. Goods are cheerfully shown, and anything in the line of furniture can be furnished at short notice and at the lowest market rates. Upholstering is an important department of the business, and furniture repairing in general will be done in a thorough and workmanlike manner at a reasonable price. Mr. Clough gives careful personal attention to the supervision of affairs, and makes it an invariable rule to allow no defective work to leave his establishment, while at the same time sparing no pains to deliver orders promptly when promised.

C. H. Fowler, Druggist and Pharmacist, dealer in Drugs, Medicines, Chemicals, Paints, Oils, Glass, Brushes, Varnishes, Perfumery and Toilet Articles, Penacook, N. H.—Every experienced physician will agree that the cure of disease would be much more easy than is now the case were the drugs and medicines sold by every dealer uniform in character. The public are apt to suspect that a physician who directs them to a certain pharmacy does so because he receives a percentage of the cost of the medicines sold, but this is so seldom the case as to be unworthy of consideration. The fact is, a physician learns that a certain pharmacist obtains his supplies from reliable sources, renews them often enough to prevent serious deterioration from age and is skillful and careful in the compounding of prescriptions. As these things enable the effects of prescriptions put up at his establishment to be more accurately prepared than would otherwise be possible, and as the professional reputation of the physician is directly dependent upon his prescriptions having the desired effect, what more natural than that he should direct where they should be compounded? Mr. C. H. Fowler is one of the most popular pharmacists in this section of the State, not only among physicians but also the general public, for he has had long experience in the business and his methods are uniformly reliable. He was born in Webster, N. H., and was at one time a member of the city council. Mr. Fowler became identified with his present enterprise in 1866, as partner under the firm name of Rollins & Co., it having been inaugurated in 1852 by Mr. J. S. Rollins, Mr. Fowler assuming sole control in 1875. A heavy stock of drugs, medicines and chemicals is constantly carried, prescriptions being very carefully compounded at reasonable rates. Perfumery and toilet articles are dealt in to a considerable extent, and paints, oils, varnishes, brushes, glass, artists' materials, etc., are supplied in quantities to suit at the lowest market rates.

J. E. Symonds & Co., Table Mfrs. and Wood-Workers, Penacook.—The enforcement of the law against selling liquors "over the bar," in Massachusetts, has already caused a great deal of comment although it was not begun until the middle of May, and public opinion seems to be about equally divided as to whether the law is beneficial or not, but at all events it is beneficial to a prominent Penacook establishment, for its proprietors, Messrs. J. E. Symonds & Co., are extensively engaged in the manufacture of saloon tables, and their trade extends throughout New England. The saloon tables made by this firm are celebrated for their strength and durability, and as they are of the most approved design and are furnished to the trade at bottom prices, it is natural that they should be in great demand. The largest orders can be promptly filled, however, for the manufacturing facilities are very extensive and work can be "rushed through" at a great rate when haste is desirable, the quality of the productions remaining uniformly excellent. This firm is made up of Messrs. J. E. Symonds and G. W. Abbott, both of whom are natives of New Hampshire, Mr. Symonds having been born in Hancock, and Mr. Abbott in Webster. Both served three years in the army during the Rebellion, and are widely known in business and social circles throughout Penacook and vicinity. They by no means confine themselves to the manufacture of saloon tables but make a full line of extension, dining, kitchen and office tables, besides doing special order work in a superior manner at short notice and at low rates. The factory is two stories in height and 200×40 feet in dimensions, and is fitted up throughout with the most improved machinery, driven by a 150-horse water wheel and a fifty-horse engine. Employment is given to thirty assistants and the business is thoroughly systematized,—no imperfect work being allowed to leave the establishment.

John Chadwick, Livery, Board and Feed Stable, Penacook, N. H.—The majority of those who patronize livery stables are not unreasonable and therefore do not expect to be furnished with horses that can trot in 2:30, or with carriages that look as though they never had been used, but even the best-natured customer may be excused for kicking when he is supplied with the lame apology for a horse and the antediluvian vehicle which some public stable keepers seem to think ought to be entirely satisfactory. It is very poor policy to force patrons to put up with such "accommodations," for it has a tendency to disgust them with hiring teams and to cause them either to give up driving or to get a turnout of their own. We think that the methods followed by Mr. John Chadwick might be profitably imitated by some other stable keepers whom we could name, for he spares no pains to keep a sufficiency of desirable teams on hand for livery purposes, and although he makes no extravagant claims, still, his rigs will compare favorably with the average private turnout in this vicinity. Mr. Chadwick was born in Boscawen, N. H., and succeeded to his present business more than twelve years ago. He was formerly assistant city marshal, and few, if any, men in this community are better known and more highly esteemed. The premises utilized are spacious and well arranged and include sixteen stalls. A general livery, boarding and baiting business is done and employment is given to two efficient assistants, so that all orders are assured immediate and careful attention. The charges are uniformly moderate and the service gives the very best of satisfaction. Mr. Chadwick is agent for the American Express Co., having served this company and its predecessor for twelve years.

John C. Linehan, dealer in Groceries, Dry Goods, Provisions, Flour, Grain. etc., Penacook, N H.—Such a stock as is carried by Mr. John C. Linehan cannot be adequately described in the limited space at our command, for it is so varied and so complete in every department that to merely name the commodities it comprises would more than exhaust our space as well as the patience of our readers. But as a matter of fact such a procedure is quite unnecessary, for the Penacook public thoroughly understand that patrons of this store are given an exceptionally large and desirable assortment to choose from, and they know that not only staple goods but also the latest novelties are well represented. It would be surprising were not Mr. Linehan's well appreciated by this time, for he has been identified with his present enterprise for nearly a quarter of a century, beginning operations as a member of the firm of Bean & Linehan who succeeded Mr. M. H. Bean in 1866. The same year the firm name was changed to Brown & Linehan, and in 1869 the present proprietor assumed sole control. Mr. Linehan was a veteran of the late war and is an active and earnest worker in everything pertaining to the interests of the Grand Army of the Republic with which he has been most prominently connected. He was Department Commander for this State in 1883–4, and Junior Vice Commander-in-Chief in 1888–9; was member of the National Pension Committee, 1884–7, and President of the New Hampshire Veteran Association 1885–6. Mr. Linehan served in both branches of the city government between 1870–77. Trustee of Industrial School since 1883, director in Loan and Trust Savings Bank, Concord. From these facts it will be seen that Mr. Linehan is well and favorably known, and it is not to be wondered at that his store is headquarters for the purchasing public who appreciate first-class goods at bottom prices. Mr. Linehan utilizes one floor and a basement, having a total area of 2000 square feet, and among the more prominent commodities kept in stock may be mentioned groceries, dry goods, provisions, flour and grain. A very large family trade is enjoyed as the goods are chosen expressly for family use, and are thoroughly reliable in quality and low in price. Employment is given to two efficient assistants, prompt and polite attention being assured to every caller.

INDEX TO BUSINESS NOTICES.

www.ingramcontent.com/pod-product-compliance
Lightning Source LLC
Chambersburg PA
CBHW021417090426
42742CB00009B/1175